A TIME

OF LIGHT

AND

SHADOW

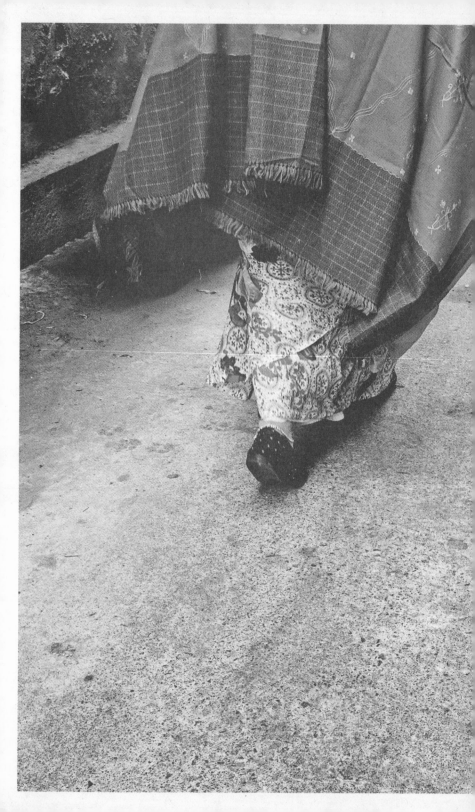

A TIME
OF LIGHT
AND
SHADOW

To Asia, Africa, and
the Long Way Home

ELLA HARVEY

RMB

For information on purchasing bulk quantities of this book, or to obtain media excerpts or invite the author to speak at an event, please visit rmbooks.com and select the "Contact" tab.

RMB | Rocky Mountain Books Ltd.
rmbooks.com
@rmbooks
facebook.com/rmbooks

Cataloguing data available from Library and Archives Canada
ISBN 9781771605694 (paperback)
ISBN 9781771605700 (electronic)

All photographs are by Ella Harvey unless otherwise noted.

Design: Lara Minja, Lime Design
Cover photo: Shutterstock/Rawpixel.com

Printed and bound in Canada

We would like to also take this opportunity to acknowledge the traditional territories upon which we live and work. In Calgary, Alberta, we acknowledge the Niitsítapi (Blackfoot) and the people of the Treaty 7 region in Southern Alberta, which includes the Siksika, the Piikuni, the Kainai, the Tsuut'ina, and the Stoney Nakoda First Nations, including Chiniki, Bearpaw, and Wesley First Nations. The City of Calgary is also home to Métis Nation of Alberta, Region III. In Victoria, British Columbia, we acknowledge the traditional territories of the Lkwungen (Esquimalt and Songhees), Malahat, Pacheedaht, Scia'new, T'Sou-ke, and W̱SÁNEĆ (Pauquachin, Tsartlip, Tsawout, Tseycum) peoples.

We acknowledge the financial support of the Government of Canada through the Canada Book Fund and the Canada Council for the Arts, and of the province of British Columbia through the British Columbia Arts Council and the Book Publishing Tax Credit.

For my mother, Mable Lawrencia,

and my daughter, Jessica Monique.

CONTENTS

– Author's Note –

I have researched, fact-checked, consulted and attempted to document the historical events accurately in this book. But memories can shift, even vanish over an expanse of time. It was my travel journals that kept me true to the story. Only a few names and identifying details have been changed to protect the privacy of the people involved.

A short portion of my first memoir *Encounters on the Front Line* (Promontory Press, 2015) is included in *A Time of Light and Shadow*. In doing so, I trust the reader will appreciate the profound impact 1980 had on my life as a young woman.

Several locations have changed their names since the 1970s. In 1995 the city of Bombay officially became Mumbai. In 1996 the city of Madras was changed to Chennai. Calcutta was renamed Kolkata in 2001. Some places I remember as small towns have quadrupled in size. In 1978 Jaipur was a quiet provincial capital of Rajasthan with less than a million people. By 2019 it was a bustling modern city of nearly four million.

ONE

Departure, 1975–1976

Come come, whoever you are
Wanderer, worshiper, lover of leaving
It doesn't matter
Ours is not a caravan of despair.

—RUMI

1

Kalashnikov Welcome

IN JANUARY OF 1976, Paris was wickedly cold, not an inviting place to be in my underheated walk-up. I preferred to be at the Brasserie des Etoiles four floors down, where I would drink a glass of red wine and read Simone de Beauvoir, or Colette, or the *International Herald Tribune*, and imagine myself the cosmopolitan woman intrigued with global affairs.

In my single room, I rolled a towel at the base of the small window to cut the draft and sat down at the scruffy table I'd covered with a bright floral cloth. The hallway telephone, provided by the *propriétaire*, rang. Probably Madame Marbot from the temp nursing agency. The first time she'd called, I'd gone all the way to Marseille by ambulance to pick up a wealthy American with a bad heart.

But it was Edwyn, an aging Welsh physician I had met over coffee at Alliance Française, the international school of the beautiful French language I struggled to master. Edwyn struggled even more and had asked for my number, which I had given him, for reasons I wasn't sure.

"I'm leaving for Beirut tomorrow morning with Médecins Sans Frontières. We need another nurse. Why don't you come?"

"Isn't there a war going on in Lebanon?" I knew that much.

"It's only for a few weeks, and we'll be safe enough with MSF."

"Tomorrow morning?" I asked, already calculating the departure.

"You have two hours to decide," Edwyn added, and gave me directions to the MSF office on the other side of town for the preliminary meeting.

I made my decision the moment he asked. I was a nurse, after all, and working on a front line aligned with my wildest dreams.

It came with a slap of pressing details. I had to inform my employer, pay the propriétaire and write my family. No point making a collect call. My mother would be sick with worry and my father would not encourage such a pursuit. I would start with Madame Marbot.

Three months ago, just after I began work at her agency, she had announced that my assignment would be with Max Ernst. "He's a famous artist, you know. You're lucky to be called," she said, tossing back her hair with theatrical flair.

I had never heard of Max Ernst and set off for the upscale neighbourhood of Montmartre where he lived. A maid opened the door to the stately building and escorted me through a courtyard and into the parlour to meet Dorothea Tanning, Max's American wife. Every angle of their elegant apartment, the staircase, sitting room and bedroom, was adorned with his art. Distorted bodies and bold images dripping with the bizarre. Max Ernst was a surrealist.

"My husband had a stroke, but don't let him fool you. He's as sharp as a tack," Dorothea said as she introduced me to the renowned painter, now an old man with unruly white hair and rosy cheeks, who smiled at us with mischievous blue eyes. The day nurse, a freckle-faced Irish woman, explained the night routine, most importantly that the patient's bedside bell always be within reach, in case I dozed on the job, a bad habit of night nurses.

My life in Paris, between Max and Alliance, soon fell into a pleasing routine. Sometimes before leaving work in the morning, I'd have coffee with Dorothea in her suite downstairs. She was an artist too, her work enigmatic, though not as disturbing as her husband's.

Some mornings I would wander in the city, bundled up with my hat and scarf in the winter weather. Crossing Le Pont des Arts, I'd watch the barges ply their way up and down the Seine. In the courtyard of the Louvre, where chestnuts roasted on charcoal grills, I'd eat fresh crepes filled with chestnut cream as the Parisians, busy businessmen or women who wore belted coats and scarves with a flourish, their high heels clicking time, walked by. It was my love affair with Paris.

On New Year's Eve, Max, Dorothea and I raised our crystal glasses of Chivas Regal to toast in the coming year. Groucho, Max's funny little Pekinese dog, lay fast asleep beside us. Dorothea doted on her husband, kissed him goodnight and I settled on the couch with Max's strange images peering down at me. In a gallery of phantasmagorical art, I mused on my New Year's resolutions. Practical everyday goals. I needed to eat less and exercise more. Practise yoga. Go swimming. Explore Paris. Visit the galleries. And improve my minimally acceptable level of French.

WHY WASN'T MADAME MARBOT ANSWERING? Would she accept my request for a month off work? I liked my night shifts with Max and did not want to lose my job. I paced the drab hallway, my mind swirling with the imminent departure until I had her on the line. In broken French, I made my plea.

"You are a lucky girl," she declared once again, not because I'd be working for Médecins Sans Frontières, but that she, in all her generosity, would hold my contract with Max.

"*Merci beaucoup, Madame.*" I could have kissed her goodbye.

I hurriedly cleaned my room, wrote a letter home that included a last will, prepared my bags, then ran to the metro for my first encounter with MSF. The office, its walls covered with maps, charts and photographs, was cold and I shivered as the director, a man with vast experience in conflict zones, gave a brief political outline.

Lebanon was at civil war, the powerful right-wing Christians in the minority and the poorer left-wing Muslims in the majority.

The Palestinians and the Syrians, accused of inciting the war, were aiding the Lebanese Muslims and threatening Israel to the south. I hardly grasped the explosive political conflict, yet quickly understood we were signing up for a dangerous mission.

The details were a blur, the circumstances sketchy, but I handed over my passport and signed the paper stamped MSF Beirut. The phone call from Edwyn, a man I hardly knew, was about to change my life in ways I could not have known then. Travel to a country I did not know had an immediate appeal, but more than that, I would be working for an internationally recognized humanitarian organization that provided medical assistance to highly vulnerable populations. I could even imagine a more heroic version of myself, making a difference in the world.

We flew to Beirut the next morning, January 30, two days after Lebanon announced its 27th ceasefire in less than a year. We were a team of four. Edwyn, with hopelessly inadequate French, fidgeted the entire flight as he couldn't smoke. Adele, an austere, middle-aged nurse with white-flecked hair tied tightly in a bun, read a book. Lucien, a physician, wearing tight jeans and a purple turtleneck, chatted amiably with me. I was wearing my wrinkled green coat, neither stylish nor suitable for the occasion, but I'd had no time to prepare.

As the plane descended through the clouds, I had my first startling view of snow-capped mountains rising sharply from the Mediterranean. The afternoon sun lit up Beirut, the city once called the Paris of the Middle East. Government officials and the media, blinding us with their flashing bulbs, were waiting at the airport, which had just reopened the day before. The bushy-haired, bearded Abdel Mowla, the Minister of Health, raised his arms in a wide welcome, rushed us through customs, then whisked us away in three sleek black cars.

Beirut was a city in shambles. Entire buildings had fallen into crumbled heaps of concrete; others had bullet-ridden, pockmarked walls and shattered glass windows. Burnt-out cars lay abandoned in the streets where armoured vehicles patrolled.

From the battle-scarred city, we drove to the luxury hotel Beau Rivage for our first night.

Abdel Mowla invited us for dinner at the classy hotel restaurant. The chicken *shawarma* and rice pilaf were served with copious cups of mint tea and glasses of wine as Abdel updated us on the volatility in Beirut. The city had been shut down for weeks, with gas stations and the electrical company opening that day. His stories were alarming – violent killings, bodies dismembered and snipers killing "*n'importe qui.*"

"Anyone?" We looked at each other with anxious glances as Lucien and Edwyn accepted another glass of wine.

"Do we need to drink more wine when your people are so poor?" Adele asked Abdel as he cracked open another bottle of French red.

"We appreciate the wine," Lucien quickly added, softening Adele's diplomatic faux pas. We had only been in the country a few hours.

I didn't sleep well my first night in Beirut but could hardly contain my excitement as we drove that morning to our destination, Bourj Hammoud, on the other side of the city. We made our way through garbage-strewn streets, having to change vehicles three times. Each time the Arab French translator explained our presence at the checkpoints, with armed guards hastily waving us on. Halfway to Bourj Hammoud, we stopped at the Armenian Embassy.

"Please be at home in our home," Mr. Nazarian, the ambassador, greeted us at his door. A tall, thin man, he wore a starched white shirt and a black bow tie. He waved us into a dining room decorated with ornate wall tapestries, insisting we eat with him and his wife. A tasty meal of *kibbeh,* lamb meatballs in yogurt and mint sauce, was served, his hospitality greatly appreciated.

"The Armenians are proud people and have maintained neutrality throughout this bloody civil war. You must be careful. There is no police force, no government and no security," Mr. Nazarian said. "We have lived side by side, Muslim and Christian, in peace. All that has changed in one year."

"Drink our coffee, it is for your strength," Mrs. Nazarian added.

After rounds of handshaking, thank you, *merci* and *shukran*, we left with an Armenian driver who took us through the Christian district where the right-wing Phalangist paramilitary snipers patrolled the rooftops, according to the ambassador. I glanced up, my anticipation laced with the shaky belief we were safe, as we drove on to Naba'a, a poor Muslim enclave in predominantly Armenian Bourj Hammoud.

A throng of men dressed in army khaki fired a volley of shots into the air as we stepped out of our vehicle into a narrow alley. Terrified, I threw my arms around the closest man, who carried a submachine gun in one arm and a baby in the other.

"No afraid, no afraid," he said with a grin. "We do Kalashnikov welcome."

2

Guns Beside Us, Prayers Below

ALI HASSAN, the self-proclaimed leader of Naba'a, waved the armed men aside and led us into our new lodgings. The rundown apartment had two semi-furnished rooms with green paint chipping off the walls, no hot water and one rudimentary bathroom. Adele and I chose the room with a small barred window letting in a sliver of light.

"Let us see our clinic. If Allah wills, we have a better clinic soon," Ali said in his loud voice. The clinic, a few doors down the street, consisted of several rooms on the upper floor of a dreary mosque. Two men smoking cigarettes, their Kalashnikovs propped at their sides, sat on a bench in the bare waiting room. I had never seen so many weapons before Beirut, having only seen my father's hunting rifle. All the men and teenage boys were carrying arms and they were all called soldiers. The two in the waiting room complained of headaches and wanted medication.

"Everyone has headaches," Ali boomed. The large Aspirin bottle in a cupboard with a broken latch was empty. It was clear we needed dressings and medications to stock the bare shelves more than the specialized surgical equipment and boxes of intravenous solutions that had just arrived in MSF cartons from France.

Miriam, the sole nurse, had lustrous auburn hair that she swept up in a ponytail. She was clearly in charge of her five assistants, young adolescent girls who were put to work to help us unpack.

"*Inshallah*, may Allah's will be done," Ali proclaimed. "My life is hard, and I will die someday, maybe soon," he said as I arranged boxes of surgical gloves on the dusty shelves. "I cannot sleep at night and my heart goes too fast." His unexpected disclosure surprised me, as I was a foreigner, a woman and a Christian, at least in his eyes.

"Take a deep breath and let it go," I said, thinking it unlikely Ali would listen. He practised three times, let out big sighs of pent-up stress, then strode off into his demanding world.

The clinic, divided by chairs stacked to the ceiling, allowed us to see our patients on one side, while boys and men wearing army-green fatigues practised drills with their firearms on the other side. From the balcony, I could see the old man, the *muezzin* of the mosque, shuffle to his ancient record player that bellowed out a scratchy call to prayer. In this haphazard clinic, with guns beside us and prayers below, we managed to do our day's work.

New patients, some seriously wounded like the man with a nasty fractured leg, filled the drab, unpainted, windowless waiting room. An unfortunate young girl, four days after a bullet wound to her abdomen, sat clinging to her mother. A barefoot boy with a fever and a deep rattle in his chest needed antibiotics, as well as shoes and socks in the cold, wet Beirut winter. There was an endless stream of patients, primarily children with eye, ear or skin infections like impetigo, soldiers with new or old infected wounds, and the elderly with chronic aches and pains.

Miriam had her finger on the pulse of every patient who hobbled up the stairs, but it was Ali who charged about, commanding attention. He stood at the doorway, tall, vigilant and stern.

Adele, a veteran of two previous MSF missions in Africa, was our queen of common sense. The young care aides jumped to her orders when they didn't know what to do. They needed training,

education, support and supplies, all of which were lacking. They
also needed security and peace, nonexistent in a country at war.
Adele could be strict, but we laughed as we faced one logistical
problem after another like the intermittent electricity or water. I
had to crouch on all fours to get a bucket of cold water from a faucet hidden under the stairwell.

The dilapidated infrastructure or attending to the patients
didn't challenge me as much as my inability to communicate in
Arabic. Patient assessment, treatment, counselling and support
were all compromised. Miriam found a young man eager to speak
English to be my interpreter. Mohammed Ghazi wore a red and
white checked Palestinian *keffiyeh* draped over his shoulders,
which hid the fact that one arm was missing.

"Too many fighting, too many guns, my brother is dead, I want
happy life." He talked rapidly, anxious to unburden his story, like
so many other stories we had heard.

IMAM MOUSSA SADR, the spiritual and political leader of the
Shiite Muslims, sat at the head of the table, the honoured guest
for dinner in the home of Abdel, the Minister of Health. I sat
awkwardly between the imam and his interpreter as he discussed
the complexities of his country. As if on cue, a blast of gunfire
erupted nearby.

"It's the men in the street saluting President Suleiman Frangieh.
They watch him on the street TV," Abdel said, dismissing the
noise with a casual wave of his hand. Lebanon was a passionate,
volatile place.

"*Rien m'impressione.*" Nothing impressed Adele, she said later
in our room as we splashed our faces with cold water. She wasn't
fooled by the ritzy apartment, the gracious hosts and particularly the charismatic Imam Moussa Sadr who had not shaken her
extended hand. "It's all half-truths," she said, not sympathetic to
the Arab perspective and praising the victory of the Israelis in the
Six-Day War with Egypt in 1967, nearly a decade ago.

"It's hard to know who to believe," I said, knowing Middle Eastern politics were among the most disputed in the world. Adele gave me a skeptical shrug and went to bed.

I threw a shawl around my shoulders in the cool evening and scribbled a few notes in my journal, trying to understand the mess of Lebanon. Bourj Hammoud, the poor Muslim–Armenian district, was on alert with talk of a Phalangist attack, the extreme right-wing Christians. We had our fears too, not unfounded. The four of us could be at risk and suspected we might be targets for kidnapping.

"What do you think, Lucien, if the Christian Phalangists kidnapped us, then demanded a ransom to return us to the Muslims?" I asked the next morning.

"*Ne t'inquiete pas*," Don't worry, he replied, though we were wary and watching everyone, even Issam and Abed our house boys, especially them, as they were armed and had the keys to our rooms. Lucien was talkative, Edwyn bumbled, Adele was glum and I jumped every time I heard gunfire, which was often.

That night we hardly slept as shots rang out till morning. "OK, OK," Issam, who carried in our breakfast on a shiny tin platter, announced. Yet in the morning two teenagers arrived at the clinic, severely assaulted by the Phalangists, their backs covered in nasty welts.

The next night dozens of armed men ran through the street in front of our building. Abed, dressed in soldier's camouflage, peered out the window. "*Fatah*. PLO. No worry. They do exercise," he said, making a muscle. I was not reassured. Three hundred thousand Palestinians had fled from the occupied territories of Israel to Lebanon. The civil war would soon be over, the officials said, but nothing was stable or resolved and was not likely to be anytime soon.

A crowd waited in the rain-drenched street outside the clinic door one morning. Wrapped in a blood-soaked sheet, a woman clung to her husband's arm. The poor woman nearly slid off the stretcher as we maneuvered it around the tight corners of the narrow staircase. Lucien banged a crooked nail into the wall to hook up an intravenous, the plaster crumbling from the wall. He attended to her, as Adele and I assisted an older woman who arrived minutes later, in labour, soon giving birth to a healthy baby girl.

The younger woman, Amina, had miscarried. Women gathered around, sisters, aunts, her mother. They held each other's hands and stroked Amina's face, arms, legs and thick black hair. The speechless husband stood nearby as Amina's eyes pooled with grief.

Miriam knew how to manage the crowd, gently leading the extended family out the door and leaving husband and wife to their private sorrow. The teenage soldiers burnt all the bloody rubbish in the side alley. It was their way to help, and help was readily given in war-weary Bourj Hammoud.

Some days Miriam would take my hand and pull me into the supply closet, the only quiet place we had to take a break from our work. "I want baby, I want peace," she said in her few words of English. In that comfortable, intimate way of Middle Eastern women, she laid her hand on my arm, an uncommon gesture in my more inhibited Anglo-Canadian culture.

When Adele and I had a lull in our work, we'd escape to the roof for a breath of fresh air. "Isn't it lovely up here?" I said, looking out on the rooftops strewn with clotheslines and TV antennas.

"Sure, in a Middle Eastern sort of way," she replied over the infernal din of the horn honking below. An occasional blast of gunfire kept us on edge.

"Our work is a drop in the bucket with a big leak. I think we should extend our stay," I said.

"We're here for four weeks and that's it. Nothing will change. We do what we can do, then we go home," Adele said, stomping out her cigarette on the concrete roof.

In the context of the Lebanese civil war, our work felt insignificant. Still, I knew it mattered. The cross-cultural exchange and the sliver of understanding and hope we offered made a difference in someone else's life, lives in danger of dying. It certainly mattered to me.

ALI, THE VOICE OF NABA'A and our go-to person for everything from safety to supplies, invited us for dinner. A large, extended family and half a dozen children lived in a modest apartment with two framed Koranic verses on the living room wall. Plush carpets and cushions brightened the room.

"*Merhaba, shokruun,*" I greeted Ali's mother Kitanna, as she extended both her hands, firmly grasping mine. Wearing a long black dress, a turquoise headscarf and plum red lipstick, she made her mark as a bold woman. She fussed over us, offering sweet red tomatoes just picked from the vine in their small courtyard.

Ali's older sisters prepared appetizing *mezze*, small dishes for sharing, that they passed around to the guests, all of us sitting on the floor. After dinner we ate baklava dripping with honey and drank strong coffee, a festive occasion in their unstable world. Ali's directive manner and ceaseless energy made him a leader, though I thought he talked too much and listened to no one. Exasperating as he was, he was committed to the Arab cause. Even Adele had come to respect him.

Our month passed too fast, and a new, enthusiastic team arrived from France. I'd requested to stay one more day in Lebanon and said a teary goodbye to my colleagues. Adele, whom I greatly admired, busied herself with her bags. She was not about to cry, though, unexpectedly, Edwyn did. I thanked him for opening the door to Beirut, a unique experience in a culture where I had received more than I had given. Lucien gave me a big hug. "*A la prochaine,*" he said. See you next time.

3

"Too Much Dangerous"

I HAD BEEN ADVISED not to visit Baalbek, home to Lebanon's most renowned archeological sites: the temples of Bacchus and Jupiter. It was too dangerous to leave Beirut and I'd no longer have MSF protection, but I was determined to go, and Mohammed Ghazi agreed to accompany me.

"No problem, no problem," he said as we caught the local *servee*, a shared taxi, out of the city. The road wound up steep hills, through villages and cedar forests, the cedar of Lebanon, emblazoned on the national flag. We drove high into the Beqaa Valley north of the city as gunfire crackled in the distance. Mohammed assured me we were safe and took me to the market in Baalbek, once called Heliopolis or the City of the Sun, to buy a shawl for the chilly February mountain air.

The temple of Bacchus, dedicated to the Roman god of wine, the harvest and fertility, was over 2,000 years old and one of the best-preserved Roman ruins in the world. With its exquisite carvings and magnificent columns, the temple was breathtaking.

Mohammed stayed close by my side, proud to protect me from harm, as we wandered through Baalbek's ancient glory to the temple of Jupiter, dedicated to the sky, which was a brilliant blue that day. By late afternoon we had to return to Beirut.

"Too much dangerous. We sleep Baalbek. No go on road night," Mohammed stated, with none of his early morning confidence. I had a morning flight to Paris and had to return to the city, even if the dangers in the war-torn country were many.

"Mohammed, let's go," I insisted as I stepped into a servee with three other men.

"*Salaam alaikum,*" may peace be upon you, we greeted each other. The driver took off at a treacherous speed into the approaching dark, but not far beyond Baalbek we were stopped at a blockade by the mountain militia. One guard shone a flashlight into our faces, while another pointed a pistol at Mohammed then at me. In an icy sweat, I pulled out my MSF identification paper and, hands shaking, handed it over. The guard, whose alliance I did not know, lit up a cigarette and examined the paper.

The last time I felt so afraid was the previous summer on the Skagit River in Washington state on a rafting trip gone wrong. The raft was nothing more than a few planks mounted on inner tubes, roped together by my adventure-seeking buddies Kiko and Ken. They expertly navigated the river, which they assured me was tame, however, rivers are deceptive. We started to spin, the raft unravelling in a turbulent whirlpool. Whirling around and around, I gulped, spit and spiralled into a vortex.

I remembered yelling, "Please, God, let me live," in some primal voice I only called upon when God might intervene. The chilly depths pulled me down three times until one lucky stroke released me. I dog-paddled to shore, climbed a slippery bank and collapsed on the wet, soft earth, my body trembling, my legs like jelly.

There would be no more white-water rafting for me after that near-death experience, though it had almost been easy – death by drowning, that is. There was a lightness to it, a sensual slipping into the void, a tender letting go. But the instinct to survive hadn't been tender. It was tough and determined and had one imperative: I was too young to die.

Terror was terror, though a near drowning was not the same as a gun pointed in my face that night on the mountain road. The moments stretched into what seemed a dreaded finality. The man with the gun barked something in Arabic, scowled then cleared us through, Mohammed muttering *Allahu Akbar, Allahu Akbar.* God is the greatest.

Half a lifetime later, I wondered why I had delayed my flight to go to Baalbek, a risky exploit that could have ended badly. Enough to be kidnapped. Or killed. Why had I taken such a risk? At that time, it had seemed a natural extension to the Lebanese mission, to see the glorious ruins, and hadn't the team taken a drive along the coast south toward Sidon? We'd been safe. But safety was not a reliable measure in a country like Lebanon in 1976. It was a lawless place. Thousands of people had died in the civil war. A hundred thousand more would die in the 15 years to come.

My Beirut immersion was a moment in time, a time that held the fate of a nation, and the fate of its people, in a violent grip. The people who had graced my life: Abed and Issam, barely 17 with their Kalashnikovs; Miriam with a dream for a better life; Mohammed, my chatty interpreter; and Ali, the boisterous, fervent leader of his people, all of them courageous in desperate times. I would never see them again. They would live their lives in a country at war. I would live mine, grappling with landmarks that were always shifting. Moving on. Travelling on. I was learning how to bridge two worlds, the somewhere in between of reaching out and walking away, holding on and letting go.

4

With or Without a Man

I RETURNED TO PARIS, the city still cold and dreary in February, and picked up my life where I'd left off one month earlier, happy to see Max and Dorothea again. Beirut became a memory that no one talked about, neither myself nor my friends at Alliance Française. Other stories preoccupied our young minds.

Five afternoons a week I went to classes. I had scraped through French in high school with my teacher Mr. Clark, a gangling man barely out of high school himself and an utter anglophone. After class, I hung out with the international student crowd who reverted to speaking English, or I went to the bistros with Jenny, my endearing friend whose thick Yorkshire accent skewed everything *en français*. We became each other's social life.

"O Paris, the city of light and lovers. Where are they?" she said.

"Well, there are the boys at Alliance. I like Norbert. We went to the Musée L'Orangerie yesterday. I love Monet and Cezanne, but Norbert's such a starving artist."

"And he's German. You said you were looking for a French lover."

"Well, you like the Aussies and Kiwis, even the Canadians, anyone who isn't from England!" I said, watching the waiter, who was sexy and I figured single.

"Could we have a cheese plate?" I asked in my best French.

"What kind of cheese?" he inquired with cool disregard. Not being French, Jenny and I could have eaten *any* assortment of cheese.

"You'd think we were dining at Maxim's!" Jenny laughed loudly in her unpretentious way. He sauntered off, not a trace of interest on his surly face.

On Sunday mornings I took the metro to Montrouge, south of the city, where Mandela lived. She was a Vietnamese Buddhist nun I had met by chance, though she said nothing was by chance. Neither young nor old, she wore a plain white robe and tended the bamboo that grew in her miniature garden. In her home, the air infused with incense, she'd serve green leafy tea in tiny porcelain cups. The Buddha, sitting by the window, smiled benevolently upon our small meditation group.

"My mind's a cluttered, messy cobweb. How can I unravel it?" I asked after meditation.

"Your mind is like a kite bobbing in the sky. It will land on solid ground when the time is right," Mandela said in her calm, caring voice. "Patience, perseverance and right-mindedness are the path. In Buddhism, we strive for compassion. It is more than just tolerance. It is tolerance plus understanding and love." Mandela was the perfect soothing balm for my restless spirit.

The human potential movement, metaphysics and spirituality drew me in, offering avenues to explore my higher self. I devoured books, from novels to poetry to the spiritual gurus of the East. I was searching for the real sacred and open to finding truth or meaning or God, wherever she or he met me on the path.

I could have pledged allegiance to my Christian heritage and pleased my mother, who had tried to maintain some semblance of religious life, taking her five children to a small white Baptist church perched on the side of a steep hill in Vancouver.

Families had their habitual red flags – money, politics, secrets and scandals. In our family the troubling divide was religion. It tore my mother and me in two. Even without a Bible-thumping upbringing, I thought I would be going to hell if I carried on in the way I was carrying on. It was never stated; it was *my* disturbing conclusion.

My Sunday school teacher saved me. "Teaching the story of Jesus and saving souls is the greatest calling," she'd said, back from mission work in Africa. I'd sit in a circle on the floor, fascinated with her colourful tales. Saving souls didn't interest me, but exotic lands became the call of my youthful imagination. I decided to be a missionary. By 15, I'd abandoned that idea, and quit the church, defying my mother's authority on all matters she considered important. I decided that heaven and hell were no longer a threat hanging over my young life, which I wanted to live as wildly as I dared.

I missed my family though I struggled with a sense of belonging – to a home, to a career, even to a country. Working in Beirut had fired my resolve to live with purpose and to care for a cause; still, I could fall into melancholic slumps or bouts of anxiety.

Then spring arrived with a flurry of cherry blossoms. The Parisians filled the sidewalk tables that had been empty most of the cold winter, drinking their *petit noir* in the morning or their *aperitif* in the evening. Lovers strolled the gardens at Tuileries, the elderly sat on the green deck chairs around the fountain and children scampered on the merry-go-round. I went to the market and bought fresh apricots and a bouquet of lily of the valley.

Every evening at eight, I went to Max's, my pleasant and predictable life in Paris. We shared a few words, never about his extraordinary life but about the little things he needed, like an extra blanket or a square of sweet chocolate. I was not a connoisseur of great art, but Max's work felt apocalyptic, as if immersed in a nightmarish version of the world. Having lived through two world wars, conscripted into the German army in the First World War, and fleeing to America as an undesirable alien while living in France during the Second World War, he no doubt was. It was in America, inspired by the works of Picasso and Van Gogh, that he became a force in the development of abstract expressionism.

Max Ernst

I'd answer Max's call bell when he needed me, but most of the time I lounged in the sitting room, its walls oozing his perplexing art, with Groucho curled up beside me on the couch. One night I asked Max to sign a book, a collection of his work I had just bought. His blue eyes weren't as bright, his hand trembled and his signature was faint. Little did I know it was the last time the famous artist would hold a pen in his hand. Max Ernst died the next day at the age of 84, on the first of April 1976.

German-born Max Ernst was a provocateur, a shocking and innovative artist who mined his unconscious for dreamlike imagery that mocked social conventions. A soldier in World War One, Ernst emerged deeply traumatized and highly critical of western culture. These charged sentiments directly fed into his vision of the modern world as irrational, an idea that became the basis of his artwork. Ernst's artistic vision, along with his humor and verve come through strongly in his Dada and Surrealist works; Ernst was a pioneer of both movements. (www.theartstory.org/artist-ernst-max)

Max's death was hard and saying goodbye to Dorothea was even harder. There were other possibilities of work with Madame Marbot, but I declined. I'd been living in Paris for eight months, a beautiful city, but it was no longer calling me. Staying did not fire my heart. Leaving did.

India was the destination that had captured my imagination since childhood, when I pored over the family atlas, dreaming of faraway places – Samarkand, Damascus, Kathmandu. I must have been 6 or 7 years old when my father, born in India during the British Raj, the son of Scottish parents, first told me stories that sparked an interest in the country of his birth.

I had to decide how, and most importantly with whom, I would travel. I began by investigating overland adventure tours, British outfits. They were too expensive and did not allow me the freedom I craved. A travel companion was the logical solution. None of my friends at Alliance were likely bets and most of them were impoverished students. I tacked bilingual ads in big print on the bulletin board: "Looking for a Travel Partner to Go to India."

A trustworthy, intelligent, adventurous, energetic and fun traveller was the unwritten subtext. Preferably male and sexy too. Replies were tacked back, and I arranged meetings with anyone who might have been a possible fit. I sat in the bistro across the street, trying to look casual and confident but feeling self-conscious, ten pounds heavier than when I'd arrived in Paris eight months earlier.

Jamil, a Turk, the first man to arrive, was smoking a foul Gitane. His clothes were ratty, and greasy hair hung over his eyes. Oh no! He wouldn't work. Two hours later, clean-shaven Bernard turned up, but he didn't have a clue how to leave home. I met others. Bruno, loud and arrogant. A turnoff. Jean-Michel, bean-pole thin wearing a red beret, told stories about big money that didn't add up.

On my second day of seeking Mr. Right, number seven sauntered into the cafe, wearing jeans and a blue leather jacket. He took my hand for a moment longer than a handshake. Gerard had all the qualities I'd imagined. I was nervous and stumbled in French, but language didn't matter. His kiss, on the banks of the Seine, convinced me I'd found my man.

"Same place, same time, tomorrow," he promised. I arrived early at Pont Neuf, waiting and watching every passerby, my old green coat wrapped around me that chilly April day. But Gerard never arrived. I plodded home, halfway across Paris, past my favourite bistros and parks, to the Brasserie des Etoiles. I lit up a cigarette, drank a glass of wine and brooded. I knew I had to be stronger than my wallowing. In Beirut, I hadn't wallowed, and I'd even gone to Baalbek. I could do it. I'd go to India. With or without a man.

5

The Orient Express

THE ORIENT EXPRESS PULLED OUT of the Gare de Lyon, the station gloomy as daylight faded into dusk. I stared out the window on the train of international intrigue, tears streaming down my face as Paris slipped away. Five Turks, amiable, older men who shared my second-class compartment, insisted on sharing their Turkish pistachios with me. Ahmed, the oldest of the group, poured cheap red wine into my cracked enamel mug.

I had considered staying in France and studying *la cuisine française*. It would have been an easier choice, a choice my mother would have preferred as she loved to cook and host dinner parties, but I chose travel.

Our last visit in Canada nearly a year ago had ended badly. I could see it in her eyes, I could hear it in her tone: irresponsible and reckless hippie, though I was a registered nurse, not in any serious trouble and only a weekend hippie. I should have known she wouldn't approve.

"Don't you have any plans for your future?" Mom had asked, days before I left on my long-sought journey.

"Of course, I have plans," I'd snapped. "I'm going to study French in Paris. And then I'm going to India," though I knew there was a wide expanse of territory in between. I didn't have a fixed itinerary. It was loose. According to my mother, I was loose.

"Well, you don't seem to care about things other young women care about," she'd said.

"Like what?"

"Getting married. Having a family."

"I'll settle down when I'm ready!" I said, slamming the door and walking away. She was bent one way and I was bent another. She was self-righteous. I was self-absorbed. I knew my mother wanted a more compliant and conventional daughter, but I was churning in a turbulent cycle of needing to be accepted, feeling judged, craving closeness and wanting to run. Still, I tried to make an uneasy peace with her those last days in Montreal as she gave me last-minute advice, from travelling with a suitable man to the unlikelihood of finding work in France.

"It's not normal to travel alone," Mom said as she drove me to the airport. Words I would remember in times when I found myself alone and feeling far from normal. Neither of us showed a flicker of gentle emotion until I walked through the security gate. Only then did tears pour down my burning face. I was off to see the world and turned back to smile, but she was gone.

We'd fought too many fights, though of course there had been good times, family holidays, Christmas dinners and kind conversations. I just had to pick up the pieces and follow my heart. I wondered how my mother picked up the pieces when her only daughter, her first-born, flew away.

I was jostled back by the train, rumbling through the night, lurching past phantom stops in France until the day dawned somewhere in northern Italy. Ahmed, who had kept me awake with his loud snoring, was organizing coffee and not-so-fresh croissants for everyone.

"Girl, no man, danger," he said. A father of three daughters, he was concerned about my safety.

"I'm OK," I responded, though I wasn't sure of anything as I stepped down from the train 16 hours later in Venice.

In the sun-drenched city of water and stone, I walked the maze of narrow alleyways with bold red geraniums tumbling from windowsills onto ancient walls. People called out to each other in melodic language, as if every Italian were uttering a great truth. Even the older women in their sombre dresses and headscarves looked like they had a story to tell. In the late afternoon, in the pigeon-filled *piazzetta*, the little square off the marvelous Piazza San Marco, I met Augustino.

"*Ciao signorina*," he said, sitting down beside me, licking an ice cream cone, the bronze winged Lion of Venice towering above us. "This is chocolate kiss, *cioccolato bacio*. You want to try?" he asked, jumping up to buy me a cone. It was as delicious as our sunny afternoon spent talking and watching the polished black gondolas glide by on the Grand Canal. My new acquaintance, who took me by the arm and led me from the piazzetta to a waterside *trattoria*, charmed me.

"I no like America. I no like Italy. I no like big money," Augustino disclosed. A communist, he deplored the corrupt capitalist regime in his country.

"I'm not a communist."

"No matter. You have pretty capitalist eyes," he said, pouring me another glass of Italian red.

He ordered a plate of calamari. We were chewing on the stringy legs of the giant squid, enjoying the convivial ambiance of the trattoria, when a strange rumble occurred. The electric lights went out, the table began to shake and a glass toppled, red wine on a white tablecloth. Fear rippled through me as a powerful tremor seized the city.

Our meal unfinished, we ran into the street along with the other patrons, servers and cooks. The square filled with people, some in pajamas, some agitated, some parents holding on to their bewildered children. Augustino gripped my hand then walked me through the narrow lanes, over a bridge and back to my *pensione*. He had lost his bravado but gave me a goodbye kiss, a bacio, on the cheek, one more time. I climbed three flights of stairs, packed my bags and went to bed fully dressed, ready to run during the night.

Later I learned the 6.5 quake occurring on May 6, 1975, was the Teremoto del Friuli, its epicentre 100 kilometres north of Venice. Over 900 people had died. I learned that an earthquake forever alters the certainties we live by. The earth was no longer solid under my feet; it could shift at any time.

6

Freight Hop

ON THE NEXT LAP of the journey through Yugoslavia, I was squeezed into a compartment with an old Slavic couple, the overweight wife fanning her ill husband with a handkerchief, a Syrian student returning to Damascus, a friendly Pakistani and an Italian businessman in a frayed gray suit. Rasheed, the Pakistani, whose shaggy eyebrows danced up and down as he talked, shared his *chapatis* with a fiery hot dipping sauce. We sat together, a band of unlikely comrades, as the cold night air blew through the open window that we couldn't close.

We crossed the provinces of Slovenia and Croatia that night and by morning were in northern Serbia, a desolate stretch of country. Farmers tilled the earth with oxen, and women in bright kerchiefs paused to watch the train roll by. In Belgrade, the station police, fat bellies bursting from their untidy shirts, came on board, demanding to see our passports. They were as solemn as their land. The land that 15 years later would be torn up by brutal ethnic conflicts and suffer one of the bloodiest battles of the 20th century.

For now, the land was flat and peaceful. The clickety-clack of the train, moving forward through fleeting landscapes moving backwards, lulled me into neither here nor there, past or present, belonging or not belonging. I could dream of adventures I'd yet to live or reminisce on those I'd had, like last summer on my great Canadian freight hop.

It hadn't been hard to stroll through the gates of the Canadian National Railway yards east of Vancouver. "What the hell are you doing here? Are y'all runaways or just looking for a free ride?" a burly man in green overalls inquired.

"We're heading east," my friend Ken said with a straight-up reply and started talking, man-to-man, about trains. "My grand-dad used to ride the rails back in the Depression years, and in his memory, I dreamed of doing the same." Ken offered his improb-able story with a boyish smile.

"Just make like I don't know you're here," the man said and pointed out the #878 to Edmonton. We climbed the rungs into the fourth engine, a sooty steel space with two leatherette swivel chairs, and counted ourselves lucky not to be sitting on a box-car floor. The heat of the engine and the noise of steel on steel propelled us down the tracks. Close to a hundred boxcars wound behind us like a snake.

I was in my summer fantasy, riding the rails, off to see the world. A little girl of years gone by, running alongside the tracks, jumped on just for the ride. She stood at my side, dreamy-eyed and daring, like it was her train, her adventure, listening to that whistle blow.

As night fell, we drank wine straight from the bottle and talked our wild vagabond talk. It was me who had proposed the freight hop, hoping to dispel any lingering fear of being a sissy on the river raft trip. No one called me that, yet some childhood myth lurked: "Chicken, Sissy, Crybaby, Girl."

Ken and I were silent for long stretches, sitting on our swivel chairs, as Saskatchewan and Manitoba rolled by, their beautiful Indigenous names meaning swift-flowing river and Great Spirit. It was a land of Great Spirits; they danced everywhere, in the wheat fields, over the wind-blown lakes and under the immense blue sky.

Or Ken would talk about his plans to hop a freighter or his revolu-tionary quests. His hero was Che Guevara. Ken was a Che himself:

intelligent, rebellious and persuasive. Following him crossed my mind, but I needed to keep my own life on track.

By our fourth day, we were crossing Ontario, a patchwork wilderness of lakes and deep, dark forest. It was moose country. A large bull with massive antlers, knee-deep in a swamp, looking like some prehistoric beast, watched the train roll by.

After more than 4000 kilometres of freight-hop freedom, we rolled into Montreal, where we had to say goodbye. "You'll be gone, and you can be my sailor at sea," I said.

"And you'll be my gypsy girl," Ken replied, pulling me close, my old jean jacket smelling like the earthy oil of freight trains.

It would be years before I'd see Ken again, but trains held me in their spell as the Orient Express snaked through Serbia, in the east of the Socialist Republic of Yugoslavia, crossing the border at Dimitrovgrad into Bulgaria. My friendly fellow traveller Rasheed shared food and colourful stories about his Pakistani homeland that he dearly missed. Like Ahmed the Turk, he was kind and generous, though Rasheed made it clear he followed his faith and did not imbibe in forbidden alcohol.

7

Sofia

THE ORIENT EXPRESS pulled into the station in Sofia, the capital of Bulgaria, a country I knew little about. I said goodbye to my fellow passengers and stepped down from the train into the crisp May evening of communist Eastern Europe.

At the Auberge de la Jeunesse, I found myself the only guest in a dismal hostel dormitory. Being a solo traveller by day was exciting, but at night strange sounds, creaking windows and skittering mice frightened me. The next morning, I woke to an argumentative voice, got out of the uncomfortable cot, dressed and descended the stairs to the sombre lobby. The manager greeted me with an unfriendly nod. She pointed out the tourist office down the main street. "You go Balkan Tourist," she ordered as if it was my only option.

In the state-run office, a woman dressed in a gray suit, her hair tightly coiffed, informed me I had to spend ten dollars a day in Bulgaria. My hostel was only two dollars a night, which left more than enough for food. A blond foreigner, I guessed American, came in, her ponytail bouncing as she walked. I thought we might be the only solo female travellers in Sofia that day.

Shirley, a secretary from Minneapolis, was spending a few days in Bulgaria for reasons that were not clear. I knew little about the country and she knew even less. Something about her didn't ring true. Her naïveté could be a ruse. Could she be an undercover agent behind the Iron Curtain? She was staying at the state-run Balkan Hotel across the street.

After a breakfast of Bulgarian *bonitsa*, a cheese pancake, Shirley and I decided to visit Sofia together, a city as remarkable as the guidebook described. It was the only city in Europe that had four different religious establishments: an Eastern Orthodox church, a Catholic cathedral, a mosque and a synagogue, all actively used in the Square of Religious Tolerance.

However, it was the Russian Orthodox Church of Sveti Nikola, with its elegant steeple, golden domes and mosaic walls, that caught my eye.

"This is the prettiest church I've ever seen," I said, pointing to an adjacent building with a good vantage point three floors up to take photos.

"We have to be careful in a communist country," Shirley cautioned.

"Oh, come on, we'll be fine," I said as she followed me up the stairs.

"What are you doing?" a man asked, finding me leaning off the well-placed balcony.

"I'm taking a picture of the beautiful church," I responded.

"Yes, it is. Maybe you would enjoy a drink of coffee," he said in perfect English, inviting us into his apartment.

Vasil, a schoolteacher, dressed in green cords and a matching wool pullover, was stylish compared to the people we had seen in the streets. Books lined one wall of his modest home. "Bulgarian, French, English and Russian," Vasil said, seeing my interest. Over a strong espresso and biscuits served on a platter, I asked about life and politics in his country.

"Bulgaria is a police state. We are not a happy country and life is hard." The Cold War had taken its toll, communism isolating Bulgaria from the progressive West where he longed to live. Vasil was as convincing in his arguments for capitalism as Augustino had been for communism.

"It's time to go," Shirley nudged me as soon as we'd finished our coffee. I could have talked all day with Vasil, a man who had taken a risk speaking with strangers from the West.

We wandered the city, marvelling at its spacious streets and green parks. By afternoon we were on the recommended Balkan bus tour, listening to a condensed version of Bulgaria's 2,000 years of history, including Greek, Roman, Ottoman and Soviet occupation. The gold-domed Alexander Nevsky Cathedral, constructed in the early 20th century to honour the 200,000 Russian, Ukrainian and Bulgarian soldiers who died in the Russo-Turkish War of 1877–1878, was massive.

I stood in front of the cathedral, the sixth largest in the world and the national pride of Bulgaria, reflecting on war and the suffering on all sides. I could feel the dark pages of human history, the mourning of mothers and fathers. The complicated beauty and violence of our world had me in tears. Shirley stood by my side, unmoved.

She was vague too about where she wanted to travel next and had a follow-along sort of way about her. My plans weren't well defined either. My desire to go to India hadn't changed, though crossing Turkey, Iran, Afghanistan and Pakistan on my own was at best uncertain. I had no idea what lay ahead and asking Shirley to join me was not an option. She was either a Cold War spy or a casual tourist. Neither would have worked.

The next evening, I hopped aboard the train for the last leg of the journey to Istanbul, the former Constantinople and Gateway to Asia. Two men were in the compartment, a quiet Iraqi and a robust Turk, who helped himself amply to the Iraqi's whiskey throughout the night as I read Dervla Murphy's inspiring story, *Full Tilt: From Ireland to India with a Bicycle*. I had hopped a freight train across Canada but was not as brave as the intrepid Dervla. She had risked it all, from living with Afghan nomads to cycling the most inhospitable parts of the globe, all for the love of wild, solitary, unpredictable travel. For me, it was enough just being on the Orient Express with Esen and Yazen, who were ever more drunk as we approached Istanbul, obscured in a fine morning mist.

TWO

Detour, May–July 1976

Reason is powerless in the expression of love.

—RUMI

8

A Kiss Crosses All Borders

TOPKAPI PALACE, once the residence of sultans, was home to the treasures of the Ottoman Empire. I had never seen such opulence, the Chinese porcelain collection was exquisite, and the guide, Alim, a handsome Turk, had green eyes as startling as Suleiman the Magnificent's jewels. He conducted the multinational group with ease, speaking in polished English, Italian and French.

"Please be my guest to visit my splendid city Istanbul," Alim said, linking his arm in mine when the tour ended. "You must try our famous Turkish cuisine and learn about my country."

"Yes…please…thank you…" I faltered as he escorted me out the palace door and into the din of Istanbul. He took off his tie, undid the top two buttons of his white dress shirt, which fit tightly over his broad back, and ran his hand through his curly black hair.

"Now I can relax and give you all of my attention," he said.

At a sidewalk *çayevi* under a purple lilac tree, we drank thick mint tea and ate *simit*, sesame braided bread. Older women, heads covered with bright scarves, and younger women, heads uncovered, wearing jeans and long-sleeved blouses, strolled by. I wore a sleeveless blouse and above-the-knee skirt that rode up my thigh when seated.

"I'll buy a shawl to wear in your country," I said, knowing I needed some adjustment.

"Let us go to the market," Alim said, taking my arm and leading the way. I chose a pink and silver pashmina that I threw over my shoulders. It was the first step to rearrange myself, to please Alim.

"I must return to work. Please promise me tomorrow," he requested in his formal way.

"Yes, of course." My face flushed, unable to hide my excitement.

I walked back to the Istanbul Hostel, floating through a park of flowering apple trees. A few backpackers were in the dorm, Europeans and Americans. We talked travellers' talk, where to go and what to do in Istanbul, but I already had my plans, thrilled they would be with a Turk.

The next day, Alim and I took the ferry up the Bosphorus, the river that divides east from west, Asia Minor and Europe. Children ran along the grassy banks of the river, waving as Alim talked about the significance of the famous waterway. In the village of Anadolu Kavaği, where the Bosphorus meets the Black Sea, we dined on fresh shiny mackerel taken from the restaurant's aquarium. I swallowed new words: *balik* for fish and *su* for water. *Lütfen*, please, and *tesekkür ederim*, thank you, were next. "Love" danced between us, not yet ready to say out loud.

To the north of the town, high on the cliffs, a medieval fortress stood under strict military surveillance. In the shadow of its history, an unamused guard interrupted our first kiss.

A kiss crosses all borders, but there were vast cultural differences between Alim and me. Public displays of intimacy between a man and woman were taboo in the Muslim world. "Do you know that girls can be stoned to death for premarital sex in our villages? A father's dignity is more important than his daughter's life," he stated as he led me down the steep slope back to the boat.

"You don't believe this, do you?"

"Of course not. I am a modern man and I believe in progress." The societal contradictions baffled me: the adherence to tradition, the position of women and the obedience to Islamic law, all of it rapidly changing in Turkey, a secular state.

It was the '70s, a time of social upheaval with new freedoms for women to determine their destinies. I wavered as this emancipated North American woman, feeling defensive with Alim, an intellectual in a fiery cauldron of his own culture. We held hands and stole kisses. Swirling in contradictions, beyond caution and reason, I was falling fast.

THE BLUE MOSQUE OR SULTAN AHMED MOSQUE, built in 1616, was the apogee of Islamic architecture in a city of 3,000 mosques. The intricate hand-painted tiles on the interior walls were the bluest of blue. The faithful sat on a row of benches in the courtyard, washing their feet in preparation for *rakat,* the ritual prostration for prayer five times a day. *Allahu Akbar, Allahu Akbar,* the plaintive call of the muezzin, rang from its six fluted minarets that pierced the sky.

Alim loved language, words and ideas. He filled me with his learned world of literature and philosophy as we walked around the mosque, side by side, his almond brown skin brushing my whiteness.

"I am so afraid of this unexpected sunrise finishing," he quoted from his favourite book, Lawrence Durrell's *Alexandria Quartet.*

"I've read Sartre and Camus," I said, attempting to impress him with my learnedness.

"That is why we must be together. It is time to move to my lodging and be my girlfriend," he declared.

"Yes," I said, knowing I wouldn't say no. Later that afternoon, I returned to the hostel where I'd been for five days, packed my knapsack and moved in with Alim. His lodging, as he called it, was a dismal basement apartment in the district of Yenimahalle, a poor, working-class neighbourhood.

In no time, I began shopping and cleaning and cooking, my travels on hold. My only concern was the cockroaches that scurried across the floor.

"Don't worry, someday we'll have our enchanted palace."

"And you'll be my prince," I said, wrapping myself around him. We fell into bed, three mice running out from under it.

Most days Alim worked at his palace, and I went to Kapalicarsi, the Grand Bazaar. I was a kid in a candy shop, in a paradise of colour, from bold ceramics to rich embroidered fabrics to exotic jewelry. Men polished shoes at gleaming brass shoe stands and women haggled over prices. A wizened old man, wearing the traditional loose white trousers and coat, cut hair at a barbershop crammed in a sliver of space between the 4,000 shops. I began to find my way in the elaborate, intoxicating maze.

"*Merhaba*," I greeted the shopkeepers, all of them men, admiring their striking carpets or copper wares.

"Please visit my shop," they'd respond and offer me mint tea that came immediately in steaming cups on a tin tray. And when it was time to go, I could find the right collective taxi, called *dolmus*, to take me home to Alim.

He would tell me stories of his life. "It is hard as a tour guide, but it was harder when I attended university. I hardly had enough to eat. There is too much injustice and oppression in my country."

"How will the country change? Will the people revolt, or will the leaders evolve?" I thought of Ken's admiration of Castro's vision for an egalitarian society and Augustino's communist passion for the same.

"I will do everything in my power to work toward social justice and economic progress in Turkey. For now, I must work with the tourists, I need the money."

Often, we dined out, as Alim would say. At our favourite roadside eatery, we sat at the plastic table on a narrow sidewalk and ate deep-fried *patlican* with garlic yogurt and grilled shrimp. Traditional music blared from a speaker a few feet away, and a stray dog stood by for scraps.

"Eggplant is Turkey's national dish and we can serve it as many ways as there are days in the year," he said, baiting me with a wink.

"*Patlican* it is, every night," I flirted as I swallowed it down with *raki*, a white licorice liquor, and basked in the unexpected pleasures of Alim.

One morning, Alim's friends Ghazi and Hussein, young intellectuals from the university, visited for breakfast. We sat on the living room floor, eating salty cheese, fried sausage, honey and *pide*, a flatbread, and drinking strong Turkish coffee. I touched Alim's hand as he passed me a plate of olives, my body close to his. He pushed my hand aside, his eyes scolding.

"In Turkey, we do not eat steak in front of a dying man," he declared after his friends left.

"What a pretense. Everyone knows I'm living with you. Everyone knows..."

"But we do not show." His words were final.

9

Captive

TURKEY, ONCE PART of the Hittite, Greek, Roman, Byzantine and Ottoman empires, was a country rich in ruins. Dr. Ethel Egerton, a British archeologist, would accompany Alim on the 16-day tour of the country. Alim had been guiding tours for a year, but he needed to ask her permission for me to join the group. The imposing Dr. Egerton must have judged me as unnecessary baggage, but she agreed. I wanted to hug her as I climbed aboard the luxury bus with a group of aging English-speaking guests. We left Ankara for the unpronounceable sites of Alacahöyük, Boğazköy and Yazilikaya, dating back to the Hittite Empire in 1700 BC.

We crossed the Anatolian plateau, past the great salt lake of Tuz Gölü. A few crops grew on patches of sparse green earth where nomadic tribes still lived, grazing their sheep and goats. Women sat by a field of golden sunflowers, their naked children playing close by, while men drank tea at the roadside çayevi. Water buffalo stood at a river's edge where milky blue grass rippled in the afternoon breeze

Alim attended to his band of earnest travellers probing the archeological wonders of the area. I listened and took note of the broad wash of history. Between stops, I sat alone at the back

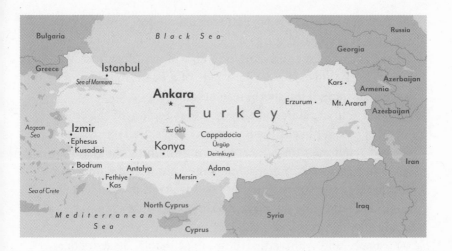

of the bus, scribbled notes in my journal and contemplated my choices as Turkey rolled past my insatiable eyes. I was captive to the words Alim whispered, yet a small voice, one I did not want to hear, warned me to be careful, be wise.

Cresting the hill of the Göreme Valley, the landscape changed to rugged cliffs and bizarre volcanic rock formations. The rocks sprouted like tall, chiselled mushrooms or bold phallic projections and were called *hoodoos* or fairy chimneys. They were formed over the eons, eroded by rain and wind, sculpting the region of Cappadocia into a breathtaking panorama.

The guests got on and off the bus, inhaling antiquity like vital air. Alim took us to mosques and monasteries, Muslim and Christian villages that had lived side by side for centuries. This was the land of the troglodyte cave dwellers. Their cave homes dotted the hilly terrain. Still inhabited, some had multiple rooms and passageways, even stables for livestock.

At the village market, a single vegetable was in season. Last week it was cucumbers in Istanbul. Green plums filled the baskets in the hamlet of Ürgüp, where a group of women waved me over. They were dressed in rough woven clothes and floral headscarves, their faces etched with deep lines. A younger woman, maybe my age, took my hand and led me into her cave home. Pots and pans, bunches of garlic and sprigs of herbs hung from the rock roof. "*Güzel*," I said, her child clinging to her skirt. "Beautiful." Her ruddy cheeks blushed a deeper shade of red. I loved these moments that were all too short on an organized tour.

I had "Tourist" stamped all over me as I followed the crowd, not all of whom I liked. The American couple, Larry and Linnie, bragged about their travels, not knowing anything about Turkey. The English were quieter, sometimes aloof and sometimes charming. I never knew which and had to juggle my role between public discretion and my private relationship with Alim. It was a facade of pretenses I wasn't good at.

Every evening, Alim settled the group with their deluge of questions about the next day's itinerary, then we'd escape to the privacy of our room and drink cool white raki. "You are becoming indispensable," he said in his proper English. We never mentioned how long I would stay in Turkey or when I would travel on to India.

"Larry is a fat fool. You'd think history began in the 20th century with Philadelphia the epicentre. The next bottle of beer interests him more than anything else," Alim laughed as he staggered across the room, rubbing his belly, imitating Larry.

"It's Linnie who drives me crazy. Me this and me that. She wears her slinky dress, flirts with the bus driver, anyone in pants, and you too, even though she's twice your age."

"Are you jealous?" he asked, pouring himself another raki. One drink had me giddy.

"I can't imagine you'd take up with Linnie if I did leave for a day or two," I giggled at the thought. "What do you think? Me travelling on my own a bit," I said, thinking it would ease the tension, particularly with the elderly Brits.

"I will tell you what to do," Alim declared.

"I will do as I wish," I said, stunned by his words.

"It is not possible. It is not acceptable. To do as you please," he spat my words back. "In the West, you are only concerned with your individuality, here in the East brotherhood is more important," he lectured.

"Alim, I'm so sorry. I only wanted to make it easier for you." I tried to reason, to comfort, to apologize, putting my arms around him. I wanted a cultural compromise, but he pushed me away and for the first time would not share our bed.

10

Water to a Desert Flower

AT THE UNDERGROUND CITIES of Kaymakli and Derinkuyu, once Christian dwellings dating back to the seventh century, there were miles of excavated tunnels, and a complex network of rooms, churches, schools, wells, wineries and even stables for livestock. Carved out of the soft volcanic rock of Cappadocia, they were able to shelter 20,000 people. The cities had been built as hiding places during times of persecution and raids in the Arab-Byzantine wars starting in the seventh century, the Mongolian invasions of the 14th century and as a refuge from the Turkish rulers of the Ottoman era, as late as the early 20th century.

We went deeper and deeper into the rocky maze of Turkey's tumultuous past. I tagged along, still reeling from the night before. I needed to excavate my heart.

After a long bus ride over the central Anatolian plain, we arrived in Konya, the town where Rumi, the mystical Sufi poet, had once lived. Rumi, known as Mevlânâ, was the master of Sufis, the whirling dervishes who danced to free their souls for sublime union with the divine. I sat in my seat at the back, where I always sat, and read his poetry.

Let the beauty we love be what we do.
There are a hundred ways to kneel and kiss the ground.

"Rumi. Please. Sweep *me* into the sublime. Teach *me* how to kneel and kiss the ground. Show *me* the way of love," I prayed as I tiptoed around Alim.

"The heat is blistering hot. If I'd only known," Linnie whined at the air-conditioned restaurant in Konya.

"Known what?" Sybil, an aged Brit who took inconveniences in her stride, quipped back.

"Let's eat," Larry interrupted, shovelling the *kofta* balls, lamb spiced with mint, onto his plate. He took a long swallow of beer then burped, annoying Linnie.

After lunch, I walked through the conservative Muslim town to the Mevlânâ Museum, my pashmina shawl thrown over my shoulders. Alim and his flock were just ahead. At the Gate of the Dervishes leading onto a spacious courtyard, a young Turk approached me.

"Would you like a guide for the museum for my own pleasure if you desire?" he inquired in his best English. I stared blankly at the boy. I hadn't shaken Alim's words of that morning. "Why do you spread your friendliness around so much? Give it to me and me alone."

"No, thank you," I hurried past the boy and on to Alim. He stood in the courtyard, commanding the attention of all as he eloquently described Islamic architecture, interspersed with quotes from Rumi. Even Dr. Egerton seemed impressed.

"You are the girl I could find oneness of soul with, just like Mevlânâ. If you give yourself to me, you will have everything you need: devotion, respect and love," he said, later in our room. He seduced me with his waterfall of words. Alim was my Rumi.

I looked out the window to the green-domed mausoleum, where the spiritual master lay. It had a numinous quality, this place where Rumi had whirled in ecstatic reverence, in and out of light and shadow. I was whirling too, in and out of love with Alim. There were a hundred ways to kneel and kiss the ground, but we weren't on equal ground. The man had the power. The woman would obey.

"You were happy, now you are sad? What is the matter?" Alim asked.

"Can we ever be equals as a man and a woman?"

"Don't talk nonsense. You are my woman and have all my respect."

"Alim, I am afraid," I said, not daring to look at him as he paced the room.

"We are worlds apart. You must go in the morning," he said, with an about-face finality. A sleepless night filled our bed with tears. He could not fathom my need to be understood and I could not fathom that he'd ask me to leave.

In the morning, I only said goodbye to Dr. Egerton, as Alim busied himself with the group. Wearing her unflattering khaki pants and her sun hat askew, she took both my hands in hers. "Go your own way. Be strong," she said. Maybe she had fallen in love with a foreign man once upon a time.

I boarded the regular bus heading for the coast and found a seat between two Turkish women. I couldn't read or write or talk or smile; breathing was hard all the way to Antalya.

"*Merhaba.*" The villagers extended a friendly hello in the town built around a picturesque harbour. I spent two days in Antalya, bought fresh fruit at the market, visited the museum and strolled the beach, my heart on hold, not yet ready to say goodbye to Alim.

On a day tour with a busload of Turkish tourists, I went from one extraordinary site to another, unprepared for the archeological marvels of Antalya, Perge and Aspendos. Alexander the Great had been given the key to Perge and Saint Paul the Apostle had been a pilgrim to the holy site. I sat on the steps of antiquity contemplating the mess of my life. A little lizard crouched on the scorched stone beside me, its eyes darting back and forth. I was darting back and forth too, unsure where to go or what to do. The gods and goddesses, their arms and heads missing, stood by in the silence of the ruins.

I returned to Istanbul. After an interminably long trip on the bus, and the sweaty, overcrowded train to Yenimahalle, I found my way back to Alim. He threw his arms around me, smothering me with kisses.

"Let me breathe," I whispered into his warm body.

"I have missed you, breath of my soul," his words like water to a desert flower. In his cramped kitchen we cooked *imam bayildi*, eggplant stuffed with onion, garlic and mint, as Alim sang Turkish love songs, convincing me we were the perfect couple.

11

Delicious as Ripe Mangos

CINNAMON DRIFTED ON THE AIR at the spice market, the crushed spices piled high in pyramids of rich golds and greens and saffron red. Every other day when Alim worked, I came to the Grand Bazaar, as vibrant a locale as I had ever seen. Often, I would meet Abdullah in the carpet market, a kind man who taught me how to know a quality carpet and the art of carpet repair. He had a head of gray frizzy hair, a generous smile and welcomed me to sit in his shop, like family, like a daughter. I practised my Turkish with him, proud I could converse on everyday matters.

"Please, you sit. Drink tea with me. My lucky day for business," he said as I stirred twigs of green mint in the small cup. Abdullah served the thick brew to his customers. I became a regular, sitting for hours, content to watch the jostling of West and East, bartering for a good buy.

"I bought a beautiful *kilim* from Abdullah today," I said, showing Alim the hand-woven carpet of gold and brown cotton.

"You are wasting your time in the bazaar repairing carpets with Abdullah. You are dreaming of other men."

"He is just a friend, like a father to me. You are my dream."

"It is not possible that a man sees you as just a friend."

"And you? Do you see every woman as someone to sleep with?"

"I am tired of your American nonsense. In Turkey, women do not repair carpets in the market."

I needed Alim more than I needed Abdullah. I promised I'd only go one more time to say goodbye to Abdullah. My fragile peace with Alim was restored.

I replaced going to the market with the *hammam*, the traditional public bath and a vital part of Islamic culture. The oldest baths in Istanbul date back a millennium and were often attached to a mosque for men to wash before prayers. The baths have evolved into public gathering places for men and women, for locals and foreigners.

I entered the hot and humid room, feeling self-conscious, wearing a pair of loose-fitting underwear provided at the front desk. The room with graceful arches and a domed roof was full of naked Turkish ladies, of all ages and sizes. A very fat lady began to scrub and scour me as I lay naked too, on a cool blue marble slab in the inner sanctum of women. I quickly overcame my reserve, surrendering to the steamy pleasure of being washed. A sensual delight unheard of in my own culture. Bristling clean, I pulled on my jeans and T-shirt and stepped back into the hectic streets of Istanbul.

In the evening, Alim and I walked the promenade on the Sea of Marmara, snacking on fresh-roasted hazelnuts. Fish sizzled on grills, caught fresh that day by the fishermen who sat mending their nets. Vendors passing in the street with their wooden carts called out their wares. After sunset, the muezzin made his last mesmerizing call to the faithful, the ritual of Islam.

At night in our basement dwelling, we drank raki and smoked cigarettes, the strong local Murads, making me cough and cry. Alim made me cry too as I tried to navigate his pride, jealousy and anger. It suffocated me.

Other times, he wanted me adorned with painted toes, scarves and jewelry, like the belly dancer shimmying at the *taverna*. I felt lovely and adored in ways I had never known, but I wanted him to admire my mind.

"My sweet queen," he said with a smile, as if he had never considered this.

BY MY THIRD MONTH IN ISTANBUL, days ran into each other, busy with cleaning, cooking, blocking mice holes, receiving uncles for tea and picking up my mail at Turk Ekspres. That day a packet of letters arrived; Mom inviting us home for Christmas, anxious that I settle down with a man, regardless of his country and culture, and my father discouraging foreign romance.

Alim came home with two matching T-shirts and 16 red carnations. I didn't say a word about Christmas, our future not yet in focus. He proposed a holiday just for the two of us, and a day later we were on the early morning bus to Izmir, Fethiye and Ölüdeniz. The luxury yachts anchored in the harbour of Ölüdeniz launched Alim onto his favourite subject: the evils of Western imperialism.

"America is decadent and in moral decline," he raved.

"Well, I am Canadian. Your perception of the West is all skewed." I hated him for hating my world.

"You are too extreme," he'd tell me, though I had to navigate our rocky relationship to avoid *his* extremes. I wasn't sure I could give up my life as I knew it and live with Alim. Even in our crucible of love. My questions tore me apart.

We travelled on by dolmus, the taxi full of village people. I'd speak in Turkish and everyone laughed. Alim praised my progress, and I savoured these moments like sunshine after a storm.

Traversing through cotton fields and citrus orchards, we arrived at the small town of Kaş, the ancient town of Antiphillus. The fragrance of orange filled the air and purple rhododendrons claimed the hot Aegean sun. We explored the ruins of the Greek theatre built before Christ, dedicated to Bacchus, the god of wine. We ate fresh village bread and cheese and fell over and over in love in our rustic room. Then I'd pull Alim into the Mediterranean waters, where we'd float away arguments under an azure sky, forgetting we'd fought the day before. In Kaş, I believed everything was possible.

Our days were as delicious as ripe mangos that grew in abundance on the roadside. Evenings quickly brought us back to our troublesome realities. The village hotels repeatedly asked, "Are you married?" Alim replied affirmatively that we were engaged, but we were frequently turned away.

"You need a certificate of engagement," a bushy-mustached hotel proprietor ordered. "Go to the police station." Alim and the man exchanged a few words in their language, a secret code between men, sizing one another up, the big man twirled his wedding ring on his thick finger. With an exchange of *lira*, we got the room. The present collided with the future. Our future. What would become of us?

Hitchhiking into Bodrum in the back of a pickup, Alim draped his arm around me, a reckless carefree embrace with a foreign woman, not the way of a Turkish couple. Maybe we had a chance in the East-West dream of love. That night he danced and sang in a local taverna and I, the only Westerner, sat watching the ways of Turkish men, feeling alone in an Islamic land.

We arrived in Ephesus, two solitudes, jostled between love and loss. The city of antiquity had been built over 2,000 years ago and was one of the most significant Greco-Roman ruins, its temples and fountains carved in marble. We explored the amphitheatre, the library, and stood before the lone pillar at the Temple of Artemis, one of the seven wonders of the ancient world.

"Tell me we will never part," Alim asked in the sacred sanctuary.

"Yes," I said, filled with irrepressible joy.

12

My Foolish Heart,
My Faithful Heart

"**I WILL MISS YOU EVERY MOMENT** of every day. I will wait for you with all my heart," Alim promised on the dock of Kusadasi. He needed to return to Istanbul for another tour of Cappadocia and I was leaving for the Greek island of Samos.

"It is only for a week," I said, holding him close, knowing we were just a breath away from a breakup. I boarded a small ferry overloaded with passengers and waved goodbye to my unpredictable man waving back to me. The boat headed out to sea, rolling on uneasy swells, adrift on international waters, tossed between Turkey and Greece.

The beauty of Samos washed over me, the air infused with the fragrance of mint, in a week filled with anguishing decisions and sulky bouts of tears. I couldn't even blame the unbreathable July heat as I toured the island on the back of a motorcycle, the hint of a breeze caressing my bare arms and legs. For moments, Alim was far away and forgotten. I could ride away, another happier me, no regulations holding me back, no orders keeping me silent.

The driver dropped me in Manolates, a mountain village with white stone houses trimmed with blue as bright as the Aegean Sea. I could see the Turkish coast not far over the sea, beckoning, and turned away to drink in the splendour of Greece – the olive groves, pine trees and vineyards terracing the slopes. A woman sat at a sidewalk restaurant on the edge of the village. She wore jeans, a burgundy blouse, several buttons left open, and a sequined scarf loosely draped over her hair.

"*Merhaba, sen turksen*?" I asked, on a hunch she wasn't Greek.

"Yes, I am Turkish," she said and offered me a seat at her table. "My name is Silaah."

Before long, our true stories spilled out, as easy as the Samos Nectar, the fine amber wine we drank. "I have fallen in love many times. Studying in Paris, vacationing in Spain, but I need my home and family. They are my roots." Silaah said, wise in the ways of love in a foreign country. I devoured a Turkish woman's perspective and she listened carefully to mine.

"If only Alim and I didn't fight so much, I'd stay in your country, with him," I said, knowing that no matter which way I tried to define home or belonging or culture or love, his country was not mine.

We snacked on a plate of cheese and olives and drank a second glass of nectar on that short afternoon that disappeared into our separate lives. She needed to return to her Anatolian man, steadfast in her commitments, and I needed to return to mine.

"Go back to Turkey and try again," Silaah said as she waved goodbye. "He is waiting."

It took two days to return to Istanbul from Samos. As the gray shadows of night descended, I hurried through the narrow streets of Yenimahalle. Arriving at our basement apartment, I knocked at the door anticipating his surprise, one day early. The door opened and his face fell. Ghazi, Alim's friend, sat cross-legged on the floor with two Western women. They were drinking raki and eating *börek*, cheese-filled pastries, bought from Ahmed the baker down the street, the same food Alim served me the first time in his home.

"These are new friends we are introducing to Istanbul," Alim said, not looking me in the eye, his face flushed red.

"Where are you from?" I said to the American girl who looked like me with her short dark hair and blue eyes.

"San Francisco," she said. "And you?"

"Canada. I live here now. With Alim." We chatted as women do. She wasn't to blame, though I could hardly breathe.

Alim waved for a dolmus as Ghazi and the two visitors walked out the door. "It was nothing," he said. I knew there would be no further discussion and let him sweep it away and shower me with sweet attention.

My days returned to solitary; only nights were with Alim. Sometimes he came back early, with a bag full of bread, cheese, olives, pistachios and a pomegranate. We'd make dinner as he talked philosophy and I shared my everyday stories, my everyday intrigue with his country. My happiness. My worries.

Sometimes he came home late, and I'd sit alone, write in my journal, cook or clean our house. I knew he met every beautiful tourist at the palace, yet once again he accused me of romance with Abdullah, whom I hadn't seen in weeks. I was sick with Alim's possessive rages.

It was the Sea of Marmara that saved us from ourselves. We strolled in the balmy Istanbul evenings and forgave each other our fierce fights. We drank beer at sidewalk stalls and spat pits of plump cherries into the street. We laughed and sometimes Alim cried his sea of tears and sang his eternal love. We talked about the baby we wanted to have, or we talked about politics, usually Alim raving about America and its many crimes. I'd agree or disagree, and he'd call me his sensitive darling, his fiery woman, his intelligent girl. It seemed a lifetime ago that we'd fallen in love in Cappadocia, in Kaş, in Ephesus.

One ordinary day, going to the market, cooking, cleaning and waiting for Alim, I knew I had to leave. Travelling to India was no longer an option. "I need to go home, Alim. We are fighting too much. It's just for a while," my voice cracked and whispered, "*Seni seviyorum*," I love you.

"You are doomed to the life of an endless wanderer if you leave," Alim said, begging me not to go. Words, words, words. I could no longer listen to his pleas. I packed my bags, along with two Turkish kilims from the carpet market and the books I'd studied diligently to learn his language.

In the taxi, en route to the airport, he had a new appeal. "Someday soon my dearest, you will return to Turkey, and someday I will live in your beloved Canada."

"You will love Canada," I said, knowing he would choose his country, not mine.

Drenched with heat and commotion, Istanbul, the city where East meets West, flew by and I flew away in a long silent wail of goodbye.

AT TOPKAPI, a prince of the palace invited me into his life. Of course, I accepted. Young and in love, his passionate, poetic world absorbed me. He wanted me to be his every goddess – the sinner and the saint – and to be his wife, Turkish, traditional and obedient. In the squalid apartment we called our love nest, I clung to his eloquent words of undying devotion.

Was it love imagined, love lived or love lost? His tears still hot on my cheeks kept me hooked for months. Then the day came to crawl out of the fairy tale forest where I had wandered too long. Alim became a faded promise, a folded letter. It weighed heavy on my heart. My foolish heart, my faithful heart.

A year had passed since I'd hopped that freight train, off to see the world, my dreams as wide as a prairie landscape, as fast as a runaway train. Only the dream to go to India had been detoured by love.

Summer turned to September and a cold wind blew. At the beach, a string of gulls sat on a washed-up log. The log, once a majestic west coast cedar, hauled by barge to the Port of Vancouver, had broken loose, been tossed at sea and swept ashore. Driftwood. That was me, washed up in the wet grayness, a drifter, in between, moving on.

The wild, random unpredictability of travel was my fastest
ticket to happiness. It would save me, I thought, though I knew
I had to land in my life, my country and my work. Nursing was
a challenging and worthy profession. I could commit to my new
position, and I could also grapple with my career. In the '70s, jobs
were easily left and easily found.

But staying home was the sensible choice. I needed Canada
like I needed my true north. I decorated a funky apartment in
an old house on the Vancouver east side and made it my home. I
listened to my favourite LPs – Joe Cocker, Janis Joplin, and B.B.
King, King of the Blues. I made dinner for friends, my favourite,
Turkish iman bayildi. I needed to nest, and the Port of Vancouver
was a nesting place. For a while.

THREE

Discovery, 1977–1979

But nothing in India is identifiable,
the mere asking of a question causes it
to disappear or to merge into something else.

—E.M. FORSTER

13

Land of the Morning Calm

THE EASTERN SKY WAS FLAMING ORANGE, silhouetting mushroom clouds that looked like atomic explosions over the rugged hills of South Korea. I was flying into Joseon, Land of the Morning Calm. And I was calm. Nothing like the final week in Canada with my last-minute anxieties leaving on a trip for Asia, where I knew no one and had no specific plans.

It had been a year since my return from Turkey, a year since Alim. I'd let him wash over me and wash away, though every day I wore the pendant he'd given me, *inshallah*, God willing, inscribed in Arabic in filigree gold. I'd made my choice. With or without God, with or without a man, I was on my way to India, wanderlust fuelling my dream.

The elderly, bone-thin man sitting beside me had slept most of the flight. "I am the chief executive of Korea's cultural exchange program," he said, munching salted peanuts. I gobbled up the condensed version of everything Korean, recounted by Mr. Kim Gi Hwan: the Korean War from 1950 to 1953, to the demilitarized zone or DMZ on the fractured Korean peninsula, to the country's relationship with its powerhouse neighbours, China and Japan.

On arrival in Seoul, Mr. Kim insisted on taking me to my hotel. His chauffeur, as old as Mr. Kim, put my scruffy orange knapsack in the trunk of a luxurious black Cadillac and we drove to the dumpy-looking downtown YMCA I'd chosen from *Asia on $5 a Day.*

"It's a national holiday week and we Koreans pay respect to our elders. Are you free to join my family to visit our ancestral burial grounds and have a picnic in the countryside tomorrow?" Mr. Kim asked, as if I might have been busy.

"I'd love to go," I said, astounded at my good fortune.

"Come to my office at ten in the morning," he said, handing me his business card, as the chauffeur carried my bag to the door.

By noon, I ventured into the streets of Seoul, a city of seven million people. School children in uniform and women with shopping baskets wove their way through the crowded sidewalks. Chestnuts, dried fish, sausage and corn roasted on small coal fires, along with unrecognizable foods in red and green sauces, smelling strongly of garlic. I didn't know where to go, what to eat or how to say please or thank you. At a roadside stand, I pointed at the food on display and ate a bun filled with an unknown ingredient. Korean food would require a strong stomach or a good sense of culinary adventure. Fortunately, I had both.

Jet-lagged, I returned to the Y, where I slept till morning. For breakfast, I ate a bowl of spicy rice with cucumber then was off to find Mr. Kim.

Impeccably dressed in a pressed white shirt and black pleated pants, Mr. Kim greeted me at the door of his spacious office. "Please meet my family, my son Ji-Hun, my daughter-in-law Soo-Yun and my youngest son Wook," he said. The three sat formally on a plush green and gold couch, the boys dressed in Western suits and Soo-Yun in a traditional, full-length, high-waisted brocade dress. I felt sloppy in my jean skirt, T-shirt and running shoes, having dressed for a country picnic.

The chauffeur, Mr. Lee, drove the five of us to the city of Cheongju, two hours south of Seoul. From there we followed a pitted country road to a small village of brick houses with bright turquoise tiled roofs and cows in tiny courtyards. We continued by foot on muddy raised paths separating field after field of rice, the yellow stalks ready for harvest.

Soo-Yun, struggling in her long dress as she waded across a small creek, reached out to her husband, Ji-Hun. He offered his hand and they both fell in. Wook and I jumped in too, splashing each other; even serious Mr. Kim and Mr. Lee joined in.

Dripping wet, we climbed up a pine-forested slope to a small clearing at the grandfather's tomb. The names of his male children and grandchildren were inscribed on the granite stone, not his female progeny, Mr. Kim explained.

"Do not give your children money. Give them books." Mr. Kim translated his father's epitaph. Ji-Hun and Wook laid out food and water on a marble slab, then bowed four times to their grandfather. I had no such tradition in my country; my ancestors, buried in places far from home or scattered to sea. It felt like something missing in my own culture and highly valued in another.

It was the formality of Mr. Kim and his Korean family that was strikingly different from my family. We were a rough and tumble bunch, at least the five of us kids who tried hard to outdo each other with acts we considered brave, like jumping off dangerous cliffs into rivers below or climbing the highest of trees, those tall solemn trees, high in the sky where no one could find me. I called myself Queen of the Cedars. I couldn't imagine Ji-Hun or Wook and certainly not Soo-Yun being so reckless.

The first-born in my family, my siblings arrived on schedule every two years. Brothers 1, 2, 3 and 4. I was displaced, misplaced and replaced – at least that's what it felt like. Mom worked hard to bring up her unruly children, and my father, the more lenient of the two, took us camping, fishing, skiing and skating, though neither of them pampered or spoiled their children.

Mom was brought up poor on the prairies during the Depression years, moving from shack to shack. Still, she was a prairie girl at heart and loved the rolling hills of Alberta, farm life and fresh cream on her morning porridge from the cows she milked herself. How many times had I heard my mother say that they were the poorest of the poor, she only wore hand-me-downs, never had proper family dinners and couldn't afford to go to the picture shows. She wanted to give her children everything she'd never had, like piano lessons and those proper family dinners, particularly on Sunday after church when we'd eat roast beef, scalloped potatoes and fresh carrots from the garden she tended. She never wasted a thing, not even a brown paper bag; the ones I had to bring back from school and use for a week of lunches. Leaving even a morsel of food on our plates was not tolerated, though we all found a way of throwing pieces of gristle to our golden lab Sheba under the kitchen table. My mother just wanted to stamp the poverty out of her life.

I remember the noise, the bravado and, in our teens, some misdemeanours with the law, some of my siblings acting out with booze, drugs and rock & roll. I partook a little, but not to any serious degree. After all, I was a registered nurse at 20 years of age.

"I want to go to Alaska," Soo-Yun suddenly said, as if she'd been preparing the phrase for some time, revealing her secret dream.

"Very exciting," I said. "And I'm going to India." The family looked at me as if I'd said, "the moon." We sat on the slope overlooking the rice fields, eating sweet and sticky rice cakes. They practised their English, and I learned *gomawoyo* for thank you. It was the gentlest of days, on a country picnic, worshipping the dead.

I SCRUTINIZED MY ENGLISH MAP, in a city without English signposts, as I walked from one temple to another. Korea had a rich 1,700-year-old Buddhist culture and the serene Bongeunsa temple with its 300 woodblock carvings of Buddhist *sutras* was well worth the long walk.

Soo-Yun had recommended the Dongdaemun food market, which I found after another baffling stroll across Seoul. Old and young women sat on squat stools, slicing and chopping food. Pig carcasses hung from the ceiling, chickens clucked in bamboo boxes and purple eels wiggled in plastic crates. A plump lady selling dried fish chuckled as I winced with the overwhelming stench.

After six days of exploring the temples and markets of Seoul, I wanted to see the country and miraculously found the right bus to Chuncheon. It was a small city I'd chosen in my guidebook as the halfway stop across the peninsula of Korea. With a ripple of panic, I walked along the main street, a conspicuous Westerner with a knapsack on her back. The utter foreignness of everything disoriented me.

"Hotel?" I asked people in the street, though no one seemed to understand. Reduced to sign language and about to cry, a man with a briefcase approached me.

"Where are you going? My name is Yong Kee Ton," he said, blushing as he stumbled over a few words in English. He took me to a *yeogwan*, a Korean-style inn nearby. The couple, surprised with their unexpected guest, showed me a modest room with a bamboo mat on the floor and a sliding rice paper door.

"*Gomawoyo*, thank you, Yong," I said to the young man, never sure if I was calling someone by their first or last name.

It was the best of evenings, sharing a meal of egg-rice and *kimchi*, Korea's hot pickled cabbage, swallowing it down with a rough brewed beer. Mr. and Mrs. Jeong and I had a delightful, impossible conversation.

By morning I was on a bus for Sokcho. My stomach lurched with every hairpin bend in the road as we wound up a mountainside with stunning sharp drops to the valley below. The mountain's sheer rock face was a climber's paradise. Just last week the first Korean team had successfully reached the summit of Mount Everest, a story I'd read in *Asia Times*.

At the seaside city of Sokcho, a city close to the DMZ and the gateway to Mount Seoraksan National Park, I met Mr. Rhee, a rotund man with a wispy mustache. At his yeogwan he showed me the cold-water hand pump in the courtyard and the outhouse that was shared by the house next door. For dinner, in their tiny kitchen, Mrs. Rhee served a large plate of small, dried fish, and what seemed to be pickled turnip. The taste was sharp but edible as I swallowed it with tea. I soon retired to my bedroom, where I could hear my gracious hosts snore loudly throughout the night.

In the morning, Mrs. Rhee laughed, her eyes crinkling in her round face, as I tried to wash some clothes on her washing board. She must have wondered how someone as clumsy as me managed laundry in my own country. Taking me by the arm, we walked down the dirt lane to a public bath, not at all like the hammam in Istanbul, with its exquisite marble tiles and carved fountains spouting warm water. In Sokcho, a few women sat naked on a low bench, washing with lukewarm water running from ordinary faucets. Mrs. Rhee and I undressed and sat down on the bench. All activity stopped and every woman looked at me. An old lady with tightly permed hair and a face full of wrinkles crouched beside me and touched my breasts. Mrs. Rhee said a few sharp words to her and handed me a bar of soap. The ladies carried on watching me as I watched them.

Early the next day, Mr. Rhee took me on his motorcycle to the entry gate of Seoraksan park. Autumn trees in vivid red and orange lined the road. "Why am I setting out alone into the forest?" I thought as he drove away. "I'll be fine. I have my water bottle, a package of peanuts, two chocolate bars and a park guidebook," I reasoned as a steady stream of cars and buses crept up the steep hill to the parking lot. A car pulled up with its occupants excitedly waving for me to join them. I jumped in.

I had never seen so much activity in a designated wilderness area, certainly not in Canada, the trails overrun with hikers on a day's outing. Children marched by in uniform, holding placards, maybe boy scouts or girl guides or a youth military brigade. Some adults barked orders with loudspeakers, maybe calling their children, or pronouncing park regulations or political slogans. It had to be a national holiday.

Mr. and Mrs. Pyo, and their three daughters Nari, Mi-Ja and Sun-Hee, were city people, Mrs. Pyo a giveaway in her high-heeled shoes. She never stopped smiling at me, her Western guest she'd taken under her wing, and I didn't let go of her girls for fear of losing "my family."

At a rocky outcrop by a picturesque waterfall, Mrs. Pyo pulled out an array of food from the packs and arranged the dishes on a cloth. There was cold bean curd with chili sauce, fish cakes, pork buns and hot barley tea in a thermos. The children sat close to me, giggling and printing their names in my journal.

Koreans were polite people, but on the return to the congested parking lot, agitated men honked their horns, gesticulated wildly and yelled at each other, undoubtedly peppered with Korean swear words. Mr. Pyo, red in the face, was yelling too. Mrs. Pyo tried to distract the girls and smiled at me throughout the ordeal. The pandemonium settled, and my lovely family drove me back to Sokcho. "*Gomawoyo*" was proclaimed by all in the Land of the Morning Calm.

14

Love on the Run

THE YONGKANG BEEF NOODLE HOUSE was a family-run affair like most eating establishments in Taipei. I sat at a crowded table, slurping noodles and drinking beer with a group of journalists stationed in Taiwan, the regulars at the Yongkang. They spoke English and French interchangeably, dotted with Mandarin. The harsh realities, social injustices and political absurdities of Taiwan were on the table. The liberation of mainland communist China was the nationalistic goal of this small island claiming to be the rightful leader of "One China." I listened intently, fascinated with global politics and the journalists who chased the stories.

Particularly Gino, an Italian freelance photojournalist on assignment in Taiwan.

"I cover all the hot spots around the world," he said to me, none too modestly.

"I've seen a few myself," I replied.

"Let me show you around then." He took my hand and led me away into the warm October evening. Taipei was a study of contrasts: half-built modernism met garish temples with ferocious dragons warding off evil spirits on streets bursting with activity. Elderly people sat on tiny plastic stools on narrow sidewalks eating from plastic bowls. Old men played board games or read the newspaper. An old woman wearing black baggy trousers stood on the corner selling bits and pieces – chewing gum, lipstick and cigarettes. She gave me a toothless grin.

The neon-lit Ningxia night market swarmed with Taiwanese eating at a multitude of stand-up stalls. Everything sizzled, from succulent braised goose to oyster omelets to steamed pork dumplings and spicy fish ball soup. Gino and I swallowed down delicacies, no matter how unfamiliar, with Taiwanese beer.

"I'm leaving for Kaohsiung tomorrow. Here's my hotel card. Find me," he said as he walked me back to the hostel, his camera with its long telephoto lens slung over his shoulder. One kiss and I decided to go to Kaohsiung.

THE ESSENTIAL PLACE to visit in Taipei, the National Palace Museum had a stunning collection of scroll paintings, porcelain, jade and ivory sculptures. The collection, spanning 8,000 years of Chinese art, captured my attention for several hours, but it was contemporary life that intrigued me.

"Come out to Snake Alley with us," Wilfred and Johann said. They were clean-cut Austrian boys, just out of college, staying at the Y. "You'll see the real Taipei."

We walked to the notorious alley that consisted of two steamy blocks of brightly lit shops selling a formidable array of Chinese traditional products, specializing in aphrodisiacs. Snack bars advertised snake soups, snake wines, snake powder and pickled snake testicles. Others sold turtle blood and monkey heads. Men who looked as slimy as their products were squeezing the heads of live snakes (what kind of snake I didn't ask) at their stands. They mixed the expelled venom with other ingredients and drank it on the spot. A group of Taiwanese and a few tourists stood about, listening to the men brag about the aphrodisiac properties in crude English.

Several scantily clad women wearing gaudy makeup stood nearby between the snake show and the porn shops. They swayed to "Hotel California" blasting from a club with a crooked sign called "The Ecstasy." The women were only girls. Two of them, maybe 16 years old, approached Johann and Wilfred, fawning over the boys. Johann gently pushed them away. One of the girls, in a flimsy pink dress, looked at me, our eyes saying what we couldn't speak: "This is my life and take care of me and go to hell" she was saying. "I understand. No, I don't understand. I wish you had another life. You are just a girl. These men are wicked. I am so sorry. I wish you a better life," I was saying. With a defiant shrug, she walked back to her corner.

"Snake Alley makes me sick. Let's get back to the Y," I said to the boys, needing to shake off the dark underbelly of Taipei. The girl in the pink dress glanced at me as I walked by. I'd remember her eyes.

I CHOSE THE TOWN OF CHIAYI, a four-hour train ride from Taipei and halfway to Kaohsiung at the southern tip of the island, for an overnight stop. A Taiwanese schoolgirl wearing floral pants and a floppy hat sat next to me eating plums. "I love you," she said in faltering English, offering me a plum. As we got off the train, she took my hand and invited me to her home.

Lien Hua lived in an unusual utilitarian house, five skinny floors high. Her father, Dr. Yang, a pediatrician, was as serious as his house, but her plump mother made up for her husband's reserve with a bubbly outpouring in Mandarin. Mrs. Yang prepared an excellent dinner of sweet bean paste dumplings and small, hard-boiled eggs, maybe quail, soaked in soy sauce.

After dinner, in the formal sitting room, we attempted conversation, seriously limited by language. After a polite interlude, Lien Hua took me up to the fifth-floor attic room, filled with dusty cartons and a cot. I woke in the middle of the night to strange noises, a whooshing sound, alive and getting louder. Not mice, nor the wind, I was scared. I crept down the unlit stairs to Lien Hua's room on the fourth floor and climbed into her bed. They were bats – flying rats in my opinion.

For breakfast, Mrs. Yang served a large helping of an unidentified stew that I ate as she hovered over me. Lien Hua and I set off on old bicycles, wobbling and weaving through Chiayi past a red-tiled temple with a ferocious dragon roof to the fish market. Motorcyclists screeched in with large sharks strapped to their bikes. Women wearing bamboo hats tied with bright coloured scarves chopped the shark into steak size pieces. Breakfast at Lien Hua's must have been shark.

"WE HAVE A FEW DAYS TOGETHER. This is all I have, it's now or never," Gino said, pulling me into his arms, his kiss insistent. I followed him up the stairs to his room. "Never" was not an option.

Morning, noon and nights were with Gino, between appointments, between stories, between pictures. I'd never seen a professional photojournalist in action. The deadlines; the urgency; seeking the story; the camera searching for the image, sensitive or intrusive; face-to-face clicking lives. He was documenting Taiwan's petrochemical industry in the country's largest industrial hub. As he got his stories, I strolled among the thousands of factory workers doing piecemeal work at assembly lines. With no unions or benefits, they earned two dollars a day. They were eager to talk, but I didn't speak their language and they didn't speak mine.

"You are my true woman, my fresh fruit," Gino said at the end of his day. His juicy words seduced me as he showered me with *amore*, though he liked to talk big about his life, his ideas and his experience. I played along, attentive and responsive until our fifth day in Kaohsiung.

"You never hear a word I say." My flash of anger was deflected with his story, his sad childhood, his sad broken marriage, his need to live now in his own life.

"I won't let anyone depend on me. You must not care about me, only love me now then leave me," he said. It sounded like an order. My resentment simmered. I could either carry it with me, like a piece of extra baggage, or throw it off like a change of clothes.

Male attention kept me in the game, though I hadn't lost sight of my reason for being in Taiwan. It was a stepping stone to India. Gino was another Alim. An international playboy. A dangerous liaison. I had a choice to live in the moment, his moment, our moment, or miss the moment. I'd toppled into loving him. He was worldly, exciting and a woman's secret desire to catch in her love nest. At least, he was *my* secret desire.

Back in Taipei, we went to Movie Row, a street with gigantic posters depicting violence and romance side by side. Throngs of people, old and young, walked arm in arm as I walked with the tough man beside me. I had no practical formula for romance and had fallen too quickly for Gino. I swung from laughter to tears.

"Don't waste your silly tears. *La vita è bella*," he said with a theatrical flourish. "You are a grand adventurer. Love your life."

On our last morning in Daan Forest Park, we watched old men with long whiskers and loose bellies stroll. They were carrying bamboo cages with birds of many colours, parakeets, canaries and lovebirds, as if they were walking their dogs. Ducks squawked, and a long-legged heron stood in the pond. A group of older women, young students and businessmen in suspendered pants practised tai chi, moving in slow motion to a timeless rhythm.

Watching tai chi was calming, the gentle push and pull, the subtle meditation of movement and rest, of mind and body. I didn't need to be anywhere else than with Gino, holding hands and holding on to our last day together. That night I'd leave for India, and he'd be in Japan.

Maybe he was already gone, onto another assignment, another conquest. That's what I'd remember, his face blurred, his words lost, love on the run.

15

The Taj

I STEPPED DOWN FROM THE PLANE into a blast of steamy heat squeezed from a cloudy sky. India! I had finally arrived at my long-sought destination, the land with the holiest of rivers, the highest of mountains and the exquisite Taj Mahal. The land where Mahatma Gandhi had changed the course of history and Mother Teresa had captured the heart of the world.

I knew long before landing that India would not be easy but hard and astonishing too, like the sacred cow loitering on the tarmac. It stood in front of a large billboard that stated in English: "Courtesy Keeps Everyone Happy."

"Well, it sure didn't make me happy last time I came to India. This country is bloody impossible," the American businessman who had sat next to me on the plane from Bangladesh said. "Do you really expect to spend six months here all by yourself?" He wiped his forehead dripping with sweat.

Little did he know that India had been on the back burner of my imagination for half a lifetime. Nor did I tell him that a year and a half ago I'd set out on the Orient Express with ambitious plans, albeit vague, to travel overland across Iraq, Iran, Afghanistan and Pakistan. Alim had ambushed all that. It was time to

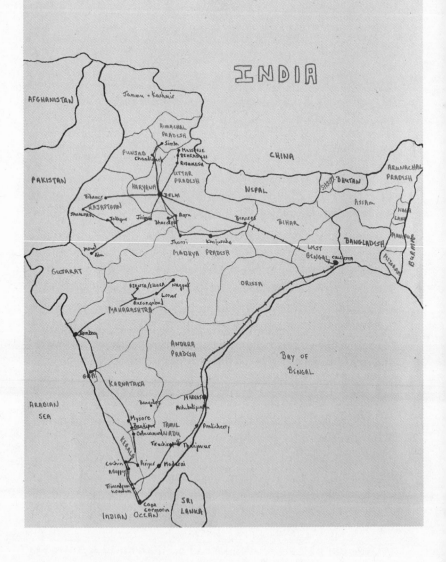

step into the din of India and put love, or what I thought I longed for in love, aside.

Tours are for tourists, and I am a traveller, I said to myself. I coveted this self-definition and told whoever might be listening that I was not the type of girl who took all-inclusive beach vacations. Still, my first full day in India, after a noisy night at the Delhi youth hostel, felt big and scary. I took a tour.

Delhi was a wave of pulsating heat, even in early November, considered one of the cooler months of the year. A mess of auto-rickshaws, black and yellow Hindustan Ambassador taxis, boldly painted rickety buses, bicycles, oxen-pulled carts and a plethora of bony cows all vied for space as I made my way to the tour agency. Mr. Dhaliwal, in a starched-white *kurta*, a long shirt that reached the knees, announced to the waiting passengers that he was a first-rate guide.

"India is a glorious civilization that is 5,000 years old," he began. "Our diversity of religions, languages and cultures is unparalleled," he said with a dramatic sweep of his hand as if looking out the bus window to the densely congested streets would prove his point. We visited several monuments of the Moghul dynasties. At the Lodhi Gardens, I had a welcome moment of silence until a band of children appeared, perfect urchins with bare feet, torn clothing and big brown eyes.

"Please, Mister, please, Ma'am. One *rupee*," they pleaded. India was already tugging at my heart. I had no idea how hard it would pull.

I MADE MY WAY to the outskirts of Delhi in a scooter rickshaw decorated with flashy images of Ganesh, the elephant god. Ganesh, one of the most worshiped deities in the Hindu pantheon, was the remover of all obstacles. He had a twinkle in his eyes, something like my rickshaw *wallah*, who gleefully wove in and out of the chaotic traffic without any apparent concern for obstacles in *his* path.

I was going to meet Dhiram and Sushali. "You will like this young couple. They are the emerging educated middle class. Dhiram is an architect and Sushali has a degree in political science," John, a mutual Canadian friend, had said and arranged the introduction. The driver made several sharp turns, dropping me at a drab, concrete building. I climbed four flights of stairs and knocked on a weathered, green door.

"Come in, come in. You are welcome in our home," Dhiram greeted me warmly. Sushali, in an emerald-green sari, shyly extended her hand. Dhiram, tall and slim, adjusted his heavy-rimmed glasses that half obscured his handsome face and offered me a seat on the floor covered with a plush carpet. One piece of art adorned their modest two-room apartment, a picture of Niagara Falls, a gift from John.

"Sushali, tell me about your political science studies and the work you will do?" I asked as she served a vegetarian lunch of yogurt *raita* and *channa masala*, a chickpea dish of North India, flavoured with fresh coriander. She pulled back her shiny black hair and looked down at the plate of food.

"The degree has achieved its purpose. She has found a husband," Dhiram replied. Sushali glanced up at me and giggled.

ARRIVING IN AGRA, Indian tourists spilled onto the platform in noisy disarray. I jostled my way through the commotion of vendors and travellers and those who made their ragged homes at the station to a guest house nearby. I threw my pack on the bed and set out for the destination I had dreamed of for years: the Taj Mahal.

Shah Jahan, the progressive and cultivated Moghul emperor, had built the Taj in the 17th century as a monument to everlasting love for his wife Mumtaz Mahal. Mumtaz had died giving birth to their 14th child. Mumtaz was her husband's constant companion and trusted confidante, accompanying Shah Jahan on his military campaigns. Court poets and artists praised her beauty and grace, despite her frequent pregnancies. The mausoleum took 20,000 workers and 20 years to build.

I walked slowly through the Great Gate; it was not a place one would rush, toward the Taj. I was instantly enamoured. The aesthetics of architecture, the mythical romance and grandeur of India all merged in the Taj. Rabindranath Tagore, India's renowned poet, wrote:

> Let the splendor of diamond, pearl, and ruby vanish. Only let this one teardrop, this Taj Mahal, glisten spotlessly bright on the cheek of time, forever and ever.

For three days I visited, sitting for a lengthy time on the benches in the landscaped gardens, capturing its many moods. The marble walls, with their delicate inlay of semi-precious stones, shimmered golden at dawn and the colour of ivory in the midday sun. By sunset, the Taj was rose and silver-blue under the moon. Between visits, I wandered around town and watched the everyday life of shopkeepers, schoolchildren and the women of Agra. With their vibrant saris, the jingle-jangle of their bracelets and the graceful sway of their walk, I thought they were the most feminine women in the world.

The poor women walked barefoot with faded saris draped around their gaunt frames. They shuffled along dusty roads with terrible loads on their backs or earthen jugs of water on their heads. Their faces were sometimes smeared with dried turmeric paste, a beauty aid for smooth and radiant skin. They looked like yellow ghosts. The younger ones, their lives not yet lost to the hardness of poverty, had sparkling dark eyes.

At the Agra Tourist Guest House, a dreary little place, I met Winston from England, a gangly, awkward sort of fellow, frequently tripping over things. He was also an authority in classical Indian architecture. Our two rooms, separated from each other with a partition that didn't reach the ceiling, allowed us to chat over the wall. Till late into the evening, the conversation jumped back and forth from the trials of travel to the moments we were stunned breathless by the magnificence of India.

16

Sex in Stone

"**NOT A GOOD PLACE FOR A SINGLE LADY.** Very, very sexy place," the rickshaw wallah said as he drove me to the station. He was referring to the Khajuraho temples with their erotic sculptures.

After five stinking hot hours on the train, I decided to spend the night in Jhansi, halfway to Khajuraho. Sick-looking cows and mangy dogs loitered on the main street. Women walked, their heads covered with drab scarves, their eyes downcast. They glanced up at me with arms and legs uncovered as I walked the short distance to the one-lone-star Hotel Elite.

At breakfast, a large lizard, not a friendly gecko, clung to the ceiling in the dingy dining room. "Boiled eggs and toast please," I said to the server, who looked at his bare feet. After a lengthy wait, the eggs arrived without salt.

"Where is the salt?" I asked, shaking an imaginary saltshaker, my voice rising more sharply than required. The waiter did not understand, or he intended to exasperate me. Five minutes later I sprinkled the salt on my cold eggs. I didn't want to be impatient in another culture and didn't admire this shortcoming in myself. Seeing other foreigners who were impatient, rude or outright furious would temporarily assuage my guilty conscience.

I read books about India, by Indians, as many as I could carry, and scribbled passages in my journal without noting their source, like "dust is the presiding deity, omnipresent and all covering, it hangs in the air and falls on the faces of the people like powder." It may have been Khushwant Singh, the prolific Indian novelist and politician, or it may have been from *Heat and Dust* by Ruth Jhabvala.

In his book, *An Area of Darkness*, V.S. Naipaul cautioned against the haughtiness of foreigners who found conditions too distressing in India.

> You might have seen the smiles of the begging children, the domestic group among the pavement sleepers waking in the cool Bombay morning, father, mother, and baby in a trinity of love, so self-contained that they are as private as if walls had separated them from you. It is your gaze that violates them, your sense of outrage that outrages them…it is your anger that denies them their humanity.

He was right. Too often I had to turn my back on the beggars. Even glancing into their expectant and smiling faces could feel like a plunge into something dark that elicited fear and shame. The encounters with extreme deprivation haunted me, then a woman would walk by wrapped in vibrant colour, her sari shimmering red, her spirited children skipping after her. The men darted about in their rickshaws with garlands of marigolds hanging off the mirrors, or bicycled by in their best pressed clothes, seemingly on a fine outing. They would look at us, perhaps bemused with our shabbiness, carrying our heavy knapsacks, looking exhausted in their world.

That morning in Jhansi, I spotted three Westerners walking toward the station and ran after them. In the overwhelming filth and chaos of an Indian train station, I didn't want to be alone. It was easier to latch on to fellow travellers. Nothing horrible had happened with Indian men. They didn't do anything. They just stared. It unsettled me. It undressed me.

"How long have you been in India?" the Englishman asked. The two unshaven, sallow-faced Frenchmen ignored me.

"Three weeks," I replied. It felt like three months.

"Do you like it?" he asked and introduced himself as Adam from Guernsey Island.

"No, I don't *like* India. Sometimes I hate it and sometimes I love India too." How could I be lukewarm in a country that never stopped clamouring for my attention? Like the little boy pulling at the Englishman's shirt, begging for a rupee. It was his lucky day as he landed a pocketful of loose change.

We climbed aboard the second-class railcar, called a *bogie*, and settled into our seats, watching the worn-out countryside roll by. The villages rose from the dry yellow earth of the same colour, the mud huts covered with dung patties. Emaciated cows, goats and pigs meandered, chewing on tufts of grass. Small children, usually naked, waved at the passing train.

At the Chhatarpur stop, we needed to find a bite to eat. The only stand was filthy, with a boy sitting on the floor cutting spinach on a dirty board. Another rolled out chapatis. A cloud of black flies buzzed around the stall, and a holy cow rubbed its dung-covered nose on Adam's shirt. I managed to eat a potato *pakora*, hoping my stomach would tolerate it, as toilets were rarely available in rural India. I had learned to wear skirts, which were easier and more discreet if needing to squat in a public place. I needed to stop eating risky roadside food and told myself I'd only eat eggs, rice, bananas and baby crackers.

We arrived mid-afternoon in Khajuraho and found a cheap hotel called the Love Palace with a bare room aside from two single beds. Hotel rooms often had two beds, more like cots, perfect for single backpackers ready to share a room, even if they'd just met. We sponged ourselves clean at the hallway sink, drank a soda in the downstairs lobby, then set out to see the famous sites.

The 22 medieval temples dating from the tenth century had a profusion of sculptures with details of daily life, such as eating, washing, praying, playing and working – the terrestrial and celestial occupations of the once-powerful Rajput warriors of the region. Many of the sculptures were explicit, with large-breasted, bejewelled women and their consorts carved into elaborate love-making positions. The carvings depicted nymphs and demons, gods and mortals caught in their passions. Khajuraho was the *Kamasutra* of erotic art.

Adam and I strolled through the temples, amazed at the intricacy of sex in stone. The sculptures broke every code of modern-day modesty between the sexes in India. Fascinating as it was, I began to stumble on our walk. Nausea swept over me in waves, and an hour later I collapsed on the ground in the shade, shivering with fever.

I laid my head on Adam's lap, his presence more reassuring than any heavenly nymph. Without him, I could have curled up and died, an unknown foreigner found dead at the temples in Khajuraho. Probable cause of death: potato pakoras in Chhatarpur.

"Let's get you to bed," he said, taking my arm. I limped back to the Love Palace where he soaked his T-shirt in cool water, wrapping it over my burning body till the fever broke.

Twenty-four hours later I boarded the packed night train to Varanasi, sufficiently recovered from whatever bug had ailed me with Adam at my side. The two of us squeezed into the upper berth of the sleeper car. In the early morning, we arrived at a platform full of station dwellers sleeping next to sacks of rice, tarnished pots and plastic bags full of their worldly belongings. A woman stirred in the light of dawn, her three children lying beside her. Only the day before I had been the one lying on the ground in a bundle of misery.

Varanasi, also called Benares, one of the world's oldest cities and the holiest of seven holy cities in India, was a destination for pilgrims in search of spiritual enlightenment. The city had 87 *ghats*, steps leading down to the most sacred of rivers. For every Hindu, a trip to the Ganges was the ultimate spiritual experience. Poor people (which meant most of India) saved for a lifetime to make the pilgrimage. The pilgrims would fill urns with the deified water to take home and sprinkle on the less fortunate who had not been able to make the trip.

The devotees performed *puja*, acts of reverence with rituals, prayers and meditation, washing away their sins and sorrow in the sacred waters. Some were *sadhus*, the holy men or religious ascetics of Hinduism who have renounced the worldly life. Others were Hindu worshipers in white robes, their foreheads bearing the three stripes of Shiva. Some were Western-dressed Indians who could have been businessmen from Bombay or bureaucrats from Delhi. Women submerged themselves, their brilliant saris billowing up on the water like lily pads.

Adam and I sat on the massive steps watching boys run along the ghats with their bright paper kites. Women were washing their clothes, soaping and scrubbing them with great devotion. The hectic intensity of India was transformed into a calm, cleansing ritual of faith in Varanasi. I felt the absence of holy waters, or pilgrimages, or traditions in my life.

Three sadhus, bathing in the morning sun, were chanting, praying and giggling. Maybe they were giggling at us, two foreigners trying to capture the holy moment. We were the white-skinned kites bobbing in the wind, holding on to a slender string of understanding.

"Do you think we could ever achieve this devotion?" I reflected.

"It would take me a lifetime and I don't have the patience," Adam, the most patient man I'd ever met, replied.

"I don't either. And which god would I worship?"

"You've got quite a choice in India. Most of us go home to our own gods, at some time or other."

"The truth seems as much cultural as absolute. I was born into Christianity in Canada. If I'd been born here, I'd be Hindu or Muslim or Buddhist. Can a relative truth be true?"

"My guess is it's in the eyes of the beholder," Adam said, pulling me up from the steps where my feet dangled in the river.

We stayed three days in Varanasi, a place not only for the living but considered the most auspicious place to die in India. Cremation on the banks of the Ganges was the supreme final blessing. At the Manikarnika Ghat, the flames of life and death had been burning for thousands of years.

A toothless old man, a *dom* or person responsible for cremations, waved us over to a burning pyre. He launched into an informative explanation in a garbled mix of Hindi and English about his duties. First, he would cleanse the body with holy water then wrap it in a white robe. A mixture of butter, rice and banana would then be put into the deceased's mouth. With these finishing touches, the dom would light the pyre and the spirit could depart on its karmic destiny.

Further down the ghat, a paunchy middle-aged man, presumably the deceased's son, scattered sandalwood powder on a body covered with white fabric and yellow flowers. He lit the funeral pyre as the male family members gathered around and recited a solemn mantra. Hindi women were not allowed at the cremation, only female tourists could observe, which seemed a heartbreaking situation for wives, mothers, sisters and daughters.

The scent of death hung in the air, smelling like autumn debris burning, an earthy decay mixed with sandalwood and sulfur. The ritual by fire allowed for a rapid departure. I could almost see the dead person's spirit drift away in a smoky sky. Public cremation, unimaginable in my own country, was commonplace, cultural and sacred in India.

From the ghats, Adam and I climbed a maze of steep paths, past temples full of celebration, outside the beggars beseeching, their hands grasping. At a tiny tea stall overlooking the river, we shared one last meal of bright yellow *biryani* rice with a steamy glass of chai. He was heading north on the night bus to Nepal; I was going back to Delhi. I pulled him close, the stranger I'd met three days before, burying my head in his shoulder. We had to leave each other in Varanasi, the city of departures. There was no expectation that either of us would change our plans. Sweet, considerate Adam was a tender link on a journey of many goodbyes.

17

The Gods Will Bless You

PEACE AND QUIET were hard to find in the second most populated country in the world, with its 22 official languages, more than 2,000 ethnic groups and six official religions. India was the birthplace of Buddhism, the homeland of Hinduism and had a deep Islamic presence, even since the partition of the country into India and Pakistan in 1947.

Persistent rickshaw wallahs surrounded me after the long trip from Varanasi, calling out "Where you go lady," or "Number one rickshaw," or "Speedy safe." I was miserable with a vise-like headache, felt at my least spiritual and muttered insults, thinly disguised, to the poor wallahs. I needed to find a room to rest, a shower to wash away my sweaty exhaustion and turn off India for a while.

"I am ashamed of my impatience, especially with the rickshaw wallahs," I confided in Dhiram and Sushali.

"Do not worry. We Indians are worse. We are a tolerant country, but we are always shouting at each other. Rich and poor. Brahmin and untouchables. Hindu and Muslim," Dhiram said as Sushali served her spicy spinach with cheese.

"Dhiram, you always make me feel better, and Sushali, I love your *saag paneer*." With them, I saw the everyday life of a young couple, an arranged marriage; two people striving to be modern in a culture still tied to its traditions, its contradictions and its volatilities. They kept my own exasperations with India in check.

I hung out in Delhi, where I'd stroll at Connaught Place, visit the temples or retreat from the intensity of the city to five-star, air-conditioned hotels, like the Taj Mahal Intercontinental. There I'd lounge at the poolside, eat papaya drenched in lime served by waiters dressed as maharajas or swim in the pool surrounded by impeccable gardens. No one knew I was staying at the hostel down the road, sharing the six-bunk room with an eccentric American couple into tattoos and a talkative English girl with her quiet husband, a Malay hairdresser. Big black beetles darted across the linoleum floor of the cluttered room.

One afternoon, as I was walking from the five-star to my no-star, a fat man wearing a shiny blue jacket over baggy pants rode by on an antiquated bicycle. "Could I have the pleasure to speak with you?" he asked in excellent English.

"Yes," I replied, startled by his request.

"My mother is dying in my natal village. I have no money for the bus," he said. "It is my sacred duty to see my mother. Please help me." Moved by his plea, I rummaged in my bag and gave him 50 rupees, an exorbitant sum, and more than my daily budget.

"The gods will bless you," he added, bowing ceremoniously.

The next day I saw the same man hustling another unsuspecting foreigner. His flawless English should have alerted me. He was a pro, and I'd been taken, a solitary female traveller being an easy target. Beggars, the poorest of the poor, settled for a rupee or two. Swindlers concocted clever stories and extracted much more.

After rationalizing my misplaced good deed, I set out for the Gandhi Museum. Photographs of the wiry little man who mobilized a nation on the principle of peaceful civil disobedience to overthrow British colonial rule covered the walls. Spinning wheels, the symbol of Gandhi's ideal for self-sufficiency, filled one room. Even the Mahatma's walking stick and spectacles were on display. Seeing the blood-stained *dhoti*, the Indian-style sarong worn by Gandhi on the day of his assassination in 1948, choked me with tears.

BOMBAY WAS A CITY in urgent need of restoration. The long rows of apartment buildings, the Bombay *chawls*, three-storied structures with a common veranda on each floor, appeared as if they would collapse momentarily. The sidewalks were crowded with shelters made of torn cloth and cardboard where entire families lived. Could I learn to not notice them, to walk on by, to not wonder how people survived such wretchedness?

I decided on a tour of the Parsi Hanging Garden high up on the Malabar Hills, a calm oasis from the teeming city below. The Parsi or Zoroastrians were a small, progressive religious community that venerated earth, water and fire. Their tradition did not permit cremation or burial of the dead. They left their dead atop their circular concrete towers of silence where bodies would decompose in the sun and be scavenged by carrion birds, usually vultures. The Parsi had practised excarnation – the exposure of dead bodies to the elements to avert contamination of the soil – since the fifth century.

The Hindu communities complained that the vultures dropped pieces of bodies into Bombay's water supply. A wealthy Parsi built a cover over the reservoir and planted a beautiful garden to remedy the problem.

It was a quintessential Indian story, odd and other-worldly. Religion, when viewed from the perspective of another faith or no faith at all, seemed bizarre, but the complex social-religious-political fabric of India fascinated me. I listened to every guide, talked to everyone I met and read the *India Times* trying to comprehend India's loud, messy and unfathomable soul.

After five days, exhausted with the city, I packed my knapsack and waved down a *tuk-tuk*, an auto rickshaw, for the station. A billboard plastered on the station wall announced, "Please Do Not Discuss Political Issues."

It didn't seem to have any effect as people pushed, shoved or shuffled about from one line to another. A boy, about 10 years old, veered toward me, propelled by his forearms in a semblance of a crawl. His twisted hips and spindly straight legs didn't bend at the knees. He was one of the mutilated for more profitable begging. I stood in the train station, disturbed, frightened, shutting down on India. The gods wouldn't bless me that day as I hurried away, the rich white lady, going somewhere far away.

GOA, A 12-HOUR RIDE FROM BOMBAY, was the ideal getaway, and the homey guest house of Mrs. Bianca de Silva Rosario in Panaji, the capital, was perfect. Mrs. Bianca, who lived with her daughter and old mother, welcomed me into the inner courtyard, proudly showing me her orchid collection. "Goa is my garden of riches and I have the best garden in town."

"The Portuguese arrived in Goa in 1510 searching for the lucrative spices of the East. They established a colony that only recently became an Indian state. It stands apart with its distinctive Christian influences, impressive churches and baroque architecture," my guidebook stated. I could see a pink brick church beyond the lush garden and smell the salty sea breeze, as I sipped cool hibiscus tea.

Mrs. Bianca leaped at the opportunity to talk. "I try to give my daughter the teachings of the church, so she can be a good girl and marry a good boy, like her father. He was a good man. He would not like our Goa now. There are too many hippies," she declared.

A group of them sat at the Bella Vista restaurant, the air heavily infused with the earthy scent of patchouli and hashish. The Western guys dressed Indian, the few girls wore long breezy skirts and silver bobbled bracelets. They smiled or giggled in a state of mystical bliss as they drifted through their day. At least it seemed that way to me as I sat at a table for one and wrote in my journal, pages of introspective ramblings about belonging or not belonging, trying to understand myself in the clash of cultures, not with India but with my own.

I didn't define myself as a hippie, though I lingered on the sidelines. I toed the establishment line back home, as a nurse, part of a bigger system, the medical world, where I didn't break the rules. Hippies rejected the materialism of the West and sought another life, more spiritual or free, stoned or not stoned. I was vaguely jealous of them and their identity as a group, a movement or a trend, not quite fitting in. But as a traveller I could choose to be nonaligned with any path that I wasn't sure I wanted to follow.

After drinking a delicious mango *lhassi,* I contemplated my choices. Goa's beaches, fringed with pine brush and coconut palms, seemed the best bet. I lay on the warm sand, looked up to a cloudless sky and let the ocean soothe me into a luxurious, drug-free peace of mind. A few Westerners strolled the beach, some of them naked, not even wearing a bikini thong. I couldn't. I wouldn't. It wasn't cool. It wasn't right. Not in front of the gawking Goan boys.

Still, I felt silly lying there in my blue striped swimsuit with its pointy darts. Down the beach, a single Japanese man seemed sillier trying to keep a sarong wrapped around his slim body in the breeze off the Arabian Sea. Goa, a mecca for free spirits, was too trendy a scene for me. Added to that, I had a dreadful cold and Delhi belly again. Mrs. Bianca boiled water for me every day and gave me bits of motherly and medical advice.

I TRIED TO BE BRAVE as I waited on the platform for the southbound train to Mysore. A horde of young urchins surrounded me, as well as men selling chai in small earthen cups. Other passengers with their old torn suitcases gathered around too. It was all coming and going, noisy and rumbling, just like the train that pulled in and out of the station. I soon fell into that state of suspended anticipation, so easy on a train, gliding over a land of rice fields, water buffalo, shabby villages and waving children.

Twenty hours later I arrived in Mysore. I felt homesick, wishing I were in Canada for the Christmas season, not in insufferably hot Mysore all alone. I walked from the station to the closest guest house, past the stately Saint Philomena's Cathedral where a group of albino beggars with skin so white it blistered red in the sun sat on the ground.

A group of eunuchs, dressed in bright saris, tacky makeup and cheap jewelry, sauntered by, chatting and combing each other's hair. Their outlandish cackling and laughing solicited attention. I couldn't help but stare. They were an altered version of everything I thought I knew about gender identity and sexual orientation.

Some eunuchs, or *hijras* as they were called, were born that way, males with altered genitalia, neither male nor female. But most had been castrated in their youth. I had heard that the practice of castration was still a common occurrence in India, controlled by the hijra mafia. They abducted boys for the clandestine surgery that was performed throughout the country.

The eunuchs had once been royal servants to the maharajas, often elevated to the position of confidante and companion to the emperor. They were particularly liked as guards for the harems. As the maharajas fell into decline, the hijras fell into a life of begging, though they had retained some of their reputation as psychics.

Between the eunuchs, the albino beggars and the stench of poverty, I dissociated into a see/not see way of being. It was the only way I could cope with the onslaught of India. I was tempted to run back to the lovely Mrs. Bianca de Silva Rosario.

18

Christmas in Kerala

I COULD FALL INTO DRIFTING from one place to another. I needed a plan and laid out my worn map of India on the table at the Kwality restaurant. Bandipur Wildlife Sanctuary, known for its small population of tigers, was only two hours away from Mysore. An elephant ride to see a magnificent tiger in the wild appealed to me. But all alone?

The bus, always an ordeal of crushing bodies, clinging heat and sweaty odours, took me to the front gate and the game warden's house. The warden, Mr. Gowda, was a talkative man in the way that Indians are a loquacious people. It was clear he enjoyed his position as the gatekeeper of Bandipur, sorting through a mound of dusty paperwork and issuing me a room at the guest lodge.

Three travellers, about my age, sat on the wooden porch surrounding the rustic lodge. The couple from Switzerland, Marie and Hermann, fanned themselves with a giant leaf in the sweltering 40-degree weather. Luc, a French Canadian, mopped his wet brow with a bandana as he drank a Limca, India's 7 Up. He'd just arrived in India the week before, his first time outside of Canada.

"You are daring to travel all by yourself to Bandipur," Hermann commented.

"Except the bus trip scared me to death."

Mr. Gowda sent us to a cluster of shacks down a dirt road for dinner. A village man ushered us into a cave-like room with an open fire range along one wall. There wasn't a table, only four wobbly stools to sit on. We shared a plate of rice served with runny *sambhar*, a lentil vegetable stew made with tamarind, using the three available spoons.

"They still have hideous problems after the cyclone in Andra Pradesh last month. Over 10,000 people died, and they still can't clean up the mess," Marie said, outspoken on all matters Indian. The stew dripped down her chin as she talked. It seemed the aid workers, from either the army or the government, were not willing to dispose of the decaying bodies because the dead were predominantly of the lowest caste, the untouchables.

We shared other shocking stories, like kids telling horror stories around the campfire. It was common travellers' talk in India, gripping or outrageous stories in a complex society. I loved the India of magnificence, the Taj Mahal, the gardens of the maharajas, and the bold, extravagant images of the ubiquitous gods. It was much harder to be enamoured with the villages in the rural depths of the vast subcontinent, where inconceivable poverty reigned.

"We could be in Switzerland where everything runs like a clock," Hermann said.

"Or cold, clean Canada," Luc added.

Walking back to the lodge, Marie and I fell behind, talking about our relationships and the web of expectations and desires they held. "Can you imagine me as a housewife married to Hermann?" she asked.

"I only met you today, Marie. But you don't seem the settling down type."

"And how about you?"

"Independent traveller becomes an attached wife. Maybe someday," I laughed. I was still holding on to a dead-end relationship with a romantic Turk, and a year later madly attracted to Gino in

Taiwan. Finding the right man felt like an elusive dance of court-
ing butterflies flitting from yes to no.

The four of us slept in one room, the single beds supplied with a
mosquito net, a sheet and a ratty blanket. Hermann's snoring kept
me awake all night long.

Mrs. Gowda, as meek as her husband was officious, served an
omelet and chapatis for breakfast, while Mr. Gowda fretted about
arrangements for an elephant outing. Two aging elephants, their
skin as furrowed as old tree bark, finally arrived. With a ladder we
climbed aboard, Luc and I sitting sidesaddle on the one named
Gajendra. The *mahout*, the elephant trainer, straddled her neck
and we ambled off in an easy rolling gait.

Once again, a little girl sat beside me, full of wonder, riding
Gajendra into a jungle of giant bamboo and entangled flowering
shrubs. She was on the lookout for wild beasts. Oh, to see a striped
black and orange tiger with fierce golden eyes! But we only saw a
dozen spotted dear, numerous brilliant peacocks and a small herd
of elephants across a swampy pond. Gajendra was her greatest thrill.

We left Bandipur on the night train for Cochin in the southern
state of Kerala. Too many people piled into the sleeping compartment meant for eight. I twisted myself every which way, sharing
my bunk with Luc and an Indian man. Maria flew into a rage,
Hermann sulked and Luc slept through it all. A glaring light
bulb swung dangerously over my head as the train flew through
the night.

Cochin was a city on the Malabar Coast, until independence
under the colonial rule of the Portuguese and the Dutch and famous as a spice trade port. From the Vasco da Gama square, a
promenade that bordered the port, we looked out to huge fishing
nets strung from bamboo poles, a "catch-all" system of fishing
from the shore. Just off the square, music blasted from the Island
Maharaja Hotel, which was hosting a Christmas Eve dinner and
dance. "Let's go," Maria said, and we followed her in.

A few women sat at a long table and groups of men hung about
inside the dimly lit room. There were Indians, a group of Polish

sailors and another group of Nigerians in Cochin for reasons we didn't know. A band crooned to "Honky Tonk Women," and an overweight Indian lady with flaming red hair, wearing a shimmy and shake dress, sang "White Christmas," though Kerala had never seen snow.

The Poles were soon drunk. The Indians danced flamenco-like with dramatic tosses of their heads and the Nigerians sensually teased their male partners, as there were not enough ladies. Maria and I were up for every dance as Luc and Hermann sat back and drank beer.

Over breakfast, we reminisced about Christmas in Canada and Switzerland. I missed not being home, but easily accepted the more exciting options in India. Luc and I decided on Periyar National Sanctuary, high in the Cardamom Hills, where they claimed to have tigers in the wild. It was worth a second try, after Bandipur, and I enjoyed Luc's easy-going companionship.

After several exhausting hours on beat-up buses, we arrived at the park, where a sinewy man in a khaki safari suit chopped coconuts with a machete. After much haggling over a cup of tea, Deepak agreed to take us to a cabin accessible only by boat.

Capsizing seemed a likely possibility in the small unsteady craft as we plowed up the lake with partially submerged tree stumps that stuck out of the water like dead sentries. From a desolate beach, we trekked ankle-deep in mud into a jungle where monkeys screeched from the trees. In a grassy area, we surprised two boars that grunted and ran away. Luc walked ahead with long determined strides, living his fantasy as the original wilderness explorer. Deepak, armed only with his machete, tried to reassure me we were safe.

A stone hut stood on an embankment above a clear green lake. I pulled on my bathing suit and plunged in. Birds chirped in the trees and mighty beasts roamed nearby as I swam in the idyllic waters. It was close enough to my wilderness fantasy.

Luc and I travelled comfortably together, usually sharing a bed, friends but not lovers. He liked to talk about his log cabin in

Canada, growing his own food and his spiritual journey. A "flower power" sort of guy, he espoused love and peace.

"Indians are cool. They live simply, close to the land," he said.

"They have no medical care, no school for their children and live such hard lives," I argued, exasperated with his naïveté. Annoyed with my comments on the endless problems plaguing India, Luc saw himself as the more spiritual one.

We debated our country's future as well. Luc believed in an independent French Canada as the only viable solution. I understood his reasons yet rejected them emotionally. He was talking about my country too. Luc could be intransigent, and I could be as prickly as a porcupine. Before long, we'd back off and laugh at our touchy friendship.

Deepak returned on our last day and paddled us down the lake where four elephants were bathing at the shore. The mother, spraying her baby with water, looked up, alert to any intrusion. We never did sight a tiger. Still, our foray into unspoiled country satisfied my longing for the wild.

CHILDREN, THEIR BODIES WET AND GLISTENING, swam in Kerala's network of backwater canals. Women in vivid colours strolled the dirt paths and slim men with bulging biceps pushed poles as they strode the gunwales of their boats. Kerala was a land of tea plantations, rice paddies and golden beaches, kissed by the sun.

On New Year's Day, Luc treated me to savoury *rava dosas*, crisp wafers spiced with cumin and ginger and served with chili sauce that cost 25 cents at the Alleppey Tea House. A father and daughter entered the festive room. "May we join your table?" the plump, gray-haired father asked.

"Of course," I replied, happy to have their company. Mr. Gopinatham was a member of the Indian Marxist party and his pretty daughter a medical student in Trivandrum.

"We are blessed in Kerala. We are the most progressive state with the highest literacy rate. Our communist party was the first to challenge Indira Gandhi's despotism. And I, myself, belong to the coffee cooperative," he said proudly. Luc fascinated Juana, Mr. Gopinatham's daughter, with his stories of Canada, and I, intrigued with Indian politics, enjoyed the lively conversation with her father.

Luc and I had been travelling together for two weeks, interrupted by an occasional squabble. Still, carrying on together was much easier than apart in a country that could overwhelm even the most seasoned traveller. In Thiruvananthapuram, or Trivandrum, the capital city of Kerala, we agreed on one thing. We were tired of hearing men gob and spit profusely in the public sink a few feet away from our table at the station canteen. I had to pee on the bathroom floor as it only had a urinal.

At our hotel, on the dumpy side of decent, I flopped onto the bed. "The mattress is too hard," I whined.

"Fuck it, I can't live with your five-star habits," Luc, usually so cool, said in a rage.

"You've got to be kidding," I retorted. I turned my back on him and reviewed my options to continue together or to move on. Solo travel had its pleasures and intrigue.

In the morning, I left for Cape Comorin, the southernmost tip of the Indian subcontinent, nearly three hours away, leaving my pack behind with Luc, who stood forlorn at the hotel door.

Kanyakumari, the Tamil name for Cape Comorin, was a significant location at the confluence of three seas: the Bay of Bengal, the Indian Ocean and the Arabian Sea. Kanyakumari, the sister of Krishna, was the goddess who removed the rigidity of our minds. I had to figure out my own mind and how I'd got myself in such a muddle with Luc.

Indian psychedelic rock screeched from a teen's ghetto blaster as I stepped down from the bus. Rows of sidewalk stalls sold trinkets, seashells and plastic figurines of Hindu gods and goddesses, and Christ on the cross too. At the door to the temple, a large billboard warned: "Beware of Thieves."

I walked over to the point, called "The Land's End," sat on a rock and looked out to the three seas. "Why am I here?" filled my thoughts. Not in Kanyakumari, but India. Was it a journey, a challenge, a shock, a test, a quest? I wanted to experience the mysterious East, walk in the Himalayas, see the home of Mahatma Gandhi, fall in love with the Taj, go to an ashram and learn to be compassionate with the poorest of the poor. I wanted to *be* spiritual.

The sun, a red ball of flame, played over the Arabian Sea and a prayer arose for sunlight glittering on water, for the noisy Indian tourists nearby and for Shiva, Krishna, Christ and Buddha, or any other Great Spirit listening. I made a vow that afternoon in Kanyakumari. "Help me, inspire me in my seeking, in my wandering, on this earth. Help me kindle the fire of truth. Help me love my fellow man, respect India and lighten my soul. And help me to like Luc."

A decrepit bus took me back to Trivandrum, where Luc sat on the beach staring out to sea. He wore a checkered sarong, no longer in his white T-shirt and shorts. He put his arms around me, apologizing over our senseless arguing. As we walked along the beach, Luc suggested a Kathakali concert being performed at a temple close to our hotel.

Inspired by the *Ramayana*, Hinduism's epic poem, the classical mime dancers wore colourful costumes and elaborate make-up. Their evocative facial expressions and delicate hand gestures swept me into the magic of Kathakali. After the concert, Luc and I strolled back to our hotel, ready to share one more night at our ramshackle hotel.

19

String of Sparkling Lights

I BEGAN A MEDITATION PRACTICE every morning sitting on the beach outside the thatched hut where I lived. In my first transcendental meditation class, Bhanu, the teacher, instructed me in the basic precepts: correct thought, proper posture and right breathing. Correct thought challenged me the most as the malicious drone of a mosquito hovered around. I knew that correct thought included the principle of nonviolence, a reverence for all living creatures and that my actions, no matter how small, could result in negative karma, according to Hinduism. The mosquito landed and I swatted it dead.

With time my daily practice drifted into a string of days, unmarked with expectations or plans. The rhythmic ebb and flow of the waves washed away the scattered fragments of my life as I watched the beautiful children of Kerala play hide and seek in coils of fisherman's rope. The men, with bodies shining like polished ebony, cleaned their nets, while the women sat with the tide breaking on the shore, sifting the sand for tiny crabs. At the Chai House an old man with a dirty pink *lungi*, a loose-fitting cloth wrapped around his thin hips, served me refreshing lemon tea at three cents a glass.

In the evening, I sat by my hut watching the sky turn brilliant pink and purple then melt into the dark. The fine lines between drifting and staying, restless and restful, played with my soul. Connections with a place and with people were the lifeblood of my travels, but the spirit of travelling was to move on and was greater than my need to stay. It was time to head north to Madurai, the city in the heart of Tamil Nadu.

I crammed into the second-class bogie with my fellow passengers, people of all colours and castes, except the Brahmins, the upper caste, who rode first class. Eight hours later I stepped down from the train onto the platform where station dwellers claimed their temporary corners strewn with straw mats and bundles of belongings. Children ran about among the beggars, the vendors and the ever-present, near naked sadhus. It was a study in commotion, adaptation and survival. The usual posters with attempts to inspire the nation were plastered on the wall: "There Is No Substitute for Hard Work."

Navigating the crowded streets of Madurai with my knapsack weighing me down *was* hard work. As well, I looked a sorry sight, my cotton blouse wet with sweat and sloppy masala spilled down the front.

I had come to the city to see the Meenakshi temple, the shining glory of South India. The temple, originally built in the sixth century, was dedicated to the goddess Meenakshi, the incarnation of the goddess Parvati and her consort, Lord Shiva. The cosmic structure was adorned with an entire mythology of stone deities, animals and demons. The central Court of a Thousand Pillars had intricately carved images, including Meenakshi's wedding to Shiva. Temple rites involved the pouring of liquids from the seven seas, symbolized by brine, water, milk, curd, ghee, cane juice and honey. I loved the temple's bold, ornate otherworldliness.

In the market, women scooped up steaming food from huge pots, wrapping the sticky coconut rice or deep-fried fish or curried vegetables in banana leaves. Men rapidly chopped greens with big knives, their Tamil chatter in rhythm with the chopping. I sampled *idli*, traditional rice dumplings served with a fiery hot peanut tamarind sauce. The vendor offered me a tall glass of sugary almond milk, called *jigarthanda,* a specialty of Madurai. It meant heart – cold, to soothe the heart.

I needed to soothe *my* heart, tripping over the disturbing sights of Madurai. A naked flea-bitten lady searched for a morsel of food in a pile of garbage. An ugly pig shovelled around nearby. An old man, his feet grotesquely swollen with elephantiasis, reached to me with an outstretched hand. I felt sick, powerless to respond. And what response could make a difference? It had to be more than a handout. The complexity of giving or helping in the face of such overwhelming need was like a heavy stone I carried or kicked about, or it sank into the swamp of my conscience.

"I can't do this alone. I need someone, anyone, to help soften the unremitting shocks in a country that feels like one big shock wave," I worried as I walked away. Luc had been there. Adam too. I vacillated between my independent spirit and need for human company, between my need to experience India and my fear.

In the evening, I rode a rickshaw across the Vaigai River as the sun dipped over the Meenakshi temple. Everyone was out, moving in a timeless stroll, rickshaw wallahs, vendors, families, boys hand in hand, girls hand in hand and always the sacred cows. I was one white face, a pilgrim of sorts seeking my path on their ancient road.

After three days in Madurai, I moved on to Thanjavur, halfway to Pondicherry, where I settled for the Thanjavur Tourist Bungalow close to the station. I was tired and needed to clean up, but the only faucet in the room had no running water. Outside some ragged children followed me down a path to the imposing Brihadishvara temple.

Built in the 11th century, the temple stands out for its size and architectural mysteries. Archeologists questioned how the temple was built, as there was no granite in the region, yet it was made with giant pieces of the hard heavy stone. A huge *nandi*, the sacred bull of Shiva, in front of the temple was carved out of a single piece of stone. It is believed that thousands of captive elephants hauled the granite from many miles away.

A noisy group of Indians was worshipping as I traipsed around. I never knew which Hindu holiday was being celebrated, but I knew I was in no mood for celebrating and dragged myself back to my drab accommodation.

A great number of birds whistled and warbled in the scrappy courtyard, competing with loud drumming in the streets as I tried to meditate, sitting cross-legged under a tree. I floated in and out of my meditative mind till I opened my eyes to bullock carts with massive wooden wheels painted pink creaking by the courtyard. Farmers were returning after a day's work in the fields, probably to their mud shacks and to their evening bowl of rice and lentils. The rose-flecked sky cast a soft light into the dreariness and dust.

At that moment I was transported into another India. Beyond the poverty, I saw families coming home from fertile fields with full carts; plenty of food to feed the hungry. The flow of humanity lit up like a string of sparkling lights. We were all connected, Black and white, rich and poor, everyone moving forward to the places we call home.

A TALL MAN in a long white robe opened the door at the famous Sri Aurobindo Ashram in Pondicherry, a spiritual mecca in South India. He introduced himself as Dieter from Germany and showed me around the premises. The devotees, Westerners and Indians, moved quietly, talked in whispers and looked rather solemn. They followed the principle of *sadhana*: the surrender to the divine.

"We left our old life behind us and began a new one here," an older American couple from Kansas stated as we ate a lunch of vegetable *korma*, rice and a banana.

"Was it hard?" I asked as I dipped into more korma.

"It is simple. We just follow the path of our guru Sri Aurobindo," the husband, once a tax accountant, said.

"Sri Aurobindo tells us that spiritual realization leads to a divine life on Earth," the wife added.

> But few are those who tread the sunlit path;
> Only the pure in soul can walk in light.
>
> —SRI AUROBINDO

It seemed highly unlikely I would be a successful convert. I didn't know how to follow a guru, nor did I want to walk in a long white robe in an ashram. Sri Aurobindo Ashram, despite its calming allure, was not *my* spiritual home. It was not *my* divine.

I left the ashram the next day and walked slowly to the train station through the baffling layers of India, its weary-worn people walking along the road with me. I would catch someone's eye, a stranger's smile, a brief acknowledgment, a fleeting curiosity, welcome gestures in a traveller's world.

Heading north to Madras, the train rolled through fields of sugar cane, then inched its way past a shantytown of plastic and cloth hovels south of the city. The slum dwellers walked alongside the tracks carrying heavy loads of bananas and coconuts, or squatted in plain sight of passengers passing through their public toilets.

It was a cruel glimpse into the stark reality of India but soon merged into the bustling core of Madras. The largest city of South India was ablaze with colour and sound. A Muslim muezzin called from the minaret, Hindu pilgrims in burgundy robes chanted on the street corner and the rickshaw wallahs honked incessantly. A car inched by with a loudspeaker on its roof blaring snatches of scratchy music from a Bollywood film to tantalize the crowd.

Madrasi women with purple sprigs of jasmine in their long hair ambled arm in arm, their saris swishing in the breeze off the Bay of Bengal. Watching them made me feel clumsy, a not-so-feminine traveller as I trudged to a hotel, knapsack on my back.

Twenty letters were waiting for me at the Poste Restante. I relished them one by one as I sat on a bench, eating crunchy cashew nut pakoras, encircled by curious children. "When are you going to settle down?" my mother predictably asked. My father was concerned about my solitary travels too. Neither said they missed me, nor inquired about the stories I'd written them, though several friends wrote, intrigued with the life I was living. Even Gino and Alim wrote.

I stuffed myself with pakoras (no matter how many children looked on), then crammed the wad of letters into my bag. Choices loomed. Should I go home and find some semblance of a regular life? Or should I stay? Five months on the road had me feeling far off normal, just as my mother had forewarned a long time ago.

My money might last another two or three months on a frugal budget. I wanted to see Calcutta, and I couldn't leave Asia without going to the Himalayas and Rajasthan too. Wanderlust and homesickness pulled me in opposing directions. I was swinging on a sea of uncertainty, but India still held me in its curious spell.

20

Calcutta: A Mess and a Miracle

I BOARDED THE CORMANDO EXPRESS, heading north for Calcutta with the fraudulent Indian Rail pass a fellow backpacker had given me. A ridiculous risk and savings I did not need to calculate into my budget, but it appealed to the rebel in me, breaking the rules.

The train rumbled through Andra Pradesh on the east coast, the area that had been ravaged by a cyclone two months earlier. The thatch shacks and their inhabitants would not have stood a chance. Twisted trees and remnants of villages strewn across the land rendered it apocalyptic.

"I am a scholar from the University of Calcutta," an Indian gentleman wearing a cotton dhoti and sitting on the wooden bench beside me stated. "Please, I would be happy for you to make the acquaintance of my wife Mrs. Gupta," he added, peering over his rimless glasses held together with wiring. She was short and plump like her husband, a glittering little jewel, adorned with gold beads and bangles.

After a chit-chat, Mrs. Gupta delved into the questions that troubled her. "Why do you send your elderly to senior homes?

Why do your youth leave their families as soon as school has finished? Why do you have such a high divorce rate?" I was at a loss
for answers. My attempts to explain sounded ethnocentric, or "too
Western" as Alim always accused me of being. Neither Mr. nor
Mrs. Gupta understood the West any more than I understood the
East – the caste system or arranged marriages. But I happily accepted the wide assortment of food Mrs. Gupta laid out on our
bench, particularly her specialty, *shukti*, a dried fish wrapped in
cloth and served with tangy mango chutney. Their company alone
was a taste of India, rich, spicy and satisfying. After dinner I fell
asleep on the upper bunk with Mr. and Mrs. Gupta snoring below.

By morning we had arrived at the Howrah train station, the
oldest and largest railway station in India, in a city I had always
longed to see. Calcutta, once the seat of the British Raj, was now a
city of profound paradox, with opulent palaces and horrid slums,
where tens of thousands lived and slept on the streets. It was
India's most populated and poorest city.

Stepping off the train into the cool January air that smelled of
stinking fish, a horde of rickshaw drivers clamoured around me.
A thin, dark man wearing a threadbare lungi with a rag wrapped
around his head helped me into his small two-wheeled buggy. I
felt odd, conspicuous and exploitive, sitting in a man-drawn rickshaw with an undernourished, barefoot wallah.

Before crossing the huge Howrah Bridge, which straddles
the river Hooghly, the wallah stopped to urinate beside a man
gutting a fish. Another man cupped water dripping from a block
of ice to wash his face and a child lay asleep on the road only feet
from passing buses and bullock carts. Pavement people sat on
their haunches in their improvised homes strung with rags and
cardboard as beautiful Bengali ladies whisked past, looking like
high society in their elaborate buggies.

The wallah, a man of indeterminate age and probably much
younger than he appeared, took me to the Paragon off Sutter
Street, a dismal budget hostel. Too tired to look any further, I took

the one spare bed in a mess of a room with other foreigners, still sleeping in what seemed a stuporous state. After a shower that dripped lukewarm water, I ventured into the streets of Calcutta.

A pervasive dust coated everything, from the crowded sidewalks to the ancient buildings that looked like they should be declared unlivable. Yet they had intricately carved wooden niches in their walls, and inside the niches miniature sweet shops. Merchants sat outside their closet-size shops on the sidewalks, reading the morning newspaper. Shiny tin stalls selling flowers spilled colour into the dinginess.

Calcutta, regarded as the intellectual and cultural hub of the country, also drew those attracted to the extreme elements of the city, like the Westerner I met that afternoon on Chowringhee Road, the wide promenade in the centre of town. After saying hello, Shane, shirtless and wearing a saffron dhoti, stated he was a sadhu studying obscure Eastern metaphysics. He was a strange, displaced individual from Vancouver, my hometown.

Solo travel offered other serendipitous moments, like meeting Chloe in a long hippie skirt strolling down the promenade. We had briefly met months ago in Delhi. I threw my arms around her as if she was a long-lost friend.

"Wonderful to see you," she said, tossing back her long auburn hair and laughing in her uncomplicated way. Chloe was the true, intrepid traveller, travelling without any apparent schedules, plans or agendas. I avoided organized, packaged or predictable tourism, but I carried a guidebook and always had a map.

"I'm on my way to a Manipuri dance concert. If you're brave enough to take a bus, come along with me."

"Sure, let's go."

The double-decker bus lurched around corners at a precarious tilt with passengers hanging off the open doors. With bodies, including ours, crammed into sweaty contact, all attempts at Hindu decency were lost. We arrived tousled but safe on the other side of town.

After a few enthusiastic but misleading directions, we arrived at the Hindu temple where the concert was being held. A woman ushered us into a room decorated with gaudy baubles and seated us on plastic footstools in the front row. The performers, teenage girls, stood on the makeshift stage looking shy, not yet grown into their elaborately made up faces and decorative dresses. An ensemble of men began playing drums, cymbals and a flute, as the dancers came to life with choreographed gracefulness. The classical Manipuri dance depicting scenes from the life of Krishna was magical.

After the performance, Chloe and I waltzed outside the temple like dancers ourselves. Two women took our arms and guided us down a back alley, leaving us at a Sikh *gurdwara*, a Sikh holy centre. The priest, who could not have been expecting two foreign women, invited us in and gave us a gooey sweet, the holy offering of *prasad*. He chatted amiably in Bengali or Punjabi, unconcerned we did not understand a word as we toured his house of worship. The cool marble floors were an intense pleasure to my hot and tired feet.

THE HUMAN CONDITION interested me more than history or museums or galleries, I mused as I set off in the morning through streets of wrenching poverty to visit the Seva Sangh baby clinic. It served Calcutta's poorest, the untouchables. Many of the babies were severely undernourished, their *kohl*-lined eyes weeping sooty tears. The one and only doctor, a quiet Bengali, saw 200 patients a day, just enough time to glance at the child and write a prescription.

I could become attached to the sad little waif I cuddled in my arms. He looked up at me with solemn eyes too big for his tiny face. "Stay" flitted across my mind, but the daunting task of working as a nurse in Calcutta overwhelmed me. I gave a small donation and said goodbye. It wasn't the first or the last time I would hold a dying baby in my arms.

In the early afternoon I visited the grand Kalighat temple. The "superior priest of the inner temple," as he called himself, greeted me with a jovial smile and ushered me into the sanctuary of Kali, the goddess of death and destruction. The sculptured black Kali, one of Shiva's three wives and the patron divinity of Calcutta, sat on a pedestal, a garland of skulls around her neck. Her three penetrating eyes and protruding gold tongue made her a fierce and frightening sight. The priest with his long white hair slicked back onto his white robe answered my questions like a doting grandfather.

"Why is blood pooling near the entrance?" Twenty goats were slaughtered daily, as a sacrificial offering for Kali.

"What becomes of so many dead goats?" They were blessed and butchered, and the meat was given to the poor.

I had many questions, never having seen such an unsettling holy site.

After the Seva Sangh baby clinic, the wretchedness in the streets and the surreal temple I was ready to retreat, but I had one more visit to make. Next door to the temple was the Kalighat Home for Dying Destitutes.

A Bengali Missionary of Charity dressed in a white cotton sari with deep blue borders opened the door. A large crucifix hung from her neck. I stepped into a clean spartan interior where the missionaries cared for 100 residents in their hospice.

Mother Teresa had opened the hospice in 1952, two years after establishing the Missionaries of Charity in Calcutta. The building, once a Hindu temple dedicated to Kali, had been abandoned, and with the help of Indian officials she opened her doors to the destitute and dying. It was a place where the poor could die with dignity, according to the rituals of their faith. Muslims were read the Koran, Hindus received water from the Ganges and Christians received the last rites.

Born in what is now Macedonia, Mother Teresa came to India in 1931, at 18 years of age. In 1979 she won the Nobel Peace Prize for her work in the struggle to overcome the suffering of humanity.

Later she changed the name of her hospice to the Kalighat Home of the Pure Heart People.

That afternoon Mother Teresa was not present, but Sister Claudette had me feed three old women, pavement dwellers, who had found their final place of rest. I scooped rice from a large steel pot into bowls and fed them, one small spoon at a time. One of the women was toothless and combatant, spitting out the food; one accepted each tiny bite with great solemnity; and the third was drifting into her final hours, her breathing shallow, her eyes elsewhere.

The next morning, I attended to the same three women, still living in that nebulous space between life and death. The toothless one grasped my hand as I sat with her. After washing the women, I dressed them in clean cotton gowns that covered their emaciated bodies. They seemed peaceful, just as Mother Teresa would have wanted for her dying destitutes.

The nuns invited me to their modest chapel with a single wooden cross on its whitewashed walls. They read a few passages of scripture then sang some hymns with joyous fervour. I felt vaguely unworthy as Sister Claudette repeatedly addressed me as *a sister of God*, though I couldn't get too serious about matters of faith. Not with those lively ladies.

In a state of goodwill, I said my goodbyes, stepped into the street and tripped up against an unsightly human being with his hand outstretched. His savagely mutilated face was the tragic outcome of advanced leprosy. I turned away only to see a naked woman walking toward me, her face covered in mud.

"Calcutta is a mad and deranged place. It punches me in the gut," I said to Chloe later.

"Yeah, it's a hellhole, then it hits you with its humanity," she replied.

"I feel forever distorted into some weird new way of seeing the world."

"That's why we're here, don't you think?" she asked. "And tonight we're going to see Ravi Shankar!"

We walked to the opulent concert hall where the maestro was performing. The city's elite, women in their stunning saris and men in their finest kurtas, both sexes dripping with gold, gathered in the lobby. Looking shabby in comparison, we found our cheap seats at the back of the hall.

The lights dimmed and the music began. Ravi Shankar's haunting sitar felt like music for a dark night of the soul, yet the father on the sitar and his son on the tabla communicated nothing less than love. I was overcome with tears.

We left the dazzling crowd and walked back to our rundown hotels. At night, the streets transformed into shadowy ghettos where one small fire after another burned, the scent of burning cow dung hanging in the air. Families clustered under their ragged sidewalk dwellings. Mothers nursed babies or called their children in for the night. Rats ran around, and a dead cat lay outside my hotel door.

DESPITE THE SIGN at the entrance, "Beware of Pickpockets and Necklace Cutters," I fell in love with the Parasnath Jain temple. The courtyard had ornate silver gilded cherubs, marble lotus flowers, elaborate mosaics and large, sculpted elephants. The inner shrine sparkled with chandeliers that lit up a golden dome. The temple was a splendidly cluttered creation, at that moment empty of devotees and divinely serene.

As I left the temple, I tried to step gingerly around the parts of India I did not want to step into, like the beggar who blocked the doorway. My stomach wrenched just looking at the tragic, misshapen human being, smelling the ever-present odour of urine and listening to the constant hectic noise of Calcutta.

"Dear God, pretend I'm not here," I muttered and imagined Vancouver, my fresh, wholesome city I had left behind. An older Bengali woman in a soft blue sari approached. She must have known I was distressed and took my arm, walking me away from the beggar and into the street, humming with life.

Talkative women filled baskets with food, spirited men enticed customers with their goods and children with the brightest of dark eyes played around the market stalls. Despite its appalling poverty, Calcutta had an unmistakable pulse that beat on every street corner. It was a wreck of a city with a whole lot of holiness. Calcutta was a mess and a miracle.

Back at the horrid Paragon, where I had been for 12 days, I inspected my itchy arms and legs covered in a rash creeping up my neck to my face. Why had I stayed in such a nasty flea-infested dump? I had to leave and get back to Delhi.

Chloe and I met for a farewell meal, choosing a popular spot known for Calcutta's famous fresh grilled fish, from the not-so-fresh Hooghly. At a tiny table squeezed into a corner we delved into our stories, hers more alarming than mine. In a hushed voice, she confided her fly-by-night schemes, some quite illegal, like dope running across borders. Her Asian trip had been financed by money she'd made transporting large amounts of hash from North Africa to Holland in the false bottom of a van.

"You're risking prison or worse. Please don't do this."

"I don't touch the stuff and don't smoke it. I only transport it. It keeps me in cash."

My cautionary words did nothing to change her mind. She was her own wild woman. I loved her bohemian company and hated to say goodbye. We were both Sagittarian souls.

21

Are You Married?

THERE WAS COMFORT in movement on a train heading for Jaisalmer, a remote town in the desert of Rajasthan. I had just left Jaipur, the Rajasthani capital, a city of pink sandstone that claimed several architectural wonders, the most notable being the exquisite Hawa Mahal with its windows of stone filigree and the stunning Amer Fort.

I wanted to meditate, a difficult discipline with the constant commotion on Indian trains. It was easier to chat with the sympathetic Rajasthani seller of garlic and onion who shared the compartment with me. He was concerned about my dreadful cold, neither of us speaking the other's language. I had run out of toilet paper, a luxury in India, but in the second-class compartment, I could blow my nose in the public sink, wipe it with the back of my hand or spit out the window.

My compartment filled with eight men, all staring at me. Two of the younger ones pursued a conversation in their schoolbook English, dotted with antiquated expressions like "hither and thither," "helter-skelter" and "over yonder." One man wore slick garish purple pants, the other dressed in bright orange, and both wore dark shades.

"Where is your husband?" Viyash, the more talkative of the two, inquired, as if my husband might have been temporarily absent. Dhanu wanted to know what my father did for a living and why a father would allow his daughter to go to a faraway land, even if she had left her parental home ten years earlier.

"I don't have a husband," I said, looking Viyash straight in the eye. He was momentarily speechless.

The two men insisted on helping me find a hotel for the stop-over in Jodhpur. I even accepted their invitation to lunch. We ate *dum aloo*, potatoes in spicy yogurt, as Viyash and Dhanu talked with the server. It occurred to me that all three were talking about my marital status.

After our meal, we went to the afternoon matinee. Dhanu sat on one side of me. Viyash, on the other, moved his squeaky metal chair close to mine. Hindi films were known for their melodrama and glorification of traditional values and this one was about the very subject we had contested – marriage and motherhood. The heroine was a sweet and devoted mother; the other woman had failed in her maternal and marital obligations. Neither was por-trayed as a real mother in a real marriage.

"Are you married?" The question most frequently and predict-ably asked of foreign women in India was a sensitive question for me. Why wasn't I married? I had asked myself a thousand times. A product of my culture, I wanted too much, dreamed of too much and wanted children, just not yet. I was lonely, though not so lonely as to sacrifice my freedom. I couldn't explain any of this to Dhanu and Viyash.

"I didn't feel any electric shock sitting next to you. You are dressed like a man," Viyash announced, spitting the red betel he'd been chewing onto the sidewalk. I wore my scruffy blue jeans, not at all like an Indian lady, and knew it would require far more than a pretty dress to bridge our differences.

I set off toward my hotel, trying to examine my values in the context of Western culture – the '70s, the sexual revolution, the hippie generation and the search for authenticity. I didn't have a leg to stand on with Dhanu and Viyash. They belonged to an Indian social structure where women didn't have the freedoms I took for granted. It had been a clash of cultures, and India would take me a lifetime to understand.

A turbaned man was squatting on a rug at a roadside stand. His sign declared, "Clairvoyant, 100% Accuracy."

"My name is Mr. Chandur Singh. Very, very good to tell your life," he said, pulling at his long white beard. He charged a steep fee for my backpacker's budget, but I let him inspect my palm.

"You are looking for a way to God. Stop your worries," he proclaimed. Psychics often spoke in generalities that could apply to anyone, yet his insights were uncanny. He named my mother Mobley (her name is Mable), and affirmed I had four brothers and no sisters.

"You are a gypsy with a butterfly heart, sometimes a broken heart." I wasn't sure I wanted a butterfly heart. I wanted a heart of gold, solid and steadfast. I didn't want to flutter about.

NOT A SINGLE RICKSHAW waited at the Jaisalmer train station in the early dawn when I arrived. Wheelbarrows for luggage were propped against the wall and a few scruffy camels stood nearby. With a handful of fellow passengers, I walked down a dusty road toward the town through a scattered settlement of twig huts where men, women and children huddled around small fires. Beyond their encampment, the walled town of Jaisalmer rose like a citadel from the barren earth. Everything was the colour of camels.

The town, carved in yellow sandstone, was once on the silk route of central Asia and was close to the Pakistani border. Delicate lattices decorated the arched gateways and murals depicting goddesses, flowers and elephants adorned the doorways, but it was camels that meandered haughtily down the narrow, unpaved streets.

The Rajasthanis, proud and fierce descendants of Rajput warriors, were tall, lean and fine-featured. The men had voluminous bold turbans and large gold hoops dangled from their ears. Striking women wore long embroidered skirts in the colours of their land: copper brown, mustard gold and saffron red. They looked like the consorts of maharajas with their jewelled wrists and ankles. We watched each other in mutual fascination.

Jaisalmer boasted one tourist office, where I met Kapaali, a boyish English-speaking guide who jumped up from his chair and stammered when he spoke to me, though his English was good. I was always surprised in remote India when I heard my native language spoken fluently, even if English was the unifying national language of India. He suggested riding out to the maharaja cenotaphs at Bada Bagh, just north of town.

We took off over a rock-strewn terrain on bicycles from another era to a site of ornately carved pavilions bordered by mango trees. Bada Bagh shimmered in its silent beauty. The next day we bicycled to the Jain temple at Amar Sagar and sat on the steps at a small pond, an exquisite place to be in communion with nature.

"Let's drink rum," Kapaali announced, pulling a flask from his pocket. He had asked me more than once if I was married.

"It's not the time for rum," I said, my spiritual moment interrupted.

We rode back to Jaisalmer, a camel and his driver trotting along the path behind us. The old Rajasthani sang a mournful song that rung out over the arid earth where black goats grazed.

That night, as I drifted off to sleep in a near-empty hotel, "Midnight at the Oasis" played in my mind. I woke up from a bizarre, erotic dream with Jimmy Carter, America's new president, and myself making love. He merged into a fantasy image of my cowboy hero swaggering down the main street of Jaisalmer, a good omen on my solo journey.

I was always arriving or leaving, it seemed, driven by curiosity or loneliness or simply the desire to move on. I decided to visit an ashram at Mount Abu in the south of Rajasthan. The bus scheduled to leave from Jaisalmer at six in the morning sat idle as passengers chatted or drank chai or ate sweets from the vendor's cart, swarming with flies.

Kapaali, his thick hair uncombed in the early morning, had come to wish me farewell. He was a single man in his tourist outpost, longing for love, companionship, friendship, sex or someone to make a solitary life a shared life. I longed for it too. My heart shifted just enough to put my arms around him for one quick embrace.

By seven, the men got off the bus, pushed it forward until the engine turned over, scurried back on and we took off. I settled into my travelling space, gazing out the window, losing myself in the heat and dust and desert rolling by.

Twelve long hours later, I arrived at Mount Abu. The small town on a green, forested hill rising from the desert was a destination for spiritual pilgrimage. It was the international home of Raja yoga, dedicated to personal transformation and healing.

I found a modest guest house and met Debbie from Ohio, who lived across the hall. She flopped into a chair in my room and spilled out her frenetic life, fuelled by heavy drugs and dissolute living. It was hard to imagine wandering around India in Debbie's fragile state. My challenging moments, usually when I was confronted with the dire conditions in the country, were hard enough.

The bright morning light shone through the window of the meeting hall where the devotees, some Indian and some foreign, gathered. People dressed in flowing white gowns looked calmly spiritual; even Debbie appeared to be at peace with herself that day. An elderly English lady talked about a golden age with sexless beings and souls of the dead dancing in limbo. An attractive Australian with intense blue eyes announced that his moments of greatest clarity were in times of celibacy and eating a strict vegetarian diet, excluding garlic and onion.

The conversation focused on God consciousness, body consciousness, reincarnation and karma. I wrote across the page of my journal on my first day of class: "Know Thyself as Soul."

I wanted a foothold in the spiritual, but renouncing my worldly life and devoting myself to God was doubtful. I was skeptical, concerned I'd fall for some obscure mysticism or cult. I believed in a greater mystery and respected those seeking it, but I resisted dogmatic, prescriptive or absolute belief systems. But yoga was an ancient and honoured discipline. I thought I'd stay a few days.

At night in my guest house, detached from the ashram, I turned to the little white New Testament that Sister Claudette had given me in Calcutta. I imagined Jesus as a compelling and friendly soul and felt closer to him than Brahma Baba, the founder of Raja yoga. Though Jesus was not an easy choice either.

My lack of religious convictions bothered me. I wanted to believe in *something*. I just couldn't pin an answer on Christianity or Hinduism or Buddhism or anything else. I snuggled into my single bed with a book of poetry and listened to the deluge of rain on the tin roof that soothed my questing soul.

On my last day at the ashram, I listened to a lecture on *samsara*, the wheel of life, and chanted with the ardent, white-robed seekers. Like a baptism, I let myself be immersed. A soft vibrational glow wrapped itself around me. All of us were in the river together, forever flowing to some eternal truth.

22

Kathmandu: The Secular and the Sacred

ON APRIL 25, 2015, a 7.8 magnitude earthquake struck Nepal, the worst quake to strike the region in more than 80 years. The death toll was in the thousands. Entire villages were flattened, terraced farmland was swept away and historic temples, both Hindu and Buddhist, were damaged. The earthquake triggered an avalanche on Mount Everest, making April 25 the deadliest day on the mountain in history.

I watched the images of destruction on CBC news. Chaos, fear and grief were the aftershocks of the Gorkha earthquake. The country was in desperate need of water, food and shelter. Rebuilding Nepal, a mountainous country with widespread poverty, poorly constructed roads and hard-to-reach villages, would take years. I sent my donation to the Canadian Red Cross. Every dollar counts, but it wasn't enough.

I looked for my Nepal journal, wanting to go back to 1978, to the exhilaration, the textures and the terrain of the Himalayas. Every step of my trek was recorded in a journal I couldn't find. It wasn't in my trunk, which was randomly packed with old shoeboxes full of everything else, my interminable paper trail more than a glimpse into the subterranean layers of my life.

"I can't have lost a memory," I worried, driving to my storage unit, not even in the city where I lived. It was up-island, three hours away in the pouring rain. It was cold and miserable pulling out boxes in an unheated, poorly lit warehouse, hoping to locate one small journal I wrote 37 years ago.

Then there it was, wrapped in a plastic Safeway bag. I held it to my heart like a prayer, a *namaste*, the divine in me bowing to the divine in you. It was my bridge back to a remarkable land, to the villages I traversed and the people I met. Maybe the same valleys and villages that were crushed by the landslides. Maybe the same people who were among the 8,700 dead.

THE BACK-TO-EARTH TREKKERS wanting to see Earth's highest peaks, and the tougher breed of mountaineers planning to scale them, headed for Kathmandu, a mecca for travellers in 1978. It was also a destination for Buddhists, Hindus and Westerners exploring Eastern spirituality. Hippies from all over the globe had swept into the city too, with its readily available ganja and a tolerant people who looked the other way.

At the Mona Lisa Café, painted in bright green and red with no other discernible Italian features, the smoke of hashish filled the air. Back home in Canada, I smoked a little pot, read Timothy Leary and loved the Doors and the ragged voice of Janis Joplin. I considered myself a halfway hippie, but I wasn't drawn to the scene in Kathmandu with its one imperative – getting stoned.

While sitting at a crowded table and drinking a banana honey lhassi, a young French man squeezed in beside me. It only took a few words to like Marc. Or trust him, like I had Adam.

We strolled through the narrow streets of the city that smelt of animal dung, cooking oil and the sweatiness of people jostling one another as street sellers called out, "Best deal!" or "Special for you!" Haphazard markets were built next to century-old temples,

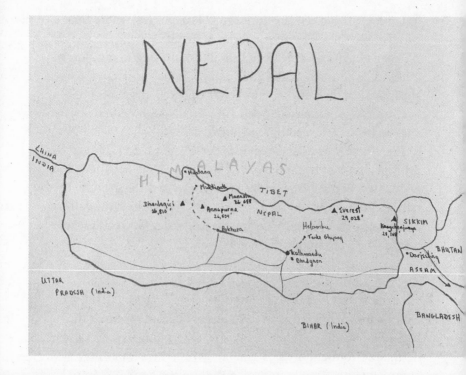

the secular and the sacred brushing sides. A multi-armed goddess sat on a pillar next to a woman selling grapefruit.

As night fell, the shopkeepers closed their shutters and the street sellers pushed their carts with leftover potatoes or onions down cobblestone streets into dark alleys. Late-night people sat at roadside stands, drinking a cup of chai or a glass of *rakshi*, the local beer distilled from millet or rice. A woman, Buddhist or Hindu, I didn't know, dressed in a white robe stood at her temple door. "The day is done, the temple has heard its last laments and the gods are at rest," I imagined she might be saying.

Through a maze of confusing alleyways and wooden buildings squeezed together in a hodgepodge way, Marc and I found our way back to the Star Hotel. One wall of the room was painted a shiny purple, the other three were a neglected yellow. The bed, like all beds in a backpacker's hotel, had a rusty metal frame, a thin mattress on a piece of plywood, a grayish-white sheet and one tatty blanket. The Star Hotel charged 20 Nepalese rupees, $1.70 a night.

One night at the Star was all we had. "I am tired of fast entanglements and fast endings," I said. But first, he whispered, "*Je t'aime*," before morning, before leaving, his gray eyes like a young Kathmandu god.

Timelessness and tenderness at the Star Hotel, call it love or lust, Marc was heading back to France. I headed out for KC's, a popular hangout with an extensive menu of Nepali, Tibetan, Indian and Western food. I could eat, drink and write in my journal, the one bought in India with its cheap plastic cover and flimsy pages stamped with mottos to live by: "Sudden acquaintance brings repentance."

Sudden acquaintances, men, and sex were easy, but it was the caring and sharing that mattered. I dreamed of lifelong, but one day and one night mattered. No regrets. No repentance. I wrote pages upon pages about the life I was living, seeking other worlds, crossing borders, with no fixed address. I was 27 years old.

A tall American, sexy in his tight black pants and black sweater, walked into KC's with a smug swagger and sat down at my table. He talked about money and deals and rip-offs, even in Kathmandu where everything was dirt cheap.

"Wanna go to Yin Yang's tonight?" he asked, slurping his drink. He knew the scene and had a hook – hashish – but I didn't bite. I couldn't go with this man from Tucson, Arizona. Too loud and full of his self-importance.

"No, thanks. I think I'll go back to my hotel and read," I said, probably the last thing anyone did or would admit to wanting to do in Kathmandu. In the hotel room, I lit up the joint Marc had left me. Immediately stoned, every thought stretched into a magnified moment; every word bounced off my brain. The room became dingy and dark, the walls closing in on me. I ran out to the busy street and climbed into a rickshaw. I thought the driver was playing tricks on me, taking me round and round, until I found myself at the central market, a place that could have been a thousand years old. Great raindrops were casting a silky shine on wet tomatoes and carrots, the scents of Kathmandu floating on the air. The sensory overload, either from the hashish or Kathmandu itself, a town of bustling intensity, lingered until the evening when I returned to my humble hotel, closed the door and fell into bed.

For days I walked around town in my new Chinese runners and Tibetan wool socks, popping into markets or temples or cafes to drink chai. I could spend hours reading or writing or talking with people who passed in and out of my life. Like Anne, a serious Swiss girl with henna red hair and inquisitive eyes, partly obscured by thick-rimmed glasses. She was an independent traveller with no fixed itinerary, just like me.

We bicycled out to Narayanthan temple just north of Kathmandu, up and down the dirt road through a terraced land of emerald fields. In the open-air temple, the reclining Vishnu, the creator of all life in the trinity of Hindu gods, lay in a small tank of murky water representing the cosmic ocean with Ananta, the 11-headed snake god in knotted coils around him. Incense curled into sandalwood air and the devotees tossed yellow marigolds to their god. I had a momentary glimpse into the holy.

Riding back to Kathmandu, I was happy, at my most holy. A woman threw water from her bucket onto a potato patch, another spun wool on an archaic wheel. A few old ladies sat on the ground, topless and smoking hand-rolled cigarettes called *bidis*, as their clothes dried on a line. We pedalled through their village and called out "*Namaste.*"

The next day we took the bus to Bhaktapur, caged chickens squawking in the seat next to us, to the Nyatapola temple. Nepali men and women circled the temple in a clockwise direction, chanting the soft hum of the faithful. A flight of stairs led up to the temple, with a pair of stone wrestlers, elephants, lions and griffins displaying their ferocity on each step, though the temple was dedicated to the delicate Lakshmi, the embodiment of beauty, grace and wealth.

Standing among the noisy Nepalese climbing the steps, lighting incense and bowing to the divine, the Nyatapola temple stirred my longing for the spiritual. The cathedrals of Europe inspired me with their magnificence but did not lead me to worship. In a sudden revelation, I saw the Hindu gods and goddesses, the Buddha and Christ all as enlightened souls leading the way.

"No religion has a monopoly on the truth. There are many paths to God," I reflected.

"You know, science and spirit come together at a certain point," Anne, a student of philosophy in Zurich, stated. "Even Einstein knew there was something more."

On another overcrowded bus, we bumped along the road from Bhaktapur to the village of Nagarkot. From there we climbed a steep path to the guest house, every few steps pausing to catch our breath and be dazzled with our first spectacular views of the world's highest peaks.

At the Mount Everest Lodge, a shack of a place that cost 32 cents a night, two young ruffians, about 14 years old with cigarettes hanging from their mouths, stared at us from the open door. They shook their heads with a sideways wiggle, amazed with two laughing, sunburnt, white girls. We shook our heads back, scolding them for smoking. Probably their whole family smoked. A few women, squatting on the side of the road, were smoking and splitting stones with hammers. It was bleak, brutal poverty, and no way for a woman to live.

The Maha Shivaratri festival, where devotees worshipped Lord Shiva, the god of destruction in Hinduism's divine trinity of Brahma the creator, Vishnu the preserver and Shiva the destroyer, had begun in Kathmandu. Anne took her pink bicycle and I took my turquoise one, and we rode out to the Pashupatinath temple, just east of the city on the Bagmati River.

Crowds of Indians, Nepalese, Tibetans, tourists and hundreds of sadhus walked the temple grounds. The sadhus, with their long beards, matted dreadlocks, stripes of Shiva smeared on their foreheads and wearing only the scantest of loincloths, mingled with the festive crowd. It was a gathering of nakedness. One sadhu, smeared with blue ash, gestured us over to his group where two men chopped wood for the evening fire and the others, lounging on the ground, smoked ganja. Anne and I tried to be cool but giggled like schoolgirls talking with the wild-eyed man.

A group of Italians, the women stylish and the men swaggering like peacocks, took photos with their telephoto lens. The smoke from the fires cast a ghostly light over us, the faithful and the faithless, all of us pilgrims, travelling somewhere, seeking something at the festival of Lord Shiva.

Pashupatinath was the most extraordinary environment Anne or I had ever encountered. As night fell, we pedalled away on our old bicycles, riding back to Kathmandu to eat cinnamon rolls at KC's.

23

The Air Between Us

THE HAZARDOUS ROUTE west to Pokhara, with sharp mountain curves and treacherous edges, would be sure death if the bus driver dozed for a second. I clenched the seat in front of me, trying to relax and imagine the adventure ahead, trekking in the mountains, though my courage to hike alone in the Himalayas flapped like a kite on the wind. It was easier to slip into my favourite fantasies, like finding a soulmate, a true love or at least a hiking partner. I'd choose different settings, plots and characters for my Himalayan hero.

Pokhara was a small village scattered across a valley, cradled at the foot of Machhapuchhre. The mountain, not a giant by Himalayan standards, stood at 6993 metres. Revered by the Nepali as Shiva's sacred mountain, it rose behind the town, majestic and powerful one moment and lost in the clouds the next.

I found a room at the Mountain View with a single bed, no other furniture and one small mouse that skittered about. The manager, Devi, an affable laid-back Nepali, played the Beatles on an old tape deck. He served me a cup of chai and told me about his life as a "businessman." Many Nepalis were hanging out signs with "Room to Rent" for the trekkers pouring into Pokhara. The

Annapurna region had just opened to tourism the year before and was a destination for wilderness travel.

Children ran after me in the dusty streets as I wandered about, not exactly aimless as I hoped to meet someone, preferably a man, who wanted to join me on the hike up the Kali Gandaki valley. No such person crossed my path, so I returned to the Mountain View, ate pumpkin pie on the patio with Devi, then retreated into my book, *The Mountain Is Young*, by Han Suyin.

A man dressed in faded jeans and a jean jacket stood by a crumbling rock wall in the vacant lot next to the Mountain View. He was Tibetan, taller than the Nepali, with strong chiselled features. He approached the patio, opened his knapsack and displayed his wares on the ground.

"Come look," he said, showing me some odds and ends, little cars and airplanes and plastic trinkets from China. I bought a yak bell because I wanted to hear his Tibetan story. He called himself Tutop.

"When did you leave Tibet?"

"1959. We walk many days. Very cold. No food."

"You were a little boy. It must have been hard for you."

"Tibetans run from China. My people very, very poor. No freedom."

"How is your life now?"

"I am a refugee in Pokhara camp. I want to live in the mountains," Tutop said, handing me a cigarette.

"Why you come to Nepal?" he asked.

"I want to hike in the mountains."

"Do you love mountains?" he asked. I had never considered if I *loved* mountains. Their towering, indomitable stature could close in on me. I liked open vistas, rolling countryside and pastoral landscapes, softer than the bold power of mountains.

"Yes," I ventured, "but I'm afraid to hike alone."

"You be brave. You sleep and eat in the villages." I took his words as my new truth, my new determination. Tutop would not counsel me unwisely.

"I stay in Pokhara camp," he said, as if guessing my next request that he accompany me.

He took me to a ramshackle store that sold used trekking equipment. I bought chocolate bars, peanuts and raisins for the hike and spent 24 rupees on a Nepalese hand-typed mountain guidebook. Tutop's daily earnings were probably much less.

A cigarette dangling from his lips, we walked back to the Mountain View, his strong mountain body close to mine. I wanted to put my hand in his and breathe the air between us, but Tutop bowed ever so slightly and strolled away.

I considered taking the 20-minute flight, a 20-seat Twin Otter that flew once a week for Jomsom. Then I'd walk for a day to Muktinath, a Buddhist and Hindu spiritual destination with one of the world's highest temples. It would be the easiest way to go, but I wanted to experience the land, the people, the mountains and do the hike that Tutop assured me I could do.

A daily meditation would help me feel calmer, I thought. For moments I'd sit still and sink into emptiness, into the void of all-knowing, then be distracted by a wedding procession with a band blaring off key walking past the Mountain View, or the men on the street corner hammering on scrap metal, or the mouse nibbling on peanuts that fell to the floor.

"Get back inside your mouse hole!" I yelled that night on my sagging cot, disturbed by the Aussie in the room next door, just a paper-thin wall away. He hacked continuously with his smoker's cough. I swore I would never smoke again as I listened to the downpour slamming against the corrugated metal roof.

The weather dawned wet and bleak, menacing, in fact. I was apprehensive about the looming obstacles I imagined in the mountains. Should I set out, or should I abandon my plans? It was Tutop I wanted to talk to, but instead I said goodbye to Devi at the Mountain View, ran out the door and caught the early morning bus back to Kathmandu.

In the city, I did the rounds at KC's, Jomaly's and the Mona Lisa. I ate one sweet treat after another while reading *Seven Years in Tibet* by Heinrich Harrer. True-life adventure stories inspired me to follow my dreams, even though my bravery was sorely in question.

I inquired about organized hikes that didn't appeal to me. I wanted to live my own adventure and go at my own pace. The trekking office told me about the Helambu trail, just north of Kathmandu, only seven days return and not so daunting as the Kali Gandaki. I swung from discouragement to bold ideas.

I was at my best cruising around Kathmandu on an old bicycle, weaving in and out of the bazaar, maneuvering through the crowds and ringing the tinny bell. I had to ride to offset my ravenous appetite, eating lemon meringue pies, brownies and carrot cake that the Nepalis had cleverly mastered.

At Jomaly's I sat down beside Susie from Miami and Birgitta from Sweden. Susie, her jewelry sparkling on her delicate wrist, tossed back her head of long blond hair, confident, chic and cute. I felt the opposite. "How are you doing?" she asked.

"Fine," I said, blushing, wanting to throw back my short brown hair and laugh, in that poised Susie Q sort of way.

Birgitta, the tougher of the two, had just returned from the Helambu. "It's pretty tough going, I'd never do it alone," she said. "We had miserable wet weather, lost the trail, rats everywhere and it was impossible to sleep close to the Nepali coughing and spitting all night long."

Sleeping at night in a Himalayan village with the poor Nepalese in urgent need of health care didn't worry me, but the rats did. It felt like I was losing face to an illusory image of a more courageous version of myself. "I need to do this hike," played on my mind like a broken record.

24

Helambu

AT THE VILLAGE OF SUNDARIJAL, green rice terraces fell away precipitously into the Kathmandu Valley below. A farmer tilled a miniature field at the side of the trail, his walk slow and steady behind his crude wooden plow pulled by two oxen. I gazed at the majestic vista, not as nervous as when I caught the bus out of town. It helped to see four Germans standing nearby.

A Nepali man standing at the trailhead agreed to carry my heavy pack for a dollar a day, then handed it to his son. The barefoot boy, named Jibadroo, turned the hip belt to a head sling and ran up the first steep hill, whistling as he went. The trail followed a cascading creek into a tropical forest with occasional splashes of sunlight.

Two hours later, my breathing laboured with the unaccustomed effort, I reached a ridge with a string of mud brick and thatched-roof houses. It crossed my mind to turn around and catch the afternoon bus back to Kathmandu. My stamina and courage were flailing, but it was no longer an option to chicken out, to forfeit a dream or to fail.

Jibadroo was waiting for me and pointed to the *chai pasal* or tea house. A tattered sheet divided the simple room in two,

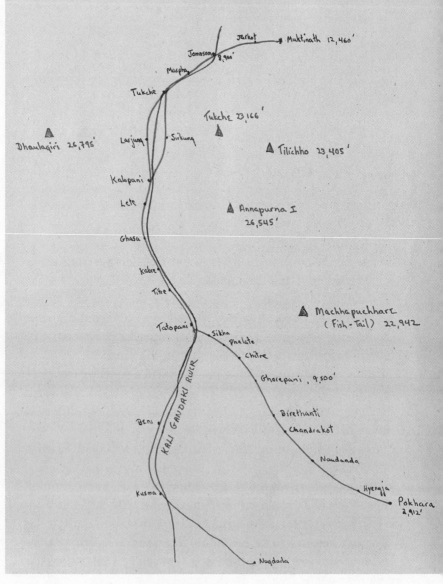

Jomosom – Muktinath Trek

Jarkot
Muktinath 12,460'
Jomosom 8,900'
Marpha
Tukche
Tukche 23,166'
Larjung
Sirkung
Dhaulagiri 26,795'
Tilichho 23,405'
Kalopani
Lete
Annapurna I
26,545'
Ghasa
Kabre
Tilre
Machhapuchhare
(Fish–Tail) 22,942'
Tatopani
Sikha
Phalate
Chitre
Ghorepani, 9,500'
Birethanti
Chandrakot
Beni
KALI GANDAKI RIVER
Naudanda
Hyengja
Kusma
Pokhara
2,912'
Nugdara

one side for business, the other side the family home. I sat down cross-legged among a group of men sitting on their haunches. The woman of the house handed me a cup of hot sugary chai, which I savoured like a precious elixir, then she served lentils and rice, *daal bhat*, which I ate with my fingers from a cracked bowl. As an acclimatized camper in Canada, skilled with campfire cooking, my first meal in a Nepali home wasn't much different.

The food and friendly atmosphere revived me. From there the trail meandered up and down hills, through stretches of open country where I had glimpses of high mountains – the Langtang Himal range. Several *chortens*, small rock structures, had been built along the path, often at the entrance to the villages, some battered by the elements. A chorten symbolized a spiritual land-mark and was believed to have a positive effect on the people who live nearby or pass through the area.

By late afternoon I dragged myself the last few steps to the pic-turesque hamlet of Pati Bhanjyang, made up of seven rock and mud houses. The largest was the village inn where Gerda, one of the Germans, showed me the narrow loft, the communal quarters for the trekkers. Jibadroo and his father would sleep below in the stable for the goats.

After a breakfast of barley pancakes, I handed my pack to Jibadroo and followed the cheerful boy into the fields and forest. I was soon on my own, needing to stop on every steep switchback. With each winded pause, I took the time to notice the flowers along the path, Himalayan buttercups and bluebells. It was exhilarating to have overcome, at least for short stretches, my trepidation in the disquieting aloneness of the mountains.

Nepali porters walking barefoot passed me carrying enormous loads. I thought they must be the world's most fit people, yet it was true that they coughed all night long. They were a nation of smok-ers, living in conditions staggeringly below any national poverty line. There was no electricity, no running water and very few goods, except those carried in by porters.

At the confluence of two rivers, I stepped into a stream, warm enough to wade in and heavenly to soothe the blisters on my feet. I'd trekked nearly 20 kilometres that day, albeit without a pack and not entirely by myself. Jibadroo, wearing my yellow nylon Korean jacket, kept me company, laughing loudly when I attempted words from my Nepali phrasebook: "*thik cha*" for OK, or "*jaani*" for let's go.

After crossing a suspension bridge made of rotting logs, we reached the village of Thakani an hour up from the river. Prayer flags, strung from the cluster of stone dwellings, snapped fiercely in the constant wind in the upper Helambu. I entered a small shrine, the interior walls adorned with painted images of *bodhisattvas*. In Buddhism, bodhisattvas are those who have reached enlightenment and postponed a heavenly *nirvana* to help others on the path. I closed my eyes, celebrating my journey on a Himalayan path.

An old couple, as old and rugged as the hillside they lived on, invited me into their home. They humbly served their daal bhat with one small potato thinly sliced on top. The simplicity of being among people with little choice but to live simply, their homes cradled in the majesty of the mountains, was good for my heart and soul. I had walked into the beauty and sorrow of an extremely poor world and was honoured to share a meal with them.

After an exhausting climb to the village of Taramarang, I collapsed in a circle of mountain women. It was the largest of the Sherpa villages in the area, with a *gompa*, a Buddhist monastery or place of worship, surrounded by prayer flags, but the central store had a serious lack of commodities. Biscuits and a gooey fudge candy crowded the elaborately carved wooden shelf. One tin of fruit cocktail sat on another shelf with some jars of tea and rice. A few decks of playing cards and kerosene lanterns completed the inventory.

Though hiking alone, I'd been comforted by the loose group of trekkers on the trail. We often started and ended our days in the same villages, that night in Tarke Ghyang, a large Sherpa settlement in the Helambu. The four Germans, one lone Kiwi and I gathered in the home of Asmita, who welcomed us with a shy smile on her weather-beaten face. We found our place on the floor, among the children, her husband and a variety of dogs.

Asmita placed a large, chipped bowl of vegetable curry before us. I dipped small pieces of chapati into the savoury stew and rubbed my tummy as a gesture of thanks. After dinner I climbed the ladder up to the loft where the six of us lay down, side by side. Snuggled up against a bale of straw and listening to the steady rain on the roof, a deep relaxation filled every tired cell of my body.

The group decided to stay put until the rain stopped and the fog lifted on our second day in Tarke Ghyang. The rain turned to sleet then to snow, the tiny courtyard blanketed in whiteness. I wrapped an old shawl around me and watched Asmita do her endless chores, children underfoot with a cold gust of wind blowing through the open door. Her husband had left before dawn to pick up goods in Kathmandu.

We had hiked over rough terrain into their villages to eat and sleep in their homes. We tried to be respectful but could also hang about like vultures, waiting for opportunities to capture the perfect image. The Germans snapped pictures. I was guilty too as I watched and waited, my camera at my side. I took one of Jibadroo, who left that morning with his father, surprised with the 50 rupees I'd given him. He grinned and waved goodbye, wearing my wool socks on his hands.

By midday the sun cast a sheen on the melting snow. The group left together, though I quickly fell back with my heavy pack, unable to keep up with the never-ending hills. Sweating inside my clothes, both hot and cold, I braced myself against the freezing wind. One moment the fog obscured the path and the next it lifted in a great sweeping rhythm rolling down the land.

By the end of the sixth day, I reached Melemchi, the last village where I'd spend a night, once more with good-natured Gerda and Urdi, her husband, before returning to Kathmandu. Our hospitable host tried to sell us Sherpa guitars, old silver jewellery, clay pots and Tibetan bells. He didn't seem interested in money, only wanting Western items like jackknives, lighters, flashlights and a manicure set. His rosy-cheeked wife Tenzin efficiently prepared dinner, squatting to cut hunks of fish into a pot hooked over a wood fire. Was the fish caught in a nearby mountain stream, or carried on a porter's back all the way from Kathmandu? I didn't ask.

Late in the evening, a group of men, women and children climbed the steep hill behind the village. Gerda, Urdi and I followed them, the indigo sky lit up with a thousand stars, to a whitewashed stone temple on top of the hill. Men sitting on their heels recited from holy books as the plaintive sounds of their drums, cymbals and one trumpet echoed off the mountains. I swayed to the sounds of the celebration while bodhisattvas, gold and red ferocious deities, jumped from the walls. The villagers became increasingly festive, the rakshi and religion stirring the deep chill of a Sherpa New Year.

BACK IN THE CITY, a wave of lassitude swept over me, no longer on the mountain high of Helambu. I was proud of myself, having hiked for seven days, but I wanted to go higher, be braver. It was the push-myself edge I craved, a place to be myself, or find myself, or lose myself, where no one could define me other than the path itself.

I walked the streets of Kathmandu only half-interested in the shopkeepers' wares, only half-enchanted with the city's allure. I turned to the one thing that comforted me when feeling alone, or lonely, or out of step with the world around me. Writing in my journal, a cup of chai and sweets at the Mona Lisa satisfied my melancholic bout.

A woman waltzed into the Mona Lisa, a pink flower in her hair. "Chloe!" I'd last seen her in Calcutta; both of us were amazed with our serendipitous encounter. She twirled her silver bangles and told me one story after another about her footloose travels, her risky adventures and her recent lovers. Chloe equally listened to mine.

"The mountains were exhilarating," I said. "Let's do a trek together."

"I want to drink every gulp of Nepal," Chloe replied, "but I can't go." Over spicy pakoras, she revealed details of her next scheme to transfer goods from Nepal to India. Her drug-smuggling, criminal behaviour fascinated but alarmed me. Walking back to our cheap hotels, I once again tried to deter her. She was enigmatic and ephemeral, something like the dusty rose of evening that disappeared into the dark.

In the morning, we bicycled out to Swayambhunath, one of the holiest Buddhist sites in Nepal, on a hillside just west of the city. Monkeys scampered up and around the temple, its golden spire glistening in the afternoon sun. Streamers fanned out from the spire, butter lamps burned and the faithful walked around the grand white *stupa*, or shrine, spinning prayer wheels. The wheels were engraved with the Buddhist mantra "*Om mani padme hum*," meaning "Praise to the jewel in the lotus."

The Buddha had mysterious eyes that looked out in four directions with a half-malevolent warning, or a half-benevolent embrace. We had our deities, entwined in our Christian upbringings and New Age wanderings. Both of us were seekers, still looking for that benevolent embrace, a steadfast faith, not yet as solid as Swayambhunath sitting on the hill.

Chloe and I said goodbye in Kathmandu, the city of dubious connections. Her mind was set, she needed to make money and I needed to get back to the mountains. "Stay safe," I said, which seemed a hopelessly inadequate goodbye for my friend walking such a reckless road.

25

The Kali Gandaki

I TOOK THE BUS BACK TO POKHARA, which looked like a Wild West frontier town, and checked into the Mountain View. I chatted with Devi as Hindu rock blared from his old cassette player.

In the late afternoon, I walked to the open-air market, a hodge-podge place of flimsily built stalls where the Tibetans shopped. The women wore colourful, striped, wool aprons, signalling they were married, and the men wore impressive sheepskin hats. The Tibetans were a tough nomadic people, coming from the highest inhabited plateau of the world.

Tutop could have been herding yaks on that windswept Tibetan plateau. Then I saw him, lingering in the square, smoking a cigarette. "Where were you?" he asked, greeting me with his ever so slight bow.

"In the Helambu."

"Were you happy in the mountains?"

"Oh yes, I was happy."

"And you?" I asked, accepting the cigarette he offered me.

"I meet the foreigners, but they don't buy, only talk."

I didn't buy either. Tutop, not a man to chat, lit my cigarette, his hand brushing mine. "Are you going to the Kali Gandaki?" he asked.

"I'm leaving tomorrow morning. For two weeks to Muktinath and back," I said. It felt like a promise or a pact with someone who might have cared.

"It is good, the Kali Gandaki, the river of the gods."

"I'm trying to be brave."

"No worry. You be fine," he said, his face crinkling into a grin.

Walking back to the Mountain View, I wondered if I'd lost all my common sense setting off into the Himalayas on my own. Dinner with Devi and a good book were good distractions. Still, I tossed and turned all night long. At least the day dawned sunny.

I had a dozen good reasons to be scared and repeatedly examined my map, hoping it might reassure me on the rattling bus ride from Pokhara to Suikhet, the start of the trek. It began as an effortless walk by furrowed fields, but my pack weighed me down and my lungs heaved on the steep inclines. At a stream, I lay down on a large flat rock, cupped water and splashed it over my head. Small and fragile buttercups sprouted from cracks in the rock in a terrain that was all rock – the houses, the canyon, the trail.

Over 300 metres higher, in Naudanda, the hillside inn was no more than a two-room mud hut. *Didi*, as one calls a woman or sister, greeted me at first with a guarded shyness that softened into what seemed like a kind concern. She offered a meal of daal bhat and a mat to lie on. After eating, I spread out my bag, climbed in and immediately fell asleep. The cost for dinner, the bed and breakfast of Nepali fried bread with honey came to 50 cents.

With a superb morning vista of Machhapuchhare, I began the sharp descent to the next village of Bhiretani. With trembling legs and buckling knees, I stumbled down the path, longing for a tea house to rest my aching body. The mountain people, accustomed to the foreigners that tramped through their territory, watched with a trace of amusement as I laboured up and down their rocky slopes.

That night in the village guest house, a cold, bare room, I bedded down with four polite Japanese men trying to speak incomprehensible English with me. A Dutch couple arrived later and wedged in too. The company of fellow trekkers reassured me, but sleep was impossible with the barking of wild dogs.

Our hostess served an onion omelet for breakfast, then eagerly collected her fees. I set out on my solitary trek, walking into wider and wilder vistas. Small pleasures kept me focused, like the chirping of birds or watching delicate butterflies hover over red rhododendrons. A caravan of a dozen donkeys, with flashy ribbons on their heads and carrying goods out of the high plateaus, ambled by in an orchestra of bells and brays. I smiled at two Tibetans leading the procession. They threw back a quick smile, softer than the hardness of their lives.

Three sadhus stopped to talk on the 600-metre climb to Ulleri. "We are saints going to Muktinath, but unfortunately we have just run out of money. We will be most grateful if you can assist us." I couldn't refuse the request of saints and bought them tea and biscuits in the village.

The mountain children appeared healthy and robust, though I knew the conditions of their lives were tough, having to work from a young age in the fields, doing chores children from more prosperous countries never do. The three runny-nosed kids I met on the path to Ulleri were scantily dressed, their T-shirts not enough for the chilly temperatures at high altitudes. I gave their mother a half-finished tin of peanut butter, which greatly pleased her as she stuck her finger into it, giving each of her children a gooey lump.

In the small hamlet of Ghorapani, I had an uneasy night with an upset stomach, the first since my frequent intestinal distress in India. I crept down the stairs, past the sleeping family, and out the back door to the outhouse. I was afraid of rats, wild dogs and snakes, but only met a blast of cold air. I crawled back into my bag for a few more hours of precious warmth with four other trekkers sleeping beside me.

Before dawn in a biting wind, the group of us climbed Poon Hill to catch a breathtaking vista of the sunrise over Annapurna, Nilgiri, Dhaulagiri, Tukche and Himchuli. The sweep of the land rising to the world's highest peaks dwarfed me into my small self. It also inspired a longing for greatness, for living a life free of pettiness and limitations and fears. I wanted to throw my arms around someone, preferably a Nepali or a Tibetan, and celebrate this greatness.

I set out with renewed determination to Tatopani, entering the semi-arid region of the Kali Gandaki canyon, the historic trade route between India, Nepal, Tibet and China. The trail wound through a forest of gnarled stumps with big black crows cawing, harbingers of bad omens in Nepali folklore. A crackling in the bush, no doubt monkeys, made me nervous. Clouds covered the sun, bamboo trees rustled in a strong wind and a lone buffalo bellowed.

Crossing a shaky wood bridge, I reached Tatopani, which meant hot water. Big orange pumpkins were popping up in fields around the village. I devoured the main dish, pumpkin pie, served for supper at the lodge, then strolled down to the riverside where a steamy mist rose from the springs. I washed all my stinking clothes and let my sweaty body relax deeper and deeper into the hot waters. Every step of the trail had been worth it for such a luxury. That night l slept like a baby.

In the warm morning sun, I massaged my feet, put on my Tibetan socks and laced up my second-hand boots. I reluctantly left Tatopani and walked on to a village that appeared to be clinging to the rubble of a landslide. I wasn't reassured by the guidebook's description of what lay ahead:

> The trail is chiseled into the face of the vertical cliffs high above the river. This stretch should be taken slowly and carefully. Although the bridges are solid and the footing secure, gale force winds perpetually howl through this narrow gorge, and the noise and constant buffeting can make it difficult to concentrate on the trail.

The panorama was wild, awesome and terrifying. I shuddered with cold when the sun disappeared behind a cloud, feeling too small in too big a place – big mountains, big skies and everywhere big rocks. Each step tested my commitment to keep going. I was frightened. I needed a village. I needed shelter.

On day five, reaching Ghasa, two boys led me into their house, a wood and mud structure permeated with the strong, bittersweet smell of yak dung. I sat down by the fire, keeping my down jacket on as three younger children sat naked from the waist down. They gaped at me, bewilderment in their eyes, as their mother, Bhadra, served delicious Nepalese cornbread with honey.

I brought out a crumpled *Time* magazine from my pack that I'd bought in Kathmandu. I read about Japan's booming trade surplus. The news seemed irrelevant, as it appeared that few goods of any sort trickled into this village on a remote mountainside. Once, the Thakali people of the upper Kali Gandaki had been successful traders with Tibet, but their economy was hit hard when the People's Republic of China closed the Himalayan border after 1960.

The family gathered around, serious and excited, pointing to the pictures of high-rise buildings. In their room full of smoke, rolled up sleeping mats and a scattering of other belongings, I wondered what they were thinking. I was sharing an alien world with them.

Bhadra busied herself in a tiny, organized kitchen, bending over the open fire, popping corn. I rubbed my tummy, indicating I loved popcorn. She added a wallop of congealed yak grease.

"How are you, Bhadra?" I asked in Nepali. She shrugged her thin shoulders and swept up her arms as if to say, "Can't you see I'm run off my feet?" She swung her baby onto her hip while giving orders to her teenage daughter for the evening meal. The girl stirred a huge cauldron of cornmeal mush.

Everyone worked, including the children. There was the plowing of fields, the sowing, reaping, thrashing of wheat, the milling of corn, the weaving of cloth, collecting firewood and milking the cows. The women had the cooking and cleaning and the raising of children, as well. There were undoubtedly a thousand other chores I wouldn't have known about, coming from a life of many comforts.

The family squatted and I sat cross-legged as we ate a dinner of the surprisingly tasty mush. They scooped up great amounts of food with their hands, then the dogs came over and licked the plates clean.

I searched Bhadra's face for moods and meaning. She seemed sad and tired with the weight of her life, then softer, a woman, once young and beautiful. She handed her brood of children some *mithai* or candy. I had two oranges in my pack but only relinquished one to the kids, who seemed both hardy and malnourished at the same time. I needed the sweet juiciness of a Nepali orange in moments on the trail when I couldn't take another step.

Upstairs in my sleeping quarters, I heard a skittering of little creatures in the bags of grain a few feet from my sleeping bag. One of them ran across my head in the middle of the night. It was only a mouse. Still, I shifted myself downstairs, stretched out my bag beside the children and cuddled close to the family in sound sleep.

In the morning, I collected the clothes I'd hung out to dry. My pink underwear had mysteriously disappeared from the line, but I didn't say a thing. I enjoyed Bhadra's cornbread breakfast, put my hands to my heart and left the village of Ghasa behind.

I was walking through the deepest valley on Earth, the Kali Gandaki, with Dhaulagiri at 8167 metres, the world's seventh-highest peak, rising sharply to the west, and Annapurna at 8091 metres, the tenth-highest peak, to the east. The desolate plateau led into Mustang, the forbidden kingdom of Nepal. I welcomed the stop in Larjung as the wind thundered up and down the valley. The small village had thick-walled houses built close together, forming tunnel-like streets. In the gloomy tea house, I felt like a climber in a bivouac, uncertain of my fate on a mountain face. I'd soon be in the next village of Jomsom, with its airstrip if I needed a fast way out.

That night, His Highness, the King of Mustang, graced the Jomsom Hotel, a cut above the usual village inns with two stories and a wooden balcony. I sat down next to him in the inner courtyard, sipping chai from a battered tin cup, not knowing he was the king. His Highness wore a black fur coat, fur hat and padded silk pants. He flung his arms in the air with great flourish and made some sort of exclamatory remark. He laughed loudly, threw me a friendly smile, then continued talking with his entourage from Kathmandu.

As darkness fell, I stepped outside into the howling wind and looked up at the night sky, astonished at its million stars. Everything astonished me in the Himalayas: the day and the night, the earth and the sky, the vast emptiness and the God-inspired fullness of it all.

26

Moksha

THE SNOW FELL HEAVILY from a stormy morning sky as I trudged up the path from Jharkot, a village with a market and a monastery. I had to rally my resolve for the final incline, my stamina flailing. I felt in tatters, like the white prayer flags that did not stand a chance in the raging winds. My head started to pound and I gulped for air, the first signs of acute altitude sickness. It was much more worrisome than the weather but, huddled in a protected corner, turning back was no longer an option. I was almost there.

I had been hiking for eight days to reach my destination of Muktinath on the edge of the Tibetan plateau at an altitude of 3800 metres. It was the last habitation before the Thorong La pass, the highest navigable pass in the world that led to the east side of the Annapurna range. Muktinath had never been a place I'd dreamed of seeing, like the Grand Canyon or Machu Picchu or the Taj Mahal. I'd never heard of it until I arrived in Nepal.

The village, a cluster of rock houses, was wedged on a steep slope and enshrouded in snow. Three teen boys wearing T-shirts and pajama pants in the wintry weather stood on the path leading into the village as if waiting for me. I followed them through a narrow tangle of alleys to a small white pagoda. Hindus called the site

Mukti Kshetra, the "place of salvation." Inside the unassuming temple a golden statue of Vishnu, the preserver of all life, stood guard. Water, tumbling from the high Himalayas, spurted from 108 carved bull faces along the exterior walls.

Devotees would bathe in the ice-cold water, as they believed it gave *moksha*, the highest liberation from earthly life granting union with the divine. Moksha, sought after not only by Hindus but Buddhists, Jains and Sikhs, was the transformation from suffering to knowledge, peace and bliss. I splashed a little water on my face, wanting to believe my journey was sacred too.

To the east of the pagoda stood a Tibetan gompa. Inside its faded whitewashed stone walls was Jwala Mai, the temple of the eternal flame. A *jumma*, a Buddhist nun, who looked a hundred years old, stood at the door and reluctantly let me in. Many gilded Buddhas adorned the extraordinary cave-like place. Scrolled cloth paintings called *tangkas*, with images of furious deities strangling snakes and breathing fire, hung from the ceiling. From one wall a trickle of water flowed from between the rocks and a jet of natural gas, a blue flame, burnt continuously from the same crevice. Pilgrims had been coming to Jwala Mai for over 3,000 years to witness this demonstration of divine omnipotence.

"*Gau! Gau!*" the jumma muttered, prodding me with her stick. It must have meant "Get out!" I wanted to stay a minute longer, for a taste of that mystical moment, the perfect silence that transcends all.

I left Muktinath with an uneasy stomach and a headache, and was anxious about the descent ahead. It took five hours to reach Jomsom, bracing myself against the violent wind that nearly blew me over. I focused on my feet, glancing up intermittently at the moonscape hills dotted with caves. Holy men had lived in these small craggy holes on the rock face. How did they survive in such bleak dwellings? Such spiritual discipline and worldly sacrifice mystified me.

That night in Jomsom, I wrote in my journal by flickering candlelight, considering the 20-minute flight back to Pokhara. I'd write lists of pros and cons when uncomfortable decisions loomed, like walking a Himalayan path or abandoning it. Why *was* I walking such a wild and windswept land and subjecting myself to discomfort and danger? Who was I trying to impress? My friends, my family – my mother who didn't approve, my father who didn't understand? Or was it myself?

I could curse every step when I was overcome with doubt, exhaustion and fear. The hike had also built my confidence as a woman alone. The mountains brought me closer to an ineffable mystery. I couldn't swim in icy cold waters for moksha, but I could walk the earth in the Himalayas. It was *my* spiritual discipline, *my* spiritual high.

Falling into a deep sleep, I dreamed that Muktinath was nestled in sunny meadows with flowers blooming and birds singing. An old lady in a long white gown, a luminous angelic presence, took me by the hand and led me into the light. I woke up early, unravelled myself from my sleeping bag and looked out the sliver of a window to dense fog and chickens clucking in the yard. But my mind was clear. I wanted to be in the mountains and walk my way home.

With renewed energy, I sprinted up and down the trail on the mist-covered slopes to Marpha. My body felt stronger, my soul lighter, dancing between boulders and the scattered juniper trees. At the chai pasal, I snacked on fresh-baked apple fritters and a bowl of roasted soybeans. Surrounded by the icy peaks the Nepali said were carved by the gods, I knew at that moment I too was blessed by the gods.

The people, particularly the yak herders, fascinated me as they walked the valleys with their shaggy beasts. A semi-nomadic people, they followed the seasons, moving up to the highest pastures to graze their yaks in the warm weather. The caravans passed me, going north or south alongside the Kali Gandaki, a world unto themselves, man and beast, the land and the sky. The scent of yak drifted on the mountain air.

Yaks were an indispensable part of mountain life. The males provided transportation, carrying cargo brought from Tibet.

It could be rock salt, tea from China, dried sheep meat, wool, carpets or manufactured goods such as flashlights. They carried rice, sugar, kerosene and cotton cloth back on the return trip. The females provided milk, essential for the tea-drinking culture of the Himalayas. The tea was not like any tea I had drunk before. Made with milk, yak butter and salt, it tasted like a pungent soup to fortify against the cold.

I imagined joining a family of yak herders, a kind of cultural immersion into an ancient way of life, just like Dervla Murphy did living among the Afghani nomads. I'd work with the women, brave the elements and be brave myself. The leap from my modern world into the unknown excited me, then I'd be more realistic and imagine working as a nurse in a Himalayan village. But that seemed daunting too and I'd return to the trail, counting the days till Kathmandu.

The yak herders didn't frighten me but getting lost did, as the path often disappeared in a field of rubble and rock. I stumbled, falling over a stone fence into prickly thistles, hobbled back to the path and found my way to Khopang.

On the outskirts of the village a schoolyard with the world's finest view was perched high above the Kali Gandaki. Barefoot girls and boys, sitting outdoors on rickety wood benches, called out words in singsong voices. The teacher, a young man, sat at an equally rickety table. A strong wind whistled in off the gorge and blew all his papers away.

I arrived at the guest house and walked in without knocking, as doors were always open to communal smoke-filled rooms. I took off my heavy pack, sat on a squat wooden stool and drank a mug of aromatic chai served by Gitali, the lady of the house. She pointed out the ladder to the loft for her foreign guests.

She had made her kitchen as cozy as the circumstances of her life allowed. Tin jars in a tidy row on rough-hewn wooden shelves contained flour, sugar, rice and lentils, the staples of life. A few black tarnished pots hung from a rack, and a kettle was steaming on the fire. I tore open a packaged perfumed towelette, cleaned my hands, then offered one to Gitali. I took her hands in mine and wiped them with the moist tissue. She gasped when I threw the disposable towelette into the fire. In her world, everything was a precious commodity and nothing was thrown away.

Gitali served potatoes lightly dusted with curry for dinner, the best I'd eaten in Nepal. I'd love to cook potatoes just as she did, though I couldn't replicate the dish without the ambiance of a Nepalese kitchen. During dinner, a calf walked into the room, a rooster crowed and a dog licked my plate clean.

A few men gathered in the evening for a drink of local brew. Each village may have had its own distillery. The village schoolteacher, the man I'd seen earlier, arrived looking like a kid himself with his runny nose, tousled hair and dishevelled clothes. A serious young man, Amrit delved into a conversation with me about the problems facing the isolated settlements, from transportation to agriculture, education and health care.

"We need a doctor, and we need the birth control pill. We have too many children and the children need to go to school," Amrit stated. "No one has any money, and we are very poor." He offered me a rakshi with a swirl of yak butter. Sitting close to the wood fire, conversing with the schoolteacher and warmed by the alcoholic rough brew, a cloak of deep calm wrapped itself around me.

"Please miss, do you wish to accompany me on a village stroll?" Amrit asked the next morning as he ate a bowl of *tsampa*, a barley porridge, at Gitali's. Delighted with his invitation, I walked with him to the humble dwelling of the jumma, another bent over old woman, a widow who had become the caretaker of the temple. Her asthmatic wheeze worsened as we followed her up the muddy trail to the temple of 100 prayer wheels. A ruddy-cheeked child wrapped in torn woolens played with the brass wheels set into the exterior wall. As the jumma opened the heavy wooden door, a shaft of sunlight illuminated an exquisite interior of bright bodhisattvas. Who would have known this unimposing shrine, built 800 years ago, housed such beauty?

The jumma performed her rituals, emptying and refilling bowls with sacred water, lighting a butter lamp and blowing on a conch shell that emitted a few raspy gasps. As we left the temple, the clouds parted into shades of rose and blue, forming a magical halo over Dhaulagiri.

"Soon the people of Khopang will be happy," Amrit said. "The apple trees are planted and there will be fruit in a year or two." I had never considered the relationship between apples and happiness. Looking out to the hills, the morning sun warming the land, everything was imbued with happiness. I stayed another night in Khopang.

27

Bowing to the Divine

MOVING ON was the natural rhythm for me. I skipped down the trail between Khopang and Kalopani, a picturesque village infused with the fragrance of pine. With each turn, I remembered a familiar tree, a stream, a mountain, letting me see with deeper eyes and surer steps. The canyon still had its eerie boulders, lurking Himalayan monsters, but they spooked me a little less.

The weather swung from clear to overcast and ominous, all in a day. I had to bend into the wind and hail that suddenly fell out of the sky. Below me, the muddy, brown Kali Gandaki moved slowly like a snake ready to spit. It was not a friendly river, and the land was not a gentle land, but grand, harsh and unforgiving. The valleys and mountains swallowed me in their silence.

Invariably, I drifted into thoughts of home, my work as a nurse, my family, the problems of the world and my own irregular life. I had every freedom and opportunity, but a faint distress rumbled in my heart. I didn't name it in 1978 but wonder now if it was my privilege that distressed me. I was too young then to understand the imperative of humanitarian work or putting one's life on the line for justice or equality or peace.

Most of all I thought about love. My repetitive stories had no beginning or end. I'd escape into dreamland, then I'd remember I was alone in the high mountains and had to be vigilant. Real dangers – an assault, threatening animals, avalanches or falling off a cliff – were all possibilities. I'd tell myself over and over that I was capable and courageous as I carried on hiking the Himalayan trail.

I distracted myself with food, imagining the next village, the next meal. In Tatopani, I feasted on pancakes, cornbread, honey, pumpkin pie and lemon tea. Lounging in the rock-hewn hot spring on a scraggy slope while my wet clothes dried on the hillside made all those steps I had cursed worthwhile.

Just south of Tatopani I came upon a fork in the trail. I decided on the trail to the right, the less-travelled route back to Pokhara that began with an impressive staircase hewn from a sheer wall of stone. Climbing the steep steps, I heard a rustling noise in the bush that emitted a loud snort then trampled away. I added a wild pig, or maybe a boar, to my list of threats on the trail.

I had decided to trust the Nepali men, as they always said namaste: I honour the divine in you. I had even trusted the gallant horseman I had met the day before while sitting by the chorten outside Dana. Trying to summon up the energy for the last hour to Tatopani, a man dressed in black and wearing a red embroidered cap cantered up to me, seated on a sleek white horse.

"Do you want to ride with me?" he asked in good English, his strong, bronzed face looking down at me. I'd never encountered such a person on a Himalayan trail and readily accepted the ride. He pulled me up onto his horse and we rode off through a sparse forest of wind-stunted trees. I held on tight, and for one wildly exhilarating moment wrapped my arms around my Himalayan hero, my Nepalese knight.

"Can I spend the night with you?" he asked, taking my hand as I stepped down in Tatopani. "I want satisfaction with European ladies and Nepalese men are very good lovers. European ladies love sex with me."

"Another time," I laughed and let him kiss my hand goodbye. Like an apparition, he was gone.

Most men ignored me, including the three standing at the village pump in Tipling. Spitting red betel juice and smoking bidis, they inspected a big hunk of raw buffalo meat sitting on the ledge. They were porters taking a break from their work, their enormous earthenware pots propped up against the wall.

The Kali Gandaki cut a wider swath through the valley from Tipling to Beni. I followed the trail well above the river shore until it stopped abruptly, having slipped over the edge of the slope. A makeshift bamboo and rope bridge precariously swung over the collapsed section. Not about to cross on my own, I waited for another hiker, a villager or a porter, anyone to save me if I fell into the uninviting river below. An hour later no one had appeared, and I had no choice but to proceed. With jelly legs and in an unwitnessed feat of bravery, I crossed the bridge.

An oppressive heat clung to the air at lower altitudes, requiring frequent stops. I stuck my entire head underwater at streams along the way. Fantasies of a cold beer or a Limca soda at the trail's end tempered my thirst. Ten men carrying a long length of heavy cable, probably for the washed-out bridge, shuffled past, one foot in front of the other.

For the last leg of my Himalayan adventure, I lay back on the rooftop of a jalopy bus with six American hippies wasted on ganja. "Have a toke," they offered. I was already high, celebrating every hard-earned step of my trek, feeling free as a bird sweeping over the hills.

At the Hotel Mountain View, I let a trickle of warm water wash off two weeks of sweat and dirt from my filthy, stinking body. In a yellowed mirror I inspected my burnt face and flea bites that covered my arms and legs. Liking my new muscled and lean body, I pulled on my clothes still smelling of village smoke and headed for town.

I had walked 290 kilometres and wanted someone, particularly Tutop, to be interested in my great trek in the Himalayas. I hung around the central square, hoping to see him, but no one was there. No one to say, "Well done." It was time to pack up a memory, a momentary namaste under the gaze of Machhapuchhare, and return to Kathmandu.

I was proud of my new identity as a solo trekker in the mountains, but my self-assurance was slapped into place the first day back in the city.

"I do the hair of the royal family and can't treat lice heads," the German hairdresser at the beauty salon unceremoniously said. "I can't risk my reputation." I walked away, infested, contaminated and stunned.

A shop down the lane had a sign on its door: "Expert Lice Treatment." Pictures of the king of Nepal, Birendra Bikram Shah, Jawaharlal Nehru, the former prime minister of India, and Marilyn Monroe adorned the interior walls. The barber, a jovial man, agreed to treat my hair. He mixed a smelly powder with mustard seed oil and lemon juice and applied it to my head for 15 minutes.

"I tell you, Madam, lice eggs all gone," he said, assuring me he had the best treatment in town.

After paying the barber, I returned to Gerda, the royal family hairdresser. "Your hair is still crawling with eggs," she pronounced on examining my head.

"Lice there is not, Lice there is not," Mr. Rajasnath repeated, shaking his head in disbelief. He proceeded to cut off my hair, which fell in fine wisps to the floor, leaving me bald.

I slunk back to my hotel and on that same day fell sick. My body ached with hot and cold sensations, my muscles trembling in painful spasms. It felt like a thunderstorm, with hail as large as marbles, pounding the walls of the Parash Hotel. I lay in bed for an entire day bewailing my body and beating up my soul.

Lice didn't cause fever, but I didn't know what assailed me. My mind raced with a multitude of tropical scourges, malaria being the most likely. I limped over to KC's and ate a bowl of rice, the only food I could tolerate.

A pretty French girl sat across the table, applying her makeup with a cultivated coquette look some women so easily achieve. I looked a sight with my peeling red skin, shaved head and deplorable state, though the fever had broken. She glanced at me, a glance that said she had no interest in either me or my heroic stories.

I walked out the door and into the streets of Kathmandu. Caught between a Himalayan high and a dreary post-fever malaise, I sat down on the steps of the pagoda at Durbar Square. Melancholy, a familiar solitude, wrapped itself around me like an old smoky blanket. All I could do was watch the comings and goings of the sturdy Nepalese and the foreigners who wandered among them. I imagined they were all in the namaste, bowing to the divine, or they could be yearning for something they imagined they needed, or missing something they thought they had lost. Could this be the human condition? Living our lives in missing?

I was missing the wild, fresh adventure of the mountains, and the hospitality of the people, fierce as the Himalayan winds blowing through their lives. I could hear the sweetness of bells in far-off valleys and see the yak herders in their vast spaces under a cobalt sky. I was walking into another time, another girl, a brave mountain girl, bowing to the divine.

28

Bodh-Gaya

I LEFT THE MAGICAL KINGDOM of Nepal and flew into Patna with a bottle of Johnny Walker and a carton of Triple Fives hidden in my luggage. No matter how small the goods, I had become a smuggler of contraband. Chloe's suggestion. Just once, for the thrill.

India would be easier on my return, I told myself. I'd go with the flow. The taxi ride from the airport to downtown Patna was a rude awakening with ten people squeezed into a car meant for five. The driver sat on another man's lap as he drove the rusty crate. Selling contraband was easier. I walked a block down the main street, exposing my bottle of whiskey and carton of cigarettes, and quickly sold them for twice the price.

Khushwant Singh not only wrote that the presiding deity of India was dust but that "the presiding deity of Patna was stench." The stink of urine overwhelmed me as I approached the railway station, the floor covered with the usual transient population of ragged people, passengers with their bags and bundles and men selling chai and chapatis. Patna brought me back to a mess of uneasy emotions, India pulling me in and pushing me away.

The plastic seat on the train to Gaya was scorching hot. I wrote in my journal, my wet left hand smearing the page and sour-sweet sweat dripping from my upper lip. From Gaya I took the short trip to Bodh-Gaya by scooter-rickshaw through countryside of wheat, rippling gold in the fields, and dotted with red, clay houses. Sitting between two men, several battered suitcases and my knapsack, I was engulfed in black fumes belching from the exhaust.

Bodh-Gaya was the most revered site for Buddhists. It was there, six centuries before Christ, that Gautama Buddha was said to have attained enlightenment under what became known as the *bodhi* tree. According to Buddhist texts, he sat in meditation for 49 days.

The central shrine was an imposing stone cone set in a garden of flowers with bobbles strung on the surrounding shrubs. In the inner shrine, a large painted Buddha, who had piercing eyes, looked angry. I couldn't help but think of Jesus with eyes that were pools of compassion. I didn't take sides. I was willing to reconsider both Jesus and the Buddha.

The Thai pagoda had an exquisite roof of golden tiles with two foreboding griffins guarding the door. The Chinese and Burmese temples were ornate, while the Japanese design was simple and serene. I most liked the Tibetan temple with its bold green, red and gold walls. Outgoing and jovial monks greeted me at the door, a glimpse into their Tibetan soul.

"Do you like Bodh-Gaya?" a man asked, interrupting my reverie as I strolled on the temple grounds. He had a trim mustache and shoes so polished they glowed.

"Yes, I do. I wish I had more time to see it all."

"Buddhism is about the impermanence of all life, so we don't need more time. We only have the present," he commented. Perhaps he was a Buddhist scholar or a contemplative Hindu.

"I am not Buddhist, I am Hindu," he said, as if reading my mind, "but the wisdom of Buddhism attracts me. Not as complicated as Hinduism. We have too many gods and goddesses."

"I'm not a Buddhist, nor a Hindu, and not a practising Christian," I replied. "But I'm happy to be here in Bodh-Gaya."

"You've come to the right place. Maybe from America?" he asked as we listened to a deep chanting echoing from the Tibetan temple.

"No, from Canada," I said, always proud to announce my nationality. "And where are you from?"

"From Gaya. My name is Prajit. Let me take you back to town and may I invite you to the cinema?" I wasn't fond of sensational Hindi soap operas, but spending an evening with Prajit seemed an excellent idea.

We left Bodh-Gaya and its bodhi tree on his old scooter. I put my arms around my new acquaintance as he weaved in a show of bravado down the long straight strip of burning asphalt. An oxen cart creaked by with its owner atop the hay, asleep under the blazing sun.

The film: Happily married family. Mother dies while rescuing son playing on train tracks. Boy is traumatized and can no longer speak. Father goes to incredible lengths to raise money for the operation to restore his son's speech. I doubt such an operation exists, though this would be irrelevant in a sensational Hindi movie. Boy survives the operation, but father falls down the stairs and loses his hearing! Son sings a song to his dad that his mom used to sing. They accept their fate, and the film ends with the motto, "Life Moves On," inscribed on the screen. A sentimental and silly film; still, it made me cry.

I had been in India for months and had yet to have a romantic liaison. Prajit was an intelligent, thoughtful man and an attraction hung as heavily as the heat between us. He saw me back to my guest house and had me promise we'd meet the following day.

Mr. Chaudry, the proprietor of the guest house, talked a lot and had a great yellow *tilak*, representing the spiritual eye, in the centre of his bald forehead. "I am very, very fond of Canadians. The Canadian government is good to Indian immigrants. It just accepts Brahmins and Kshatriyas as they are the only reliable and fair-complexioned Indians." Mr. Chaudry stated affirmatively.

I didn't think the Canadian government had such a policy and arguing would not have advanced any cause for social justice. I ordered a third bottle of pop, the only way to combat my thirst in the baking weather as I waited for Prajit, who had to work that day at his administrative post with the Indian civil service. A tiresome bureaucratic position, he'd said.

"My marriage fizzled after three years in England." Prajit recounted his life over a dinner of *chokha*, the Gaya specialty of spicy mashed potato and smoked red chili. "The miserable wet winters nearly killed me. I came home," he said, a careworn look on his face.

"I've never been married but can imagine how a marriage fizzles," I said.

"I understand why you are choosing independence before marriage," he said, with an uncommon sensitivity on a touchy subject in India.

The Buddha Rest House, a two-star hotel, was above the restaurant. "Do you wish to accompany me upstairs?" Prajit asked after dinner in his formal English. "My boarding house is not a proper place to bring a lady. There will be very much gossip."

"Sure," I responded, not wanting to appear too nervous or too eager.

Prajit and I sat on the bed for a few awkward minutes. He ensured that the concierge hadn't followed us to pry at the door, turned off the overhead bare bulb light, then kissed me with a solemn reserve. Slowly he undid my blouse and my skirt fell softly to the floor. The gentle ritual surprised me after his wild abandon on the scooter and daring invitation to the Buddha Rest House. Laying in his arms, breathing his musky scent, my first Indian lover seduced me.

The next day I returned to Delhi, Prajit and I leaving each other on the note that we'd meet again. Staying in Gaya to have an affair with Prajit was an improbable option. He too seemed relieved we would part without making promises we could not keep.

Twenty-one hours on the Delhi Express with several stops along the way was an ordeal. Red-turbaned coolies pushed and shoved the anxious passengers into any available space. My compartment filled with men, including a bare-chested sadhu with dreadlocks to his waist. An intense discussion escalated into a shouting match among them. To make matters worse, I had to make several runs to the toilet, always a nasty predicament on an Indian train.

On arrival in Delhi, my stomach was hurling revenge. I was scared and needed medical care, so grabbed a tuk-tuk to take me straight to the East-West Clinic. The competent Dr. S. Chawla, wearing a turquoise turban, diagnosed me with bacillary dysentery. "You are a lucky lady to find the East-West. You require immediate rehydration with intravenous and antibiotics."

Being alone and sick in India was unsettling; not the gastrointestinal distress but my hospital roommates, all of them men. They were dressed in olive-green pajamas and one, a disturbed Swede, talked to himself all night as he paced back and forth in the room that had eight beds.

The nurses wore short skirts, most unlike other Hindu women who were well covered in their saris except for bulging exposed midriffs. The women, all about my age, attended to their routines, yet none stopped to chat. Nothing much comforted me, even the memory of my fling with Prajit only nights before. It was the kindness of Dr. Chawla that made the difference. I recovered, a skinnier version of my former self, and five days later was discharged, only to faint in the street outside the clinic door.

29

Not Here, Not Now

"I AM VERY MUCH COMFORTABLE in communicating with foreigners and breaking the ice," Sanjay said in his father's jewelry store where I browsed, looking for a silver anklet.

"Do you break the ice with all the foreigners you meet?" I asked.

"Oh yes," he said, waggling his head in the characteristic Indian way that seemed to say both yes and no. "Please be so kind as to join me for dinner? Let's go to Moti-Mahal." I jumped on his scooter and held on tight to my chubby new friend. At the popular restaurant, we snacked on deep-fried spinach pakoras and drank fresh lime sodas.

One evening led to another with Sanjay. We ate at delicious eateries, followed by promenades on the stately streets of New Delhi. I loved the Rajpath, the city's grand boulevard, where statesmen and women, Indira Gandhi being the most famous, held their ceremonial parades. Men in flowing white kurtas and their wives in dazzling saris strolled without touching. Only the single men walked hand in hand among baby strollers, bicycles and balloons. The atmosphere was festive, the boulevard lined with *dudh* wallahs, ice cream vendors. Sanjay ate mango and I ate coconut cream, my favourite, in the luscious warmth of a Delhi evening.

"Let's have a whirl around," Sanjay said after dinner. All vari-
eties of cycles, scooters and rickshaws were whirling by too, the
drivers and passengers so close their scent of aftershave or per-
fume wafted on the air. As I leaned into Sanjay, holding him just
a little tighter, he swayed, colliding with a rickshaw. Tumbling to
the ground, I landed hard on my back. Sanjay helped me to my
feet, apologized profusely, then kindly let the trembling driver go.
Reporting him, no matter who was at fault, could cost the poor
rickshaw driver his livelihood.

We righted the scooter and drove back to Mrs. Chandra's guest
house. Standing on the stairwell, both of us black with exhaust
and grit, Sanjay stole his first kiss. Oh dear, I had been spending
far too much time drinking far too many fresh lime sodas with
him. I suspected Sanjay's wealthy father had been encouraging his
son to pursue me, with the hope of marriage to a foreign girl. I
was fond of Sanjay and loved his big heart, but he was not my
husband-to-be.

Dhiram and Sushali often invited me for dinner, serving the
most delectable North Indian dishes, biryanis and masalas cooked
with a subtle blend of spices. Glass jars of cumin seeds, green cardamom pods, red peppercorns and golden turmeric were lined
up in the small windowless kitchen. A stone mortar and pestle
sat on the counter. Sushali could transform the simple potato into
aromatic dum aloo.

Her domestic boy, Badhu, stood nearby, submissive and obedient, his eyes cast downward. The boy, not even a teen, did all the
menial tasks, working from dawn to dusk. He should have been
out playing ball with the other boys. Did he consider himself a
fortunate boy, having food to eat and a place to sleep?

After Sushali's excellent channa masala, I found Badhu squatting in a corner of the laundry room like a forlorn puppy crouch-
ing for scraps. I tousled his hair when Sushali wasn't looking. He
didn't smile and I didn't speak his language. If only Dhiram or
Sushali had given him a book or taught him how to read, but it was
not the way with servants.

I relayed my travel plans to Dhiram and Sushali every time I went to and from Delhi. It reassured me that someone knew something about my whereabouts.

"You must meet my younger brother Ajey when you visit Dehradun. He is a good chap and most full of opinions," Dhiram said, and called his brother to make arrangements.

I left the next day, terrified on the bus as the driver played chicken with every approaching vehicle, including bullock carts carrying massive loads of hay. He gesticulated wildly and laughed with the ticket collector, unconcerned with the task of driving a bus. I sat in the unfortunate seat #1, with a perfect view of every potential calamity.

Dehradun was a small town that lay in the cup of a green valley. I found a room at the Prince – hardly fit for a prince – and waited for Ajey. He arrived promptly at seven, a spirited young man with a soft, melodic voice. Over chai, we talked about politics and religion, frequently disputed topics in a country that had a history of both great tolerance and extreme violence. His eyes were searchlights probing the meaning of life.

Like his brother, Ajey was a Jain and promoted nonviolence just like the Maharishi Mahesh Yogi, the founder of Transcendental Meditation. The Maharishi was all the rage in India, at least among Westerners, but angered Ajey.

"He is a fraud because he drives an air-conditioned limousine that George Harrison gave him." The Beatles, the Maharishi's devotees, had brought him fame and fortune. "An air-conditioned limousine is only for government leaders and is not fitting for a holy man," he claimed.

"Yes, I doubt Mahatma Gandhi drove in a limousine," I agreed.

"Please be assured I am your assistant in India should you need any help," Ajey graciously said as the evening ended. He rode off on a silver scooter, his long white scarf billowing out behind him.

I had come to Dehradun to visit the Kusht Ashram leprosy home, situated a short distance from the town. Like the Home for Dying Destitutes in Calcutta, I had come as a nurse to understand another layer of India, the complexities of the poor and most marginalized drawing me in.

Leprosy had grave social as well as physical consequences. Though not highly contagious, the disease elicited fear and panic. Whether from a village or city, from the privileged or impoverished class, the tragic victims of leprosy were most often abandoned by society and a frequent sight on the streets of India.

The rickshaw pulled up at a small hamlet of modest stone dwellings and a garden of leafy trees. It had an air of tidiness, not like most Indian villages. Agnes Kuntz, a warm-hearted German woman who ran the colony, greeted me at her door. "Welcome," she said.

"It was hard when I first came to India. Now it is my home. I'm too old to change, so I stay in my chosen country and with my chosen work," she laughed as I asked her about her life.

"We have 130 adults at Kusht Ashram, several have remarried, and we have 40 healthy children." Agnes took my arm and showed me around. In the factory, colourful hand-dyed skeins of cotton hung from the ceiling and attractive homespun shawls, rugs and bedspreads were displayed on a table. "For their work, the men and women receive free accommodation, medical attention and the promise of a better life. This is their home," Agnes explained. "Their wages cover food and transportation to town. The bus costs five cents a trip."

When I saw the most mutilated of human beings begging in the streets, I had wanted to flee. At the ashram, I wanted to stay. Its residents, many with disfigured faces, part of their nose absent or an empty eye socket, greeted me with a smile. I strolled in their calm and industrious village, praised their fine work and admired their gorgeous children who gathered around.

My need to work in a humanitarian capacity with the less fortunate of the world was stirred. My days of solitary wandering needed to come to an end. Many times I had considered working, not at Kusht Ashram but anywhere and everywhere in India. Most of all, Calcutta. I had vacillated between staying or leaving, but every time the commitment seemed too big.

"Not here, not now," I said to myself, once again finding a dozen good reasons not to stay. Instead, I bought three woven tablecloths I knew wouldn't fit in my knapsack and returned to Dehradun.

The heat was unbearable, like being trapped in a sauna. It made me irritable, and I fought with the rickshaw wallah over a couple of rupees. Even if the poor man had been trying to swindle me, his actions were forgivable. My haughty assumption he was a thief shamed me.

Everything annoyed me, the filth, the smells, the men who stared, but my greatest concern was my overdue period. Could I be pregnant after one night with Prajit? A tight, anxious band pressed down on my chest as the possibility raced through me.

"This can't be happening," I repeated over and over, knowing it could be, knowing that one mistake could change the course of my life. I longed to be a mother, but motherhood seemed a scary fate when I wasn't ready to change the course of my life. For all its challenges, it was the life I was choosing to lead.

I tried to imagine being a single mother, as I could not imagine any sort of arrangement with Prajit. Getting married and living in Gaya, as he would undoubtedly propose, was an unlikely arrangement no matter how good a man he might be. I was on the precipice of grave consequences, every one of them overwhelming me. I thought of all the young women who had gone before me, forced to give up a child or forced to marry men they did not love. It was a crime against half of humanity, a crime against motherhood.

"My cycle's just late," I rationalized, not surprising after such a highly eventful month. I'd hiked high in the Himalayas, travelled in the suffocating heat to Bodh-Gaya, endured long distances on death-defying buses, been sick in the hospital, fallen off a motorcycle and been pursued amorously by two men. I tossed and turned all night at the Prince. By morning, I was a wreck.

I needed somewhere or someone to calm me, at least enough to make a clear decision. I'd go to the sacred city of Rishikesh, on the holy Ganges, only an hour away.

30

Come Dip Your Tired Feet

RISHIKESH WAS A TOWN of temples and ashrams, built on steep slopes on either side of India's most revered river. Saffron-robed sadhus, Indian pilgrims and several foreigners walked its busy streets on their path to enlightenment. I wasn't seeking enlightenment but looking for immediate answers to my uncertain condition, making contracts with God asking that my dilemma go away.

At the Maharishi Mahesh Yogi Ashram, I met Koshy, an initiate of the International Science of Creative Intelligence, and the man responsible for translating the Maharishi's writing into English. "Thousands of people worldwide follow my guru, the Maharishi," he said, as he sat on the ashram's balcony combing his glossy black hair that tumbled down to his waist. Bright-eyed and jolly, he espoused his philosophy.

"My dream is to play forever on the banks of the Ganga and be blessed with her holiness," Koshy said. "We call the Ganges the Ganga in Hindi. She is my teacher. Let me teach you how to detach from anxiety and promote harmony." He seemed to know that I needed exactly that.

After an introductory session on breathing to calm the distracted mind, he left me to meditate at the riverside. Trailing my hand in the muddy water calmed me for a time, till my thoughts strayed into the distressing scenarios I faced.

A skinny white sadhu of sorts sat down on the ghat. His hollow cheeks were covered with a sparse beard and a flimsy loincloth accentuated his bony skeleton. He looked like a sick scarecrow carrying a walking stick and a small pail for *baksheesh*, the alms he would need to get by.

"G'day. How are you?" he asked, his accent distinctly Australian.

"Fine, and you?" I replied.

"I'm well. Life is calm here; the Ganges is my home," he said, twisting his matted hair on a finger.

"It doesn't look like an easy life," I ventured.

"It is when you know your path. I live a simple life as I am nothing."

"What do you mean you are nothing?"

"I dedicate my life to liberation from the cycle of life and death. It is only God I seek."

"Where is he?" I asked, always curious about definitions of God.

"God is everywhere. He's here in the river."

"Do you miss your country?" I wondered how someone could drop out of their own country to disappear into another.

"Not often. It floats away, like a leaf on the river," he said, with a long-muffled giggle.

Sadhus giggled a lot, and I giggled with him. Had I judged this strange man as displaced, or maybe delusional? He was good-natured and on his chosen path. I was the one losing myself on mine.

Back at the ashram, Koshy and I drank jasmine tea. His charismatic discussion on the Age of Enlightenment as proclaimed by the Maharishi was as spirited as the monkeys that played in the nearby trees. But my troubling predicament overrode any path to wisdom. On my third day at Rishikesh, I told him I thought I might be pregnant.

"Motherhood is a sacred step to the divine. It is not a subject to be taken lightly. Accept it as your path," he said in his wise and compassionate way. "Parvati is our goddess of mothers. Her love will surround and protect you."

At that moment, my fear lifted. A decision crystalized. I would have the baby. I would write Prajit.

The following morning my cycle announced itself, with relief flooding my body like a waterfall of grace. I wanted to celebrate my good fortune and made a vow that I would be kind and wise like Koshy. But later that day I snapped at the barefoot server who brought me a pot of murky, lukewarm tea, then hurled recriminations at myself.

"Listen to my mental temperature. Too much indecision. Too much impatience. Too many obstacles on this journey." I needed to go home, yet another voice, the voice of the Ganga, called. Come dip your tired feet in my cool waters and play.

What was I afraid of? A life of continual travel, or a commitment to home? Could I go home as the same person, just one year older, one year more travelled? That couldn't be, not after India, the land where life brushed close with death and a river was home to the gods.

"Go home. Love my own country," my spirit whispered, but I wanted more. More experience. More patience. More wisdom. More love. I said goodbye to Koshy, bought my ticket for Delhi and waited, the interminable wait for the bus.

In the searing heat, everything pulsated and jiggled like a mirage. Just like me, suspended in a quandary. I couldn't hold a thought, a decision or a direction. Returning to the ashram, surprising Koshy, and swimming in the river tempted me. I jumped off the bus and pleaded for a refund, the startled ticket vendor yielding to my request. The driver gave the horn a loud aggressive honk. I panicked, bought the same ticket and jumped back on. We took off in a trail of dust for Delhi.

The clattering rattletrap of a bus jostled me with every bump in the road. Sweat poured out of me, soaking my clothes. At a stop, the stench from a pissing wall smacked me in the face. A beggar girl pleaded for alms. I handed her a few flimsy rupees. "God save *me* from this wretched poverty," I said to myself. "And have mercy on the poor," I added.

In Delhi, I couldn't imagine the heat being any hotter, even inside Mrs. Chandra's guest house that had no air conditioning. Very few places did except for deluxe hotels. The fan didn't help and even the cold water ran hot. A knock at the door interrupted my attempt to cool down with a warm-water splash.

As if I had beckoned him from Gaya, I opened the door to Prajit. I threw my wet arms around him. "Let's go on a holiday," he said, looking uncertain about his proposal, and with no resistance we fled the city for the cooler hills.

At the bus station, we bought our tickets, pushed through a disorderly crowd and climbed onto the northbound bus for Shimla. It didn't matter that I'd just returned from Rishikesh not far from Shimla the day before.

"Sir, would you kindly vacate this seat as we have tickets for two," Prajit asked a neatly turbaned man.

"Do you want a tackle? I know what kind of character you are," the man yelled at Prajit, looking at me.

"You be careful, sir," Prajit replied with his fist clenched, a show of force I hadn't imagined in him.

"It must be the heat," a sadhu said, patting me on the shoulder. Everyone settled down, though the bus driver drove like a maniac all the way to Shimla.

Seven hours later, we arrived in the town that was once a hill resort for the British, now an escape for upper-class Indians. We promenaded among them in the exquisite pleasantness of the crisp evening air.

"Prajit, for a week I worried myself sick that I was pregnant," I finally confided. "All is fine, now."

"I would have requested that you become my wife and we live in Gaya together," Prajit responded with great solemnity.

Prajit was a progressive man with a sensitive temperament, yet we could fall into trivial arguments, rocking our fragile liaison. We would disagree about the benefits of reading fiction or nonfiction, or how Canada's parliamentary system differed from India's, a subject neither of us knew much about. We were also good for each other on our six days together. To call us either a casual fling or a love affair would have been untrue. A genuine attempt at friendship seemed the most fitting description as we listened to each other's lives.

"I feel like a misfit in my own country. I want to be more than a civil servant in Gaya," he said with a sigh. "I dream every day of a better life. I worry about what will become of me." His worries felt achingly familiar.

We returned to Old Delhi, where we had to say goodbye. I watched him walk away, his shoulders slumped, something resigned in him. I waved down a scooter, feeling resigned myself, contemplating the state of my heart. I didn't know the way to love. I didn't know the way to stay. And I didn't know the way home.

I had to see Dhiram and Sushali before I left the country. They served fresh lemonade, welcoming me like an honoured guest. Badhu's father, a sweeper in the slums of Old Delhi, arrived to visit his son that same day.

"I'm a poor man and can't raise my son. Please accept him as your own," Sushali translated his sombre plea. An old dhoti hung from his gaunt body in the same way he hung his head in shame. I hadn't seen Badhu treated as one of the family and knew he had little if any attention to his needs. The young boy's situation concerned me, but I had to be cautious with any comments on an irresolvable caste system that affected every aspect of Indian society.

After the father left, I gave Badhu a T-shirt I had chosen carefully, an appropriate gift he could use. He looked down at the floor, not daring to accept it. My display of interest in her servant embarrassed Sushali, who took the T-shirt and set it aside. She sat down on the floor, tossing back her shiny hair that she massaged daily with coconut oil, in her lady-like way. I sat cross-legged and ate several syrupy *ladoos*, my favourite sweet. Badhu cleared the plates and did not look me in the eye.

MAY WAS THE HOTTEST MONTH of the year in India. Sanjay insisted on taking me to the airport in his father's car that he borrowed for the occasion. First, we stopped for one last ice cream on the Raj-path and strolled in the muggy Delhi evening, a goodbye taste of the colourful, spicy India I loved. I thought of all the dirty, dusty roads I had walked and all the infinitely diverse people I had met. Sanjay, who was always affectionate and generous, shuffled along, his usual exuberance gone.

At the airport, he took both my hands in his. "Please don't go. Stay in India and we will marry," he stated in one last romantic plea. The unexpected proposal, following so soon after Prajit's, disarmed me. I hated to leave him broken-hearted and fiddled my way through a final goodbye, both of us in tears.

I walked through the gate with a hundred other people and slumped into a seat in the departure lounge. I imagined going home and my mind went blank. I kept expecting the unexpected to happen. The wild card to change my mind. I considered can-celling my flight and turning back to India. Just like Rishikesh. Jumping on and off the bus.

An immaculately dressed Japanese man wearing black and white polished shoes sat beside me. "My name is Hiroyuki," he said, extending his hand. I extended mine limply. "India is a perplex-ing country," he continued as we watched a middle-aged couple sitting across from us argue loudly in Hindi. The lady flashed her arms covered in gold bracelets as her husband sat diminished in the presence of his angry wife.

"I am a student of economics at Jawaharlal Nehru University, and I have experienced some difficulties in India," Hiroyuki con-tinued. I wasn't in the mood to talk, having said goodbye to Sanjay only minutes before.

"I am lonely, I need to understand myself, I need to understand this country." His candour took me by surprise.

"Me too," I said, as much to myself as to Hiroyuki. Intense, heart-tugging, complicated India had me crying again.

"Strong experiences bring tears," he said, and Hiroyuki handed me his neatly folded cotton handkerchief.

31

Vancouver

VANCOUVER. In transition from world traveller to displaced Canadian. Reverse culture shock. Fighting anxiety, fighting depression, fighting lethargy. Sad, sad, sad. At loose ends, scattered, not belonging, longing. A desperado waiting for a train.

"You are not being responsible. Endless travel is reckless," my mother says, the voice of convention, the voice of judgment. I burst into tears. We rip into each other, worse than an *Autumn Sonata*, Liv Ullmann as Eva, so clear in her rage. Reading her memoir, *Changing*, I come undone, her soul-searching resonating with mine.

I may have been reckless or restless; both were probabilities. A life of inconsistencies. Nurse in Lebanon. Lover in Turkey. Seeker in India. Hiker in the Himalayas. Now I stutter and stumble, make mistakes. A friend tells me I am mature and accomplished. A compliment riddled with holes.

My passport flies me in and out of international intrigue. Still inside my travels, I can't make decisions about work or a place to live, my belongings scattered all over the city. All played out. Skin is splotchy, body is itchy, must be carrying some Asian bug.

Don't want to be on the sidelines. I want to contribute, be involved, be a nurse. But can't see work as more than a one-year commitment. Meditate, take care of myself, be strong, be creative, write a story. I am beginning to understand that the decisions I make now affect my future.

Dinner with Dianne and two men. Anxiety attack, my heart pounding, all the stresses of the month spilling out. Switch to poised and calm. This is taking a toll. "You'll write a book some-day," Dianne says, supporting me through my troubled times. She's my confidante, my best friend.

Move into my new apartment. Apprehensive about my new job. A shadow of my travel self, I shake off my anxieties like a layer of dust. Flashback to India. A road, a train, a scent, a smile, a woman, a man, a child. I am walking among them.

I walk by the sea. Alone. I write in my diary. Alone.

Work in intensive care. Some days I love the urgency and successful outcomes. Patients recover and go home. Some doctors are competent and caring. Some are neither. One is treating Tiana, a Yugoslav immigrant, like a cow. She's dying. His arrogance is obscene. I don't know what to say. An air of impending disaster. Intense. Chaotic. Tiana. A flurry for the ventilator, her eyes wide with fear. A little morphine; sedate her.

Distressed, I try to meditate, eat and write, all on my 30-minute break.

At night I phone California. Chloe, my companion in Calcutta and Kathmandu. "I can't cut it. I miss India," she says.

"Want to go back to your Emerald Palace or my filthy, flea-infested Paragon?" We laugh.

"I'm eaten alive with restlessness. I can't sit still. I'll cut a few more deals, then I'm out of here."

"This is serious, Chloe."

"Yeah. So what saves you, Ella?"

"I need to untangle myself. Need to reconcile with my ordinary life. Need to find some balance between travel and home. Can't be only one or the other. But I worry about you, Chloe."

"Don't worry. I'm born under many lucky stars."

"Yeah, waltzing around Asia."

"Maybe it's my last waltz, but I want this dance."

"Take care," I say to the wildest woman I know.

I am waiting for my next dance too and write down my goals: Travel to remote areas of the world. Find love. Be spiritual. Have a baby. Buy a piece of wilderness land. Attainable and unattainable. Lofty and down to earth. Lost and found. I flutter.

The phone rings. A man I met in Delhi. A friend of a friend. He calls from Paris. Wants me to meet him in Rome. Can't understand that I can't leave my work at a minute's notice. He has charm, lots of money and it's sexy to get extravagant proposals from international men, but I'm not falling, I'm not flying away. I dream and desire and wait. For someone else. I'm 28 years old.

Months after returning home, a man arrives on my doorstep. "Why are you visiting Canada?" the customs official asked him at the Canadian border.

"I drove 1,000 miles for love," Gino answered.

"I love you," I say, though it seems a bourgeois concept for this man of steel.

"I came close in Taipei," he says about love, then tells me some big stories, the photojournalist who has been everywhere, done everything.

"Women are magnificent creatures. But no one will ever hold me."

"Hold me," I say. We only have a day. With his work, writing, deadlines, deals.

"I'm impossible to live with," he says, as we rush through traffic to send *his* story to *Time*.

"Do my stories interest you?" I ask.

"I cherish every word you say. You're a dreamer, a poet, a woman of the world."

"If only we had more time." Lovesick.

"Don't complicate reality," he says. And he's gone as fast as a Taipei taxi ride.

"Hit this pillow," a counsellor says. Stage fright. I freeze. I'm faking me, burning tears, drowning in yesterdays. "Integrate all parts of yourself – the little girl, the international woman, the nurse, the achiever, the dreamer, the good girl and the bad girl. Listen to your inner voice. Let go of societal expectations."

He makes it sound easy. I vacillate, assertive and shy, composed and uncertain, successful and floundering. I fall both ways, like fibreglass: taut, tense and transparent.

I leave in distress, run to the railways nearby. Sit by the train tracks. Downtown Eastside. Existential angst. Breathing. Calming down. Quiet.

I surface into sentimental, savour a few pleasures in my funky apartment. Asian keepsakes, a bundle of love letters and my Indian cookbook. I invite friends for full-course Indian meals.

Spring blossoms, pink and white. Beach walk, sand and sea. Snow on the North Shore Mountains. Magnificent Vancouver.

A year has passed since leaving Asia. I have a boyfriend. Scared of breaking his heart. Scared of breaking mine. Time with friends and family. My days aren't without happiness as I move through everything. Restless to settled, loneliness to love, introvert to extrovert. Quickly. Tangential. I find another interest, another direction, another adventure, my heart beating wildly with wanderlust, again.

FOUR

Despair, 1980–1981

Overcoming poverty is not a gesture of charity.
It is an act of justice. It is the protection of a
fundamental human right – the right to dignity
and to a decent life.

—NELSON MANDELA

32

A Pivotal Year

CERTAIN YEARS ARE PIVOTAL over the course of a lifetime. 1980 was that year. It came sweeping through my life, leaving a multitude of raw, gritty and heart-wrenching experiences in its wake.

It began with a six-month assignment with the International Red Cross in the Cambodian refugee camps immediately after the fall of the brutal Khmer Rouge regime. From 1975 to 1979, under the murderous rule of Pol Pot, Cambodia, known as Kampuchea, became the Killing Fields. In late 1979, humanitarian organizations poured onto the Thai–Cambodian border mounting large-scale relief efforts for refugees fleeing their homeland. By February 1980, I was a nurse in a camp on that war-torn border.

Thirty years later I would write a book about my experience with the Cambodian refugees, about their suffering and hope and my passionate involvement with them. My first memoir, *Encounters on the Front Line*, was a small offering to that memory.

I remember driving across the Thai countryside of rice paddies with bright green shoots dotting the watery earth, past the last village, through the barbed wire gates and arriving in the camp. A dense throng of people crowded the paths amid tightly packed shacks made of plastic and scraps of cardboard. Sixty thousand refugees were living in a field of filth and stench. This was not a town. It was not a village. Mak Moun, Camp 204, was the most abysmal human habitat I had ever seen.

A wave of despair rolled over me like an ominous cloud filling a clear sky. I was just beginning to grasp the atrocity the Khmer, the Cambodian people, had endured. The systematic destruction of a culture. The forced labour camps. The mass killings.

At the thatch and bamboo hospital, there was one big room with 50 cots occupied by a forlorn group of men, women and children. The patients, wearing threadbare clothes, their skinny arms and legs exposed, were malnourished, extremely ill or near death. The most common problem was malaria, the patients suffering from severe chills and violent shaking. The children, the ones who were skin and bones or those with big bellies full of worms, stared at us with empty eyes.

The emergency room had a bloodstained mosquito net to separate it from the big room with 50 cots. There was no electricity, no water, no oxygen and no equipment other than a box of bandages. Dirty instruments were washed in a bucket of Dettol. A canvas stretcher stood in the centre of the room and one wobbly plastic table served as a work area. I signed up as the ER nurse the moment I arrived.

Most days I arrived at work to find several wounded Khmer, both refugees and the anti-communist rebels still fighting to free Kampuchea, sitting on the ground outside the ER.

There was no paperwork, no introduction and no common language; the injured simply turned up with fresh injuries and old wounds. They waited in silence to be bandaged up, only to be sent back to the squalor of the camp, or the fighting in the forest, or to be thrown into the back of a pickup for Khao I Dang, 45 minutes away. Khao I Dang was the largest of the refugee holding centres "inside Thailand" that had an operating room where surgery could be done.

Some days we heard terrifying blasts, mortar shells or landmines or gunshots. When they would occur, or how close, or how far away, we never knew. When a mortar shell fell, the sick mothers and their skinny children would jump up from their cots on the ward to peer through the bamboo slats into the forest beyond. Old men with skinny, hairless legs looked out too, perhaps contemplating the folly of war, having been soldiers once. They were now dying for other reasons: malaria, tuberculosis and typhoid.

The landmines, as many as five or six, exploded each day in the jungle periphery of the camp. They would tear up people, particularly their legs. It was hard, tiring work to poke and clean up the debris of shrapnel embedded in torn flesh.

I remember a soldier, a ragged rebel warrior wearing torn jeans and runners with both toes missing, who staggered into the room, blood oozing down his tattooed skin. He had shiny gold loops in both ears and an automatic rifle slung over his shoulder. I washed his body, which was covered with cuts, filth and blood. Sweat ran down my face, dripped onto his chest, drop by drop mingling with his. He was my age and a soldier, a refugee, an insurgent, a hero, a casualty, his life a catastrophe.

There were times the work was too difficult to bear: the filth and flies, the daily stream of bloody wounds, the oppressive heat, the sweaty, stinking bodies, including my own, and always the heart-racing anxiety of not knowing what the next moment held. At the end of the day, I'd wave goodbye to our workers, concerned for my ER assistant and translator, Sam Ath. His baggy clothes hung off his skinny body as he stood at the shack of a hospital door like a sentinel. He always had a wide grin, as if he was a happy young man. But he was a refugee who could neither enter Thailand as a free man nor return to his devastated homeland. He had to live his broken-down life in Mak Moun.

The heat of April fell like a vertical wall wrapping itself around me. Even breathing was a hot activity in April, the hottest month of the year, the month Mak Moun fell. We were told an attack would occur before the monsoon, but it happened after the heavy rains began. The camp had been shelled all night, the hospital looted and burnt to the ground, the Thai soldiers told us at the military checkpoint. Over 100 people died and tens of thousands fled through the forest and the fields laced with landmines to other border camps, north to Nong Samet and south to Nong Chan. It was undoubtedly international news, however, on the front lines, we weren't sure who was fighting whom. The Vietnamese who controlled parts of Cambodia? The Khmer Rouge guerrilla forces in their jungle enclaves? We only knew that rocket-propelled grenades hit Mak Moun. I was seething with anger at the man with the gun, at the Khmer Rouge, at the Vietnamese, at people at war.

The Thai soldiers and Red Cross delegates didn't give us security clearance for two days; an agonizing wait at the checkpoint until our team was transferred to Nong Samet. Our vehicles crept into the camp, the refugees clearing a path, waving and smiling as if we might make a difference in their traumatized lives. I searched the throng for a familiar face from Mak Moun as I handed out our meagre supply of high-protein biscuits and cans of sardines.

Attacks on the camp occurred frequently, with refugees having to flee in the middle of the night. In such unstable conditions, we worked out of our vehicles setting up mobile clinics, as the Nong Samet field hospital was no longer secure. We'd find a clearing and rig up blue plastic between the truck and a tree for protection from the sun. Dozens of people in dire need of aid waited patiently while we kept an ear cocked to the walkie-talkie that hung on the mud-splashed pickup. With the violent afternoon storms, pools of water collected on our improvised roof that often collapsed. We'd huddle together against the torrential downpour, our Khmer workers and our team of three or four nurses, the force of the monsoon slashing through our wild and unsafe lives.

"Khmer Rouge are here," our workers whispered some days, their eyes full of terror, looking to us for the security we could not give. A volley of frightening shots would crack the air. The Red Cross teams needed to evacuate. Our Khmer workers managed to say goodbye, wet clothes clinging to their trembling bodies. They were the brave ones, enduring all manner of hardship and suffering as we rode off to safety.

The cycles of attack and re-establishing a relative calm in the camp continued throughout our six months on the Cambodian border, then it was time to leave. I sat under a tree with Sam Ath, searching for something reassuring to say, as a crowd gathered around. There were always crowds in the camps, as people without villages or fields or farm work had time on their hands. Sam Ath was the face of his people, of his lost land, a refugee brought to the border with nothing yet with everything to live for.

BY LATE SUMMER I returned to Canada for the debriefing with the Canadian Red Cross. I talked about our work, the challenges and the accomplishments, but most of all about the fatigue. The fatigue that lies deep in the bones from bearing witness to a tragedy. The tragedy of Cambodia was a foreign atrocity that sifted into my psyche as vicarious trauma.

Home in Vancouver I gave multiple slideshows to friends and family, needing to communicate about refugees, dire circumstances and mortar shells falling. I wavered in that ambiguous state of reverse culture shock, trying to seek a connection in my disparate worlds.

I imagine now what I may have needed then: a less stormy relationship with my mother, a closer relationship with my father, a solid community of friends and a regular partner with plans to settle down and have a family. My life moved in and out of the social norms of the times. Part of me pursued conventional choices and part of me longed to pursue a career in global disaster relief work.

I was tough and resilient on the surface, and I was vulnerable too. I watched over and tried to protect the softer sensibilities in a battle that played out in insomnia. My sleepless nights tormented me. I tried herbal remedies or sleeping pills, which I swallowed with a nip of brandy in the middle of the night. Before Cambodia, sleep had been an easy bed to fall into, no matter the psychic temperature of my life.

Our house guard with his Kalashnikov, standing beside the Cedar of Lebanon and below the photo of Imam Moussa Sadr.

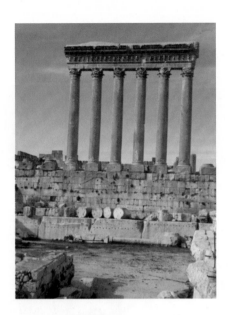

Temple of Jupiter, Baalbek, Lebanon.

Russian Orthodox Sveti Nikola church, Sofia, Bulgaria.

Göreme valley, Cappadocia, Turkey.

Mevlana Mausoleum of the spiritual master Rumi in Konya, Turkey. PHOTO: WIKIPEDIA

Author in the Thar desert, Jaisalmer, Rajasthan.

Taj Mahal, Agra.

India on $5 & $10 Day.

Erotic sculpture on a Khajuraho temple. PHOTO: WIKIPEDIA

In Varanasi, also known as Benares, the holiest city in India.

Bus stop in Kerala, India's southern state.

Rickshaw wallah in Cochin, Kerala.

A street in Calcutta.

Boy at food stand.

Mother with leprosy and her healthy child at Kusht Ashram in Dehradun.

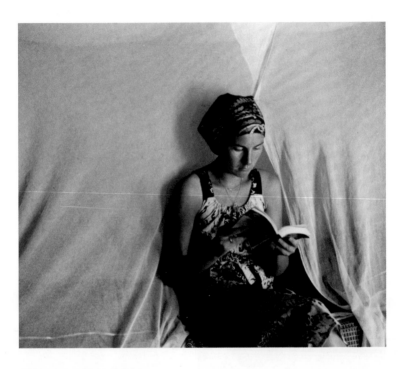

Author, always with a good book.

Barefoot rickshaw wallah in Calcutta.

Swayambhunath Stupa, one of the holiest sites in Nepal,
revered by both Buddhists and Hindus.

A sadhu, a Hindu holy man, at the Pashupatinath Shiva festival.

Young porter on the Kali Gandaki trail.

Woman threshing grain in Helambu village.

Boy at Buddhist prayer wheels in Khopang village, Nepal.

Two Issa girls.

Yaks in the Kali Gandaki valley.

Djibouti landscape.

Issa woman in front of her rock hut.

Afar girl from northern Djibouti.

Inside the feeding tent.

Malnourished girl in a feeding tent.

Feeding tents near Ali Sabieh.

Author assessing a patient.

Drying goatskins to use as water gourds.

Worker from Djibouti Red Crescent distributing cooking oil from Saudi Arabia.

Nomadic woman building her toukoul.

Girl grinding millet in Ali Sabieh camp.

Camel carcass, one of several strewn across the land.

Black tarps provided by UNHCR, at Ali Addeh camp.

Back roads travelled with Land Cruiser 4WD.

Girl at remote Lac Abbe in the region of the Afar Depression.

Yemen's capital, Sana'a, considered one of the oldest cities in the world.

Yemenis in Sana'a market.

Yemeni village.

Yemeni girls.

Yemeni man with khat, the narcotic leaf chewed as a stimulant drug.

Ganesh, the Hindu god revered as the remover of all obstacles.

Tibetan monks at the Baha'i Lotus House of Worship.

Colours of India.

Snack seller in Jaipur.

Sugar cane press in Jaipur.

Photo op at Amber Palace (Amer Fort) in Rajasthan.

Shop beside Hawa Mahal in Jaipur.

Pietra Dura at I'timad-ud-Daulah in Agra.

Taj Mahal, Agra.

In the autumn of 1980, I had been home from Cambodia for only ten weeks when the telephone rang. "Ella, would you like to go to Djibouti for six months?" George, the CEO of the Canadian Red Cross, asked.

"Djibouti? Where on Earth is Djibouti?"

"Famine-ravaged East Africa. Drought. Nomadic population. Provide medical aid and food." The conversation went something like that.

My breath caught in my chest. My mind swirled with uncertainty. No, I can't do this. I can't go. I'm not ready. I need time. I need normal. I need sleep. But somewhere between my gut and my head, I said, "Yes."

What was the distance between no and yes, and how did I leap across that ambivalent divide? Living a life outside ordinary, however I defined ordinary, called me. A call to meaningful experience fired my soul, more than the need to stay home and restore my psychological and physical health. The international arena had me hooked. I wasn't political, nor was I an activist. But it was in my character to fly away to Africa and be on the front lines. I went to Djibouti.

33

Djibouti

THE ROAD CUT ACROSS the wide plateau of black earth, dotted with sparse brush. The only landmarks were distant mountains rising sharply from the flat terrain and dry riverbeds, the *wadis*. I sat beside our Djiboutian driver, who recklessly defied the desert tracks, jets of dust swirling behind the Land Cruiser, pure white like snow. A clear blue lake appeared on the horizon, steaming heat ringing its sides, shimmering then receding further and further the closer we got. An eerie apparition. My first mirage.

We arrived at a small hill with a cluster of stone huts built on its slope. The hill, the huts and the earth were black; the only splashes of colour were the women's bright cotton clothes. A woman sat on the ground with a large flat rock between her outstretched legs and ground millet to make *dora* – a fried patty, a staple of their limited diet. She raised her arm against the blazing sun and squinted at us, four strange white faces. The children, skinny and covered in flies, clung to their mothers. The men, leaning on their walking sticks, watched us with guarded interest. A sharp, hard wind tossed sand into everyone's eyes.

Mouloud was an encampment of several hundred victims of the drought that plagued East Africa. The people of Mouloud were of

Somali descent, nomads of the Issa tribe, traditionally crossing borders and only seeking camps for the dire necessities of food and water. The camp looked as bleak under the burning noonday sun as an Inuit igloo under a frigid arctic wind.

Only days ago our Canadian Red Cross team had left Toronto in a November snowstorm. We flew to equally chilly Geneva, the bureaucratic headquarters of the International Red Cross, for our one-day orientation. "The problems in Djibouti are twofold," said Monsieur Antoine, the man responsible for operations in East Africa. "*La sécheresse et la guerre,*" the drought and the war. Thousands had died in the last two years and if the rains did not come soon thousands more would die.

The war between Ethiopia and Somalia had resulted in the exodus of Somalis living in Ethiopia to Djibouti, a small country at the mouth of the Red Sea. The former French Somaliland, Djibouti was strategically sandwiched between Russian and American interests and protected by the French, who had a sizable military presence in the country. It had just gained independence from France in 1977.

Monsieur Antoine outlined our assignment to provide medical care and distribute basic staples of rice, oil and milk to the Issa population in the southern half of the country. That was the extent of our political briefing, our psychological preparedness and health care information for a country I had never heard of three weeks earlier. We bundled up in our winter coats, about to fly to Djibouti, one of the hottest regions on Earth.

Our team consisted of two English Canadians, Chris the doctor and me, and two French Canadian nurses, Claire and Cecile. Chris spoke fluent French. My lousy French, no better than three years ago in Paris, embarrassed me. We seemed a disconnected group, a not unusual situation with newly formed teams flying into disaster zones of the world.

With our interpreter Ahmed, we walked around the encampment assessing needs, particularly of the children, and calculating the resources we'd need. In the back of our Land Cruiser, we had a first aid box, bottles of water and a few tools of our trade: a stethoscope, a suture kit, an otoscope and two baby scales. We needed a card table and chairs, otherwise we'd be sitting on the ground.

By midday, tired and sweaty, we stopped to eat oranges and nuts in the shade of our vehicle. I stood on that black hillside, overcome with the staggering work ahead of us. Like Cambodia, I knew I'd arrived where I wanted to be.

In the late afternoon, returning to Ali Sabieh, our driver, Abdi, raced across the desert like a madman. He was after his *khat*, the euphoric narcotic leaf chewed by the men of East Africa. A pickup truck filled with branches of the leafy green plant arrived daily from Ethiopia to meet the need of the national male pastime.

Ali Sabieh, a small town more like a large village, would be the place we'd call home for the next six months. We were temporarily lodged at La Gîte d'Étape, an African-style hotel, a sandstone structure on a desert plain a short distance from town. A few palm trees in the courtyard provided a respite from the relentless heat. For dinner we ate vegetable and mutton stew, swallowed down with a beer. After sharing a few stories with my team, I went to my room and collapsed into bed.

At breakfast, over strong black coffee and pastries from the Arab bakery, we had a meeting with Husain, the chief delegate of the Croissant Rouge, the Islamic Red Crescent, the counterpart of the Red Cross. We had met him our first night in the capital, Djibouti Ville, at dinner with other high-ranking dignitaries, dining on Arab African specialties of spicy couscous and fish from the Red Sea.

Plans were prioritized. Cecile and I would work in the largest camp on the outskirts of Ali Sabieh. Chris and Claire had acquired an old Land Cruiser for the outlying camps, Mouloud, Holhol, and Ali Addeh. Excited to have "our" camp, Cecile and I, carrying our Red Cross bags, walked to the densely crowded site of 6,000 refugees. Barbed wire fencing separated it from the village of Ali Sabieh.

The camp dwellers lived in *toukouls* – domes of woven mats, pieces of cardboard, plastic tarps and chicken wire. A few old men sat on the ground, their yellow eyes staring into space, not paying us any attention. The women, many with babies wrapped on their backs, cautiously looked at us. Feeling like a person of privilege among the poorest of the poor, I pushed a tinge of guilt aside, got down on my knees and let the children grab my hands. I tousled the curly hair of a toddler who screamed and ran back to his mother's arms.

We needed assistants and translators who knew the complexities of the nomadic Issa culture. The local Croissant Rouge provided us with five workers. Loula, a slim beauty with bright eyes and a quick mind, worked alongside Rakieh, who smiled readily but was slow and unusually overweight for a Djiboutian. There were three men: Farah, a gentle boy of 18, Abdullah with six fingers on one hand, and Bashir, who had three wives. The team had a dismal lack of training and inconsistent motivation, though two of the workers spoke a little French. Only Loula shone.

Our initial attempt to register the children under 5 was haphazard. The mothers declared more children than they had, their ploy to receive a greater ration of food, and gave vague birth dates, often a season or a year. We had one card table, two plastic chairs, our scribblers to record our notes and a baby scale that hung from the wobbly tent pole.

Gradually, our *centre nutritionnel* took shape, if a messy tent under the intolerable sun without a breath of moving air could be called a place of work. Hot gas fumes from the burner and the baby smell of vomit hung in the air. Milk slopped everywhere, which attracted a swarm of flies.

The women were fearful at first, but we welcomed them, touched their arms and held their babies. They smiled when we used our few words of Somali. "How are you?" was too vague, so we learned the words we needed to know for their children. "Fever? Diarrhea? Cough?" Then we'd add, "A little or a lot?"

We had three meals a day for the severely malnourished, about 10 per cent of the children, and two meals for the moderately malnourished, about 30 per cent of the children. We called the severe category "*les rouges,*" or the reds, and those in the moderate category were "*les jaunes,*" the yellows. None of the children were well nourished, as the diet of the nomadic people was grossly inadequate, lacking fresh fruit and vegetables.

I loved working with the little "jaunes," the ones who had a chance at survival: Youssef, Ali, Khadija, Salima and Ibrahim. There were about 30 of them, none doing well, though they were maintaining their weight. Knowing what to do with a sick child – how to treat an infection, start an intravenous or comfort the mother with a touch, a word or a smile – reassured me, but the "rouges," their wrinkled skin hanging off their bones, didn't respond, as if their tiny bodies were simply preparing to die.

Our Red Crescent team did not always turn up and required frequent supervision or encouragement. It presented unending, unexpected difficulties. "Abdullah, please put a bucket of water in the tent to wash our hands," I had to say several times a day, or I'd try to teach Rakieh how to boil rice and mix milk, as she'd been assigned the role of cook. She'd mess up the meals and sat most of the day on the plastic chair, like the high priestess of the camp. Only Farah, a sweet boy, and Loula, a serious girl, were attentive to their work.

Day by day, we heard their stories, usually their troubles of everyday life – no money and not enough food to feed their families. One morning, Loula revealed to Cecile and me that she had endured childhood female circumcision like nearly all the other girls and women. She disclosed her story without elaborating, without emotion.

We knew the horrific practice of female genital mutilation (FGM) was common throughout parts of Africa, the Middle East and Asia, with millions of young girls experiencing excruciating pain and having lifelong complications, particularly in childbirth. FGM reflected deep-rooted gender inequality, extreme discrimination and was a violation of human rights for women and girls. Yet, that morning with Loula, it was not our role to challenge FGM. The three of us just looked at one another and hung our heads in shame.

Apart from the feeding centre, Cecile and I saw 20 to 40 sick children a day in our makeshift clinic in the corner of the tent. We recognized all the common ailments, from eye, ear and skin infections to whooping cough, pneumonia, dysentery and one case of meningitis. We didn't have a background in tropical diseases, let alone the resources we needed to diagnose and treat such a vulnerable population, but we were conscientious and caring and did our best with what we had.

"This tent is a furnace," I complained to Cecile, knowing my life was immeasurably more comfortable than those of the women who showed up every day to feed their undernourished children.

"It's time for a break," Cecile said, wiping her clammy face with a towel. We retreated to the coolness of the storeroom, a window-less concrete block where the rats had gnawed the bags of grain. We ate an orange, out of sight of the women and children. The nomads must have eaten juicy oranges when they followed their traditional trading paths, but as recipients of food aid, they primarily ate millet or sorghum, or rice. Some days one of their men brought back a slice of tough goat. Slabs of slaughtered goat hung from hooks in the market of Ali Sabieh, the butcher beating off the flies.

A man with no flesh on his bones, wrapped in a tattered robe, came to the tent one morning. In a quiet, withered voice he told his story. "My eldest daughter died yesterday, and my baby boy died a week ago," Loula translated. I held his hand, not knowing what to say. We had heard that a young girl lay sick in a far-out toukoul and had intended to visit her, then decided not to go, as the walk was too far and we didn't have a vehicle.

"There is too much dying here. No wonder all we hear is *inshallah*. We should have gone," I said to Cecile.

"There's nothing we could have done. It's not our fault," Cecile said, though we both felt guilty we hadn't found a way to reach her.

The experience of Djibouti left me all at odds: the stark, unforgiving desert, the impoverished lives and my own battle with hopelessness or hope for the nomads. As a team, we talked about what to do, not about what we felt in the face of such destitution. At our best, all four of us were strong and resilient and committed to the cause. At our worst, we were short-tempered in the deadly heat, finding petty things to argue about. Our work seemed like a small Band-Aid in the political-economic-environmental mess on the Horn of Africa. Every night I went home to La Gîte and cried.

34

A Wavering Commitment

WE RETREATED FROM THE STIFLING CAMP to the shade of a white stucco house to eat our sardine sandwich lunch. We'd been eating there for days under the striped awning when that day a man opened his door to find Cecile and me sitting in his yard.

"Come in, have a glass of wine," the Frenchman said. With the demands of our work, we hadn't considered wine.

"*J'aimerais bien un verre.*" I'd love one.

"Come for supper tonight. I'm cooking porcupine. It's illegal to hunt, but it's a very good dish."

Pierre, a science teacher at the local school, discussed communism and French cuisine with fervent commitment over dinner, while his friend Alain boasted of his conquests with the local girls. His drunken arrogance disgusted me. Pierre might be the only intriguing man in Ali Sabieh, I thought, apart from the French Legionnaires, a tough lot of men better to avoid, and he cooked a fine porcupine.

Dinner with Pierre became my evening routine, but his opinions on all matters African were cynical, especially concerning stories of corruption at the local and national level. His skeptical views on the benefits of humanitarian work in such an environment led to fiery disagreements. Still, I let him pick me up in his red Jeep at my lonely desert lodging and drive me away.

By Christmas, I'd moved in with him. We threw a party on New Year's Eve for the Red Cross team and the expat teachers in town. With lots of carousing and flirtatious liaisons, I could let my precipitous move into Pierre's settle as an amiable arrangement.

As night fell with only the stars to light the way, our guests ambled off. I waved goodbye, then slumped into the rocking chair and reminisced on the year we'd just toasted goodbye. It had been a year of powerful encounters, drama and danger on the Cambodian border. I remembered my last day in the camp, kissing my Cambodian friends goodbye. In Djibouti, we didn't kiss the Issa. We held their hands, trying to find a way to say "hope your day is going well," which sounded stupid and inappropriate.

And I thought of home, remembering my mother, my father and my four brothers. Fiercely independent as individuals, the five of us had become the scattered siblings of divorced parents. Did I know them? Did they know me and who I'd become?

Who had I become? A wanderer of the world? A nurse with a strong yet wavering commitment to the cause? A seeker who could see both the beautiful sweep of life and weep at its ugly realities? Questions with no obvious answers troubled me. Why did I work in such hard and desolate places and when would I call a place home?

"You are doomed to the life of an endless wanderer," Alim had said. His words were too close to the truth. Words I didn't want to hear. Home was always far away.

IN THE NEW YEAR, Pierre and I flew into North Yemen for three days. It was a stone's throw away across the Bab-el-Mandeb, the strait connecting the Red Sea and the Gulf of Aden. The Biblical Queen of Sheba once ruled in the ancient kingdom of Arabia in the area now called Yemen. Sana'a, the capital city, was a mythical place, its mud-brick buildings painted with elaborate white geometric designs like Islamic lace. The unique architecture didn't hide the grittier town with haphazard construction underway on every street corner. I clutched Pierre's hand as we stepped into the crazy traffic.

Yemenite men carried impressive knives attached to their belts, looking proud and fierce. They approached us, Westerners being rare in Yemen, wanting to practise their few words of French or English. "Hello. Where you from? Need taxi? Need hotel? Come with me!" said in one breath. The women, in head-to-toe black *burkas*, peered through gauze veils that covered their eyes, their peripheral vision and movement significantly limited. Our radically different lives were impossible to bridge, but I smiled and wondered if they smiled back.

As the only woman in a restaurant, I became the object of every man's attention. Their stares unnerved me as I sat unveiled, talking casually with Pierre in a public place.

"Just ignore them, they're only curious," Pierre said, dipping into the *saltah*, a traditional potato, egg and lamb stew with unidentifiable spices.

"Easy for you to say. No one's staring at you."

The next day we decided to leave Sana'a to visit the surrounding countryside. As a taxi driver who had enthusiastically agreed to take us there didn't show up, we hitchhiked. The first car screeched to a stop. The beaming driver seemed to understand that we wanted out of the city. He drove across terraced valleys cultivated with khat and coffee, transporting us into a medieval realm.

We stopped at a little village on a steep hill where the local men crowded around, eager to talk. They led us into a courtyard of several houses built into a rock cliff. Children played, chickens pecked at grain, dogs sprawled in the shade and a donkey was tied to a post. Three women wearing loose floral scarves quickly covered their faces in front of their unexpected company. They hurried into their cave-like homes to reappear with glasses of tea, a thick mint brew we drank sitting with the men on the swept earth. The women stood by, smiling.

A stocky man, perspiring profusely and carrying a worn leather briefcase, arrived in the courtyard. He introduced himself in impeccable English. "My name is Mr. Husani Gamal. I am an Egyptian expert in demographic studies. I am on assignment in Yemen." Mr. Gamal's appearance in a small village on our single day in rural Yemen was remarkable.

"Can you tell us about your studies?" I asked.

"The reality of life here is dire," he began. "The standard of living is primitive, the life expectancy is low, the literacy rate is abysmal and the infant death rate is high." We could have been at a conference with Mr. Gamal, yet we were sipping mint tea among the subjects of his study.

The demographics were not unlike Djibouti's, though Yemen gave the impression of movement, activity and work. In Djibouti, everything was suspended in the heat, in inertia, waiting for Allah to intervene.

35

Destitution and Dying

THREE MONTHS WERE OVER, with three months to go. I could work for three years in Djibouti and wondered if it would make a difference. This was how I felt, but still I had to find the courage to believe. To believe that every child I fed was a meaningful act and that every mother needed care. Especially when the children of Holhol were all sick, a measles epidemic ravaging the camp and leaving six children dead in two weeks.

I crawled into a rock hovel on my hands and knees, the smoke from the fire making my eyes smart, gagging on the stench of rancid goat, sour milk and body sweat. A mother sat on a mat wearing a single piece of bright cloth knotted at her sunken chest, her breasts dried up with no milk for her baby. I cradled the head of the tiny, dehydrated girl swaddled in rags and gave her a sip of water. I tried to unwrap and sponge her feverish little body, but the mother held on tight and pulled the dirty rag back over her daughter as her age-old belief told her to do.

Before the end of March, 25 children died. The deadly combination of measles, malnutrition and unsafe traditions still encouraged by the *mirabou*, the traditional witch doctor, all contributed to the deaths. The immediate cause of death was usually severe diarrhea caused by milk made with water from the stagnant green pond.

Maybe the little ones died in the middle of the desperate nights. I didn't see them die, nor did I see their burials, but it weighed on my heart. We were there to save lives, but death was a cruel reality of the disaster in East Africa. I had to cope, be strong and be a competent nurse. It was the reality of working on a front line.

We acquired a second decrepit vehicle that I drove every morning to Holhol. Any mishap could occur – sinking into the sand with the wheels spinning or getting a flat tire – and I couldn't push a Land Cruiser or change a tire by myself. I'd offer lifts to Issa nomads walking along the track, though they carried machete-type knives in goatskin holsters. Imagining a nomad and myself working the jack in the loose sand and rubble made me laugh.

By nine in the morning, with the temperature close to 40 degrees, my bottled water was too hot to drink. A crowd had gathered for the distribution of the monthly provision of rice, pasta, powdered milk, oil, sugar, tomato paste and, once and a while, lentils. Sometimes it went smoothly; that day people were pushing and yelling, accusing each other of taking more than their share. A grandmother, face like a shrivelled prune, took my hand, kissing it when she received her ration, and I kissed hers back. Tears running down the furrows of her face, we looked up at a French military plane flying low overhead.

The children were dressed in shorts and T-shirts, donations from foreign countries. A boy about 10, so thin he could hardly stand, wore a top with "Expensive" stamped in big gold letters on the front, "But Worth It" on the back. There were seven or eight other kids like him, all with those big eyes that said, "I'm hungry." The irony of our work felt enormous. We were giving all we had of our energy, resources, skills and care, yet nothing much changed for the beneficiaries. After the rations were received, the women filled their gourds with water, wrapped their babies onto their backs, put packages on their heads, then walked off in a slow stride to their desert toukouls.

"Baby is coming. We go," Farah said. News travelled in ways I didn't know. We drove straight out across the rough terrain on tracks that disappeared into the sand. Two women were in a smoky hut, one lying on filthy bedding breathing hard.

Aicha looked 60, though may have only been 40. Squatting with her back arched, she reached her hands overhead, clutching the side of the hut. It was her ninth pregnancy and the baby came quickly. The old woman of the toukoul put a few stones in a piece of rag, tied the sac to the umbilical cord and tied rags around the mother's ankles and wrists. Before long, Aicha stood up and walked away barefoot over the hot black earth, her baby slung in a cloth across her back.

I was happiest when I drove home from Holhol, fast, alone, across Le Grand Bara, a wide empty sand flat with scrub vegetation and where the occasional gazelle or camel grazed. I knew the road well, its miles of rock-strewn flatness and areas of torn-up tracks. I loved the last stretch of road that wound up and over the hill and through the gate of Ali Sabieh, which served as its single stop sign, patrolled by a sleepy guard. The village lay in the crook of the valley below, cupped in the evening sun, the hills highlighted in shades of rose.

I picked up my mail, a bundle from Canada with one letter from Khao I Dang, the Cambodian refugee camp in Thailand. Sam Ath's letter ricocheted me back to another continent, another culture and another Red Cross mission less than a year ago.

Dear Ella,

How are you dear sister? Wish you have a best time at Africa. You will surprise as hearing I'm settling my life at Khao I Dang in the real name refugee. I just arrived at Khao I Dang with hard travel through many obstacles in the forest at nighttime. Me and my wife Rady must escape from the trouble camp immediately. Vietnamese still occupy and show communism like the dark time that I had enough tasted five years ago.

Before I never thought my body was a refugee. It suddenly came to my mind that I would find a peace place to have alive. I wanted to go back to Kampuchea. However, I fed up communist either Pol pot or Vietnamese. Fourteen months I have been struggle along the border. Now my life in reduced circumstances and unpleasure but it's much better than at the border.

I think my people know the hard time and are going to pull together in one idea someday to get freedom. If I have chance, I'm going to immigrate to the third country in the future for living peaceful and freedom.

I want to say hello to everybody with best regards. Never never forget good act of them and in the hard times together. How much I miss you. I will never forget you and Rady like to see you and talk.

Sincerely, Sam Ath

RECORD RAINFALLS were ripping up the roads and filling the wadis with fast-flowing currents. For two weeks I hadn't been able to go to Holhol due to the washed-out road. Instead, the four of us, our small overstretched team, went to Ali Addeh.

Hundreds of small black or blue plastic domes, improvised toukouls, were hunched on a rocky slope resembling a hill of alien mushrooms. Families with their entire belongings on their backs arrived from Ethiopia and collapsed on that horrid hill, some of them sick with malaria or possible tuberculosis.

That morning a young boy had been swept away in a sudden river. I hiked for an hour with a group of Issa looking for his body, which we never found. I didn't understand the few words uttered. Grief? Anger? Heartbreak? The men trudged back to camp as if resigned to their way of life, their way of death, the way of Allah. *Inshallah.*

An old blind lady had fallen into a well. She lay unconscious, her face bruised and battered, in her family toukoul. The air hung like a thick musty fog inside the hut. I cleaned her as best I could, pouring water from my water bottle onto her bloody face, stitched up the gouges on her head, and helped carry her into the Land Cruiser. At the hospital in Ali Sabieh, a rudimentary place at best, her son would wait with her until she regained consciousness or until she died.

We took others there regularly, the seriously unwell or wounded, and left them at the hospital gate. The male health care workers, who called themselves nurses, were often lying under a tree, their cheeks puffed up with big red wads of khat. They chewed the fibrous leaf for the longest time, swallowed its juices then spit out the residue.

"Please find a blanket for this man," I asked Dayib, the cross-eyed care worker. He didn't move.

"I want a blanket now!" I yelled. With the utmost insolence, Dayib rose from the ground, found a blanket and threw it over the old man, who was too sick to notice.

Working in an environment of destitution and dying asked more of me than I thought I had to give. My discouragement tormented me. Either I fought back tears or snapped at a lazy worker, or struggled with exhaustion from the heat, the work and my frequent sleepless nights. There would be sweet moments too, like watching Loula as she gently coaxed mothers to come to the tent for care. Or Farah as he hauled boxes of cooking oil stamped with "Saudi Arabia" onto the truck for food distribution, always working with a smile.

36

Dear Liv

LIV ULLMAN, the Scandinavian actress and ambassador for UNICEF, would be visiting Ali Sabieh – a most out-of-the-ordinary event! She was not only a famous actress; she was *my* favourite actress. I'd seen all her films: *Persona*, *Scenes from a Marriage*, *Autumn Sonata*, and more.

I tossed and turned all night, dreaming of Liv, and even with a sleeping pill couldn't sleep. In my dream, I was running after a white limousine that finally stopped to let her step down. Dressed in a luminous robe, she shone next to me in my faded jeans. I needed to protect her, as she seemed too delicate for Djibouti. We began to walk, side by side down a long country road. Soon we were friends, drenched in the afternoon rain, a precious event in the parched desert.

Liv arrived by helicopter with an entourage at the Gîte D'Étape. I hadn't met many "stars" in my life and expected to feel a sense of awe. Instead, I felt a sense of familiarity, as if we knew each other. I couldn't speak to her directly as the media, Dr. Yasir from the hospital and government officials hovered around.

Everything had been prepared for the grand occasion – the arrival of a celebrity attached to donor money. I followed a few steps behind the officials who were guiding her to see what she must see, to hear what she must hear. Several times Liv looked at me and smiled. Overcome with shyness, I couldn't speak.

I watched her every graceful move as the Norwegian blonde beauty reached out to the destitute in the camp at Holhol. The mothers, who could not have known who Liv Ullman was, looked puzzled or uncertain till Liv coaxed a smile from them.

Dr. Yasir, fawning for her attention, helped her into the Jeep to return to Ali Sabieh. She jumped out and ran over to me.

"I wish you the very best with this hard work," she said, taking both my hands in hers. Our eyes held each other; it seemed in mutual admiration for one another's life. I couldn't imagine living hers. She was a movie star and I doubt she'd have wanted to live mine on the brutal front lines of Djibouti. I carried on with my day's work, jostled with the tough reality of all my malnourished kids held a little softer in the glow of Liv.

At the end of the day, the convoy of three Jeeps returned to Ali Sabieh where the helicopter waited. She climbed in, the blades stirring up biting gusts of sand. I ran out and handed her a note I'd scribbled on a scrap of paper.

Dear Liv, I dreamed about you last night. I wanted to share it all with you today but couldn't. Your films and your book *Changing* moved me immensely. Keep up your good work for the people that need you. With love, Ella.

She was gone like a mirage, and I stood there, choking back my dusty tears. Did it cross my mind then that my work was important too, though I wasn't rich and famous and sure didn't have a helicopter flying me around that desolate land? Did I value who I was, a Red Cross nurse on a disaster mission, and how hard I worked in those tough times?

37

Farthest Corner
of Our Startling Earth

ONCE UPON A TIME, Pierre was *un chasseur de sanglier,* a wild boar hunter. Djibouti had plenty of game – gazelles, hyenas, porcupines, wild pigs and gophers – but hunting was forbidden. He recounted his stories under a solitary thorn tree where we had a picnic of bread, cheese and sausage. The sweltering heat and a glass of *vin rouge* had me spinning.

We drove the five-hour rugged desert track to Lac Abbe, a saline lake on the Ethiopian–Djiboutian border into the territory of the Afar, the semi-nomadic people of the western region. The men were tall and slim; the women wore colourful cloth wraps. Both men and women walked in a way I hadn't seen before. A slow, noble stroll over their hot, inhospitable earth. Goats and camels grazed close to the nomad encampments that were few and scattered along the way. Camel carcasses, victims of the drought, were frequent. We saw one, still alive, on the ground, his long neck twitching. If we'd had a gun, we would have shot it, put it out of its misery.

Lac Abbe is the centre of the Afar Depression, where three tectonic plates of Earth's crust are slowly separating. It is considered one of the most inaccessible areas of the planet. As we approached, the lake lost its shoreline in undefined boggy salt flats. Geothermal limestone chimneys, up to 50 metres high, spouted clouds of steam that disappeared into a bright blue sky. It reminded me of Cappadocia in Turkey, but Lac Abbe was a more severe apocalyptic place.

Pierre's red Jeep provided the only windbreak for our tiny pup tent that looked pathetic in the severe environment. Over a spaghetti dinner I made the day before, we drank wine and talked into the night that fell quick, dark and foreboding. Pierre had a practical, concrete mind, while I was pensive and idealistic – an unlikely couple. Encircled by Lac Abbe's eerie pinnacles, I had arrived at the farthest corner of our startling Earth.

Throughout the miserable night, we were bitten alive by ferocious mosquitoes that may have been carrying God knows what tropical disease. We woke up irritable, only to be greeted with the finest of morning spectacles. Hundreds of pink pelicans flapped their broad black wings, taking flight over Lac Abbe. The stunning feat of nature brought me closer to believing in a divine presence, more than any church ever had.

After our morning meal of instant coffee and chocolate, we left for the difficult drive home. I had become an expert driving over or around loose boulders and sharp inclines on terrain only maneuverable by four-wheel drive. When Pierre took the wheel, I put my hand on his knee, reassuring my rugged companion that I cared. Our lives had become intricately interwoven in Djibouti.

Back in Ali Sabieh, I watched him make his simple house, provided by the Djiboutian Ministry of Education, into a home. He made a lamp from an old wine bottle, sewed a curtain, repaired a door. Often, I would drag home from work in a state of collapse and after dinner go straight to bed.

"You're too involved with the nomads," he'd say, not wanting to hear the daily gruelling details.

"I'm not involved enough," I'd reply, annoyed Pierre didn't understand that working in a disaster zone with the most abject poverty was the reason that brought me to Djibouti.

"You smell like a camel," he said one evening when I came home from the camps. I laughed as he stripped me down to take a cool shower.

"*Je te demande trop*," I ask too much of you, I said, knowing that our temporary agreeable co-locating wouldn't last, knowing someday we would leave each other.

"*Tu ne demandes rien*." You ask nothing, Pierre answered, quick to take the blame for everything. He was hard, he said the desert made men hard, but infinitely more patient than me. He was cynical and I was hotheaded. I wondered what a "normal life" meant between a man and a woman. Had I ever known normal? I had lost all perspective, yet we were lucky to have found each other.

Then one day I fell in love with the only man who set my soul on fire: Jacques Brel. I learned every song he sang by heart. When I played "*Ne me quitte pas*" (Do not leave me) on the ghetto blaster, I had to go peel potatoes to not break down and cry.

I had three weeks left in Djibouti. The heat held me in its grip, bearing down, intolerable, inescapable, as I worked for six hours a day. Nearly all my "jaunes" were losing weight and half of them were throwing up. The mothers would sit, beaten down with the weight of their lives, their chronic malnutrition. Their babies with big vacant eyes lay on their laps. I tried to explain gently, sweetly, firmly, whichever way I could, how to give their children sips of rehydration fluid or milk or spoons of rice and they would nod. When I turned my back, they stared at the tent walls. Sticky milk ran down the chests of the little bodies with protruding ribs.

It had been easy to love the kids, but the country was impossible to love, its injustices screaming at me, echoing back their irresolvable issues. I questioned if we had done anything in our challenging six months that made a difference. Had our work been effective or sustainable? Had we helped develop the capacity of the Issa nomads to return to their traditional, resilient ways of living? It was not developmental aid; it was disaster relief and there hadn't been enough of anything – money, supplies, resources, energy or time. Guilt and shame were emotions I did not know where to put or how to handle. Was the devastation from a drought, or was an unconcerned world to blame? I knew I would return to my rich country and all my little "jaunes" and "rouges" would die.

As evening fell, I walked behind our house on the hill overlooking the village. An immense sky filled with stars, and I saw everything just as it was: the unique beauty of the desert, the ravages of Djibouti and the struggle of life, including my own. Six months of witnessing the horrors of poverty and starvation. The drought, the nomads, the dying.

38

Africa's Hottest
New Travel Destination

Djibouti is out of this world. It's a claim no travel writer should ever make, but it really is as if a great chunk of Mars has been carved out and jig-sawed on to the Horn of Africa. Seated on the Afar Triple Junction – the meeting point for three of the Earth's tectonic plates, which are pulling slowly away from one another – Djibouti is a jostle of black volcanic rock, flat plains haunted by dust devils, and a brilliant-blue coastline bulging out into the Gulf of Aden.

—*THE TELEGRAPH*, 2015

FOUR DECADES AGO, Djibouti was not a place for tourists but a wasteland cracked dry with the drought, yet it was everything the tourist literature describes. It was and is *out of this world*. I try to imagine taking an expensive guided tour to remote Lac Abbe, and with new tourist eyes seeing the country where I once lived.

I have no intention of going back to Djibouti, but I need to go back to the memory I reconstruct as I write a book. I try to step into the story, into the heat and the gritty sand winds that blow. I try to be steadfast and patient and have great faith in my work. I try to believe that our work matters, that every person's life matters, even for those living lives of profound poverty. Especially for them. They are not expendable commodities. They are not collateral damage.

Today, international aid workers and foreign correspondents take incalculable risks in a more volatile world. Different risks than we took. I never feared kidnapping or terrorism or torture or a tropical disease like Ebola or AIDS. I never feared dying. My worries were about my capacity for compassion and my strength to get the job done in the intolerable heat, in the stench of a toukoul and in the eyes of a mother or father who had no tears left to cry.

The risks I ran led to emotional burnout and traumatic stress. I had experienced two disaster zones on two continents in one year, leaving me with sleepless nights and a troubled soul. I learned how to build a protective wall around my vulnerability, or thought I did. I compartmentalized. I sought out pleasures to forget the pain. I had the invincibility of youth on my side. I wrote in my journal. I escaped.

My insomnia eventually subsided, and life resumed its course: marriage, family, studies, travel and work. Nursing continued to bring me close to the bone – working with poverty, trauma and suffering, in my own country, in my own small town.

With time I understood the impact of that year in Cambodia and Djibouti. It was a window into tragedy and the extraordinary resilience of refugees. How could I ever again be indifferent to the displaced and the disinherited? Being human, I can. I hold all possibilities: capable of acts of great kindness, or turning away with cool indifference. I appreciate the comforts of a privileged life, and

I can be drawn into the eyes that haunt a conscience, the despair that breaks a heart.

No matter the political, economic or environmental forces at play·in a place like Djibouti, we were needed and responded to a heartbreaking humanitarian crisis. In some small measure, we had made a difference. In providing care and assistance, I learned that caring is not a distant act. Feeding a sick child or reaching out to touch someone in need is immediate and it matters.

I watch a documentary on Djibouti and see that nothing much has changed for the Issa nomads, still living in camps with limited livelihoods and dependence on foreign aid. The drought of 1980 continues to ravage the country. I carry my distant memory around with me like a piece of tattered baggage, a reminder of our imperfect world and our imperfect responses to it. I make charitable donations to sustainable aid projects: Because I Am a Girl, a global initiative to end gender inequality, provide education and lift millions of girls out of poverty; and Water Aid, an NGO bringing clean water to rural Africa. Both are in memory of Djibouti.

I'd like to send my Djibouti manuscript to Liv Ullmann, living in Oslo, Norway. She is 80 years old now, a film director, still lovely, still elegant. I imagine she may remember that day, that it will surface from her multilayered life as a gifted actor and an advocate for refugees, working globally at the UN in Africa and Asia.

I remember the helicopter beating up a storm of sand, blades glinting silver in the afternoon sun. Running to her, shy though not hesitant. I'd like to sit and talk, just her and me, sharing a few stories, authentic stories, women's stories. We were both doing what we knew how to do best, caring in our own ways.

Most of all, I remember the Issa. The women carrying huge loads of firewood, backs bent, with goatskins full of water, and the children with beautiful eyes knowing hardship way beyond their years. The men, tall and proud, leading their camel caravans across the vast parched plains, would call out hello to a woman: "*Nabad naya,*" and I'd call back hello to a man: "*Nabad waraya.*"

39

Two Fishes

THE VINTAGE TAXI stalled twice along the way from the airport into Nairobi. Claire and I, squeezed between two other passengers, got out at the roundabout in the centre of a green, clean town that looked European. We found the Glob Hotel, which must have once read "The Globe." The chilly breeze was a shock after the infernal heat of Djibouti.

Kenya, a country considered a showcase of Africa with its majestic scenery and wealth of wildlife, gained independence from Britain in 1963. It was Jomo Kenyatta who led the fledgling nation of many tribes under the national motto, "Harambee," a Swahili word meaning "let us all pull together." He remained president until his death in 1978.

Men in business suits and women in Western attire walked briskly in a city on the move, so unlike Djibouti Ville where men sat on the sidewalks chewing khat and the French military dozed at sidewalk bars, not a breath of air stirring. Neither city was the Africa of my imagination. At a gift shop I bought a silk batik of bare-breasted Samburu women, from north-central Kenya, sitting under a baobab tree. For me, they were the Issa, the women I knew.

"This is hard, Claire," I said, eating a greasy hamburger at an upscale restaurant playing Western rock. I'd taken her hand on the plane the day before, thinking we needed each other, but she was strong and independent and hadn't cried, at least not in front of me. I was a mess, though I'd shut the raw, stinging tears down.

After Nairobi, we flew on to Mombasa and quickly toured Fort Jesus built by Vasco da Gama, the Shree Parshva Vallabh Jain temple and a bustling market smelling of rotting fish. After one night at a shabby hotel, which turned out to be a brothel, we took a bus to the luxurious beach resort called Two Fishes. I was looking for something – an oasis, a fresh sea breeze, international dining, a bridge – anything to leave Djibouti behind.

"This place is slick. Too much cocktail chatter, schmoozing and easy money. I don't fit," I said as Black waiters in crisp white shirts served us drinks and skewered shrimp at the poolside bar.

"Neither do I. We are no longer serving, we are being served," Claire responded. We were the Two Fishes out of water.

Claire spent the day lying on the beach, while I strolled up and down. Wealthy businessmen talked or flirted with us, the two single women at the resort. A British diplomat dressed in an African safari suit invited us for dinner at the hotel club. I was dressed in my old ratty red sweater, worn in the cool African evenings, that didn't match my pink Indian skirt and orange flip-flops. I danced, drank too much champagne and laughed along with everyone else. Surely, this man could see I was elsewhere, already gone.

"I need to get out of here, Claire. Two nights is enough." I was restless, somewhere in between leaving and not having arrived anywhere to let go of the leaving.

"A safari will be better than a seaside resort," Claire said.

We left on a bus for Tsavo East National Park, excited we'd be seeing the "big five": elephants, lions, leopards, buffalo and rhino. Villages with dome-shaped thatch and mud homes were scattered over grand expanses of hilly grasslands. I took a deep breath and closed my eyes. I could feel the swoosh, the shedding of tightness, in my chest, over my heart. Drought-ridden Djibouti, its hills of destitution, swooshing away into wild and wondrous Africa.

At the lodge, we joined a tourist group in an open-roofed van and were given strict instructions from Mustafa, the knowledgeable Kenyan guide, on how to respect the environment and the animals that lived there. Zebras, giraffes, impala, ostrich, wildebeest, hippos and rhinos roamed the land. I was in awe of elephants. They romped and rolled in red mud, sprayed themselves with red water and kicked up clouds of red dust as they strode the plains. Mustafa told amusing tales of elephant scatology and the five-footed elephant male mating with his immense and impressive appendage.

On the second day, we approached a lioness as she stealthily stalked a baby gazelle. She must have been alerted to human smell and the noise of camera-clicking tourists but appeared unconcerned as our vehicle traversed her territory. The lioness crept closer, poised for the kill. An unsuspecting prey. A successful slaughter. A snapshot of life and death on the vast African savanna. Partly obscured in the mist, Kilimanjaro, Africa's highest peak, towered beyond the border in Tanzania.

40

Inshallah

THE DELUXE CRUISE BOAT *Osiris* was docked at Luxor, the ancient city of Thebes, on the greatest of rivers, the Nile. We had flown in from Cairo to visit the Valley of the Kings, a last-minute decision to explore Upper Egypt, the land of magnificent temples and tombs built to honour the pharaohs millennia before Christ. The pharaohs were believed to be mediators between the gods and the human world. After death, they became divine, passing on their sacred powers to their sons.

Claire and I relaxed on the deck chairs as the sun rose on the river and sentimental American love songs played on the stereo. A man wearing a white robe belted with a black sash served us tropical fruit, olives, yogurt and Egyptian crispy flatbread. From the deck we looked out to the fertile banks of the river, the morning heat cooled by a gentle breeze. After breakfast we filed off the boat with the other tourists onto an air-conditioned bus for the temple tour.

The first stop was the Karnak Temple. The construction of Karnak began about 4,000 years ago and was considered the largest ancient religious site in the world. Under a brilliant blue sky, I walked through the grandiose complex, awestruck with the colossal columns designed in the shape of open and closed papyrus flowers. I scribbled historical notes in my journal – details of design, dynasties and pharaohs, but the lengthy descriptions from our scholarly Egyptian guide eluded me.

It was the colour that held my attention. The sun rendered everything a burnt yellow, rising from a desert of the same hue. In Egyptian mythology, yellow represented the eternal and indestructible, the colour of the sun god Ra, and made manifest with gold. Karnak dazzled me.

South of Karnak was the temple of Luxor. The two temples were once joined by a mile-long avenue lined with stone sphinxes, guardians of the gates to the underworld. Massive statues adorned with hieroglyphics stood guard at the entranceway to the temple.

The next day we sailed down the Nile with papyrus growing on the river shores and villages of mud, brick and straw clinging to its banks. Women dressed in long, black *abayas* carried water jugs on their heads and men worked the fields of sugar cane and sesame, a scene that seemed a thousand years old.

We disembarked at Denderah and boarded another minibus. Looking out the window, I longed to be a traveller, not on a tourist bus. I wanted to be sitting in the village square, drinking strong Egyptian coffee and greeting the villagers with *"Salaam alaikum."*

In the small town of Esna, at the temple dedicated to Khnum, whom I had never heard of, I slipped away to the village market nearby. Women wore scarves draped loosely over their heads and carried baskets full of produce. With exquisite eyes, they looked at me as if to say, "We are happy you are among us," and offered me an orange. Floating on some exotic fragrance, perhaps frankincense or myrrh, I said, *"shukran."*

After our three-day tour, we flew back to Cairo. Known as the Triumphant City, Cairo had a glorious past as the cradle of civilization. Still a vibrant city of artistic, intellectual and political importance, it overwhelmed me with its noise and intensity. A gray smog hung in the air.

The city's ten million people filled the streets, the shops and the sidewalk cafes. I snapped pictures from the taxi window and remembered Istanbul. That was five years ago, when I never took taxis but hot tram rides to Yenimahalle, bodies pushed against one another, Alim and I on fire.

With so much to do and see in Egypt, I knew I was skimming the surface and had come unprepared for the wealth of riches in the country. As Gustave Flaubert wrote, "Egypt is a great place for contrasts, splendid things gleam in the dust."

The staggering display of King Tutankhamun's collection at the Egyptian Museum needed days to explore, time we didn't have. The pyramids of Giza, built some 4,500 years ago, were a marvel to see. The construction of the monumental tombs with stone blocks weighing as much as two tons continues to baffle Egyptologists. We hardly had time to contemplate their magnificence when the camel drivers arrived with their ornery animals. It was a once-in-a-lifetime event, riding a camel at the pyramids of Giza, though my betel-spitting driver was in a hurry to nab his next tourist. We had a momentary pause at the mythical Sphinx with its partially eroded head of a pharaoh on the body of a lion, standing guard near the pyramids.

Claire and I had a day to visit Cairo and three of its many mosques. Slivers of light illuminated their vast spaciousness. There were no pews, no paintings, no human images, Islamic law forbidding the representation of living beings. In the echoing emptiness, Allah could fill the room.

I wanted to see Alexandria, the Greco-Arab city named after Alexander the Great and once the home of Cleopatra. Even the name Alexandria evoked beauty and intrigue. Two young men on the street corner of Liberation Square approached us as we walked to the bus station to buy tickets. "We will go to Alexandria with you. We are your excellent guides. We are free," Gamil and Hamin insisted.

The city curved around the Mediterranean with a waterfront road and promenade, the Corniche. Men and boys fished off the breakwater and women bathed in the sea water fully dressed.

Alexandria with its sea breeze, more breathable than Cairo, was a glimpse into once elegant architecture falling into disrepair.

We strolled with our new friends, medical students skipping work for the day from Cairo Hospital. Gamil with his soft voice clung to my side, while Hamin took to blond and blue-eyed Claire. "I want to take pictures of your eyes," Gamil said in a sweet romantic gesture, though he seemed bewildered finding himself with a non-Egyptian woman independently travelling in his country. After dinner *falafels* at a market stand in the *souk*, we waved goodbye to our amiable Egyptian company, on the night bus back to Cairo.

I could lose myself in Alexandria, I thought, sitting on the terrace of the elegant Cecil Hotel drinking coffee, Egyptian style, wearing my earthy musk oil bought at the market and writing in my journal. It was the life I imagined living.

As I write this book, unearthing stories of a time long gone, devouring old journals, I find a seed of my desire – the first stirring of my writer's soul on the terrace of the Cecil Hotel, the same hotel where W. Somerset Maugham had stayed. It had even served as a headquarters for the British Secret Service during the Second World War. It may have been at the Cecil where Lawrence Durrell called forth his Mediterranean muse to write the *Alexandria Quartet*. Scrawled across the page of my journal I'd written, "Someday I'll write a book. Something grand about my life."

ON EL OROUBA STREET, while bartering unsuccessfully with a cab driver, a tall Egyptian man walked toward me. "Hello, may I offer you a ride to wherever you wish to go?" he said in perfect English. He was wearing pressed pants and a long-sleeved blue shirt, well dressed on a hot day, and looking very much like Omar Sharif. I took his offer as a gesture of Arab hospitality and jumped in.

"My name is Khalid. I am a professor of history." We talked about argumentative Egyptian cab drivers and cold Canadian winters.

"May I please invite you to join me for dinner and dancing?" he asked formally as I stepped down from his car.

"*Shukran*," I said, thrilled with an invitation from an Egyptian man.

He returned as promised at seven that evening, looking sophisticated in a white shirt and tie. My shabby travel wardrobe was hardly fitting for the exclusive Cairo nightclub, its long driveway lined with palms and luxury cars. A live American band blared rock and roll at the glossy establishment.

A belly dancer shimmied up to us as we ate a dinner of succulent lamb kabobs drenched in mint sauce. She winked at Khalid, who was too serious to play into her seductive gestures. When the band switched to a Western "slow," we danced, his hands holding me firmly at just enough distance that our bodies did not touch.

Khalid liked to talk about Islam, the sacred Koran and his strict obedience to the prophet Mohammed. "Peace be upon him," he whispered each time he uttered the prophet's name. "Islam is the way of truth. *Allahu Akbar*," he proclaimed.

"You in the West are preoccupied with money and with sex. You have fallen from the faith. The punishment for extramarital sex for either a man or a woman should be death. They have broken a holy covenant with God." I remembered my fiery arguments with Alim five years ago, though Alim, who considered himself progressive and secular, didn't argue religion, only politics.

"We can't agree. We can't be friends. Take me home!" I yelled over the noise in the club. Still, it took two hours to get back to my hotel, parking here and there in the dark alleys of Cairo, Khalid shifting our location every time he saw the roving police. He drew me close, our first kiss passionately entangled with the dictates of Islam. "In the eyes of the prophet, peace be upon him, I will hold you forever."

He picked me up in his black Fiat to take me to the Red Sea the next day. Hundreds of abandoned tanks, sombre relics of war, lined the flat, boring road out of the city. The brilliant blue water of the Suez Canal, rebuilt after the 1973 war with Israel, was the only thing that sparkled in a landscape drained of colour, bleached by a merciless sun.

We followed a rutted gravel road to a deserted beach that Khalid must have chosen as the least likely place to be seen in public. He shyly took off his clothes, his swim trunks already on. I changed in the car, as there were no trees, then ran to the sea and plunged in. We swam in and out of the cool water, a relief from the blistering heat. Lying on our separate towels, we talked about the same subjects as on our dinner date the night before: Khalid's Islamic ideals, his fight for Palestine and his ardent passion for finding the woman he wanted to marry.

"I wish to propose to you even if you are not Egyptian. Please marry me," he asked, giving me a piece of watermelon.

"I can't marry a Muslim man; I can't be a Muslim woman." I attempted to laugh and make light of his surprising offer.

"It won't matter, as long as you believe in God and follow the licenses of good and bad, right and wrong." Khalid's declarations were solemn and righteous.

"We'd fight too much," I replied, red watermelon dripping down my salty skin.

"Maybe," he said with a pause. "Life is a struggle, but there will be love."

I ran to the water and swam out against the waves, engulfed in the sudden romantic madness. Khalid swam out after me, the waves tossing us together and apart. He took my arm in a heroic gesture and I let this man, the living soul of Islam, pull me back to shore.

"There are no rules in your life. You follow your own heart and now you are suffering. You don't need to jump anymore. God will give you the rules. God cares about you," he said as we rearranged ourselves on our towels. His burning idealism kindled mine, but I couldn't accept absolute convictions on the meaning of life, death, God and the entire order of the universe.

"Why isn't God helping the Palestinians? There is no mercy, no caring and he doesn't care about me."

"God is whispering there is love," he said, the words of a believer. We walked back to the car over the hot sand, hand in hand, the red sun of desire setting behind the hills.

Night descended onto unlit roads as we wound our way back to Cairo. He left me at the hotel door, our goodbye torn with longing. The creaky elevator with an accordion door carried me up to the room where Claire had fallen fast asleep. Her bag was packed, ready for an early morning start to the airport and a flight to Israel. I collapsed on the hotel bed, talking to God who had no answers.

41

The Children of God

I HAD LEARNED TO DART ACROSS the frenzied streets of Cairo, then arrived in Tel Aviv where I stood on a street corner, waiting for a pedestrian light. Israeli soldiers with machine guns were on one side of me and chic Israeli women in shorts and high heels were chatting on the other. I could be a Western woman in Israel and, at the same time, be surprised after Egypt to see them so scantily clad.

In Israel, two cultures, Palestinian and Israeli, collided in one of the most disputed areas of the world. Both sides claimed the small parcel of arid land dotted with olive and lemon groves as their own. Since the state of Israel was declared in 1948, violent conflicts and uneasy peace agreements had been all too frequent.

Claire and I decided to go our separate ways for a week, giving each other more space to be the independent travellers we wanted to be. We agreed upon a final rendezvous in Tel Aviv before our long trip home. I left by bus for the Sea of Galilee, as Tel Aviv was not the place to explore my Christian heritage. On arrival at the guest house in Capernaum, an old Jewish gentleman with friendly eyes that crinkled in his sun-weathered skin offered me a plate of olives drenched in oil.

"Please come to my boat. My captain will show you our beautiful Sea of Galilee. He will take care of you." He took my arm and led me down to the dock. Captain Yuri wore smart white trousers and a white T-shirt highlighting his muscled, tanned arms. He welcomed me aboard his small passenger ferry, saluted his uncle Joseph and pushed off the dock.

To the west were the hills where Jesus had walked and to the east, the Golan Heights where UN peacekeeping forces watched over Israel's hostile neighbours, Syria and Lebanon. Yuri talked of historic and modern Israel as he ferried us back and forth between the two.

After the boat emptied of tourists, Yuri invited me to the upper deck, where I stretched out on the blue and white deck chair, and offered me a glass of rosé from his uncle's vineyard. No matter how tempting his flirtations under the burning Israeli sun, I could hear Khalid's religious invocation of only three days before. "Women are not merchandise, and we will be faithful to each other." Both men were improbable encounters in my irregular life, one trying to seduce my body; the other had tried to seduce my soul.

The following day, Yuri and I visited the Mount of Beatitudes, believed by many Christians to be the site where Jesus had preached the Sermon on the Mount. From the garden of palm trees and flowering shrubs, we looked down on brown hills and the Sea of Galilee that sparkled like sapphires. Israeli army planes flew overhead, peace not yet a reality in a deeply divided land of Jews, Muslims and Christians, the same people who bowed their heads in prayer. *The children of God.*

The Bible claims that John baptized Jesus by the Jordan River that flows into the Sea of Galilee. I stood at the shallow reedy estuary, Yuri at my side, and tried making a sacred wish. Nothing seemed particularly sacred, as Yuri swooshed me around like a glass of fine wine.

I was tiring of Yuri's advances and halfway through the second day he abruptly lost interest in me too. After he dropped me on the curb in Tiberius, I took the 20-minute bus ride back to Capernaum, packed my bags and left for Nazareth.

At the German guest house, I talked with Sister Gertrude, a silver-haired nun intent on communicating her devotion to Jesus. After a thought-provoking conversation on the power of faith, I had a few hurried hours to explore the small cobble-stoned town. The Church of the Annunciation stood over the grotto thought by early Christian tradition to be where the archangel Gabriel had told the Virgin Mary she would be the mother of the Son of God. Standing at the grotto, I bowed my head in prayer, present to the very heart of Christendom.

I remembered Sunday school as a little girl, wearing my best red dress with a white bow on the bodice and black polished shoes. Obedient and too shy to talk to grown-ups, I sang along: "Jesus loves me, this I know, for the Bible tells me so." I wasn't certain Jesus loved me, but wide-eyed I listened to the missionaries, home on leave. The places they'd been, Bolivia and Borneo, filled me with wonder and I dreamed that someday I'd go too.

I stepped out of the cramped space into the busy street, the midday heat beating down. I needed to pick up my bags, catch a bus and move on to the next destination, Jerusalem. Maybe there I'd find a glimmer of faith, as Sister Gertrude encouraged, and settle my soul.

Jerusalem was the spiritual centre of Judaism, Islam and Christianity. Orthodox Jews wearing broad-rimmed hats over long curled sidelocks, Muslims in flowing *djellaba* robes and Christians carrying wooden crosses along the Via Dolorosa, the path Jesus trod on the way to his crucifixion, all jostled to assert their faith. It was a city of stone with shafts of light playing on its walls and dark shadows in its alleyways.

I tagged onto a group touring the shining gold Dome on the Rock, a holy site for Muslims, Jews and Christians, and Jerusalem's most recognizable landmark. The guide talked like an encyclopedia, the Koran, the Torah and the Bible rolling off his tongue. At the Church of the Holy Sepulchre, considered by many as the site where Jesus had been crucified and buried, a throng of noisy, picture-snapping tourists arrived. "Hurry up, hurry up," the church police said. At the holiest of Christian churches, we were herded out the door like a flock of sheep.

On my second day in Jerusalem, browsing in a bookshop, a man wearing a *yarmulke*, the traditional Jewish skullcap, approached me. "You are new to my country. I will show you a side of Jerusalem where the tourists do not go." An intriguing proposal by a religious man, I followed him into the street, wondering if he ever let the sunshine on his pale skin. He muttered a few words as we walked a busy street that turned a sharp corner into an alley. I was vaguely uncomfortable, not knowing why he had invited me or why I had agreed. His guise as a religious man didn't ring true. I slowed my pace then at the next corner abruptly turned around and ran away.

The maze of cobbled back alleys may have led to treasures of a sacred land, but I felt burdened, reeling under the weight of a cross, my spirit buffeted by the cross-currents of Jerusalem. Overwhelmed, I collapsed on a step of ancient stone. Maybe Jesus had stopped there, laid down his cross for a moment before he walked on to Calvary.

The exhaustion of my travels rumbled in my gut, from the six months in the desert of Djibouti to the African savannah, to the temples of the upper Nile, and to the affairs of my heart. And then Jerusalem, the City of Peace, timeless and pious, divided and torn.

In the evening, I strolled, the heat softer, the air gentler. I let an infinitesimal fraction of Jerusalem's weighty history waft over me like a fresh breeze. Families, couples and friends, people of all faiths walked by sharing the balmy June night.

My visit to Jerusalem concluded at the Yad Vashem – The World Holocaust Remembrance Center. Photographs of victims of the Holocaust, newspaper clippings and posters of neo-Nazi groups covered the walls. It was a chilling statement of a tragic history. I knew every country had its own brand of atrocity, but the display was disturbing. The guide, wearing his yarmulke on a head of curly hair, spoke to his version of the Jewish solution.

"The state of Israel must exist to prevent another Holocaust. Soon the Jewish messiah will arrive. He will lead the world to a new era," he fervently proclaimed. Would it be the second coming of Christ? I didn't dare ask.

I needed to see Bethlehem before my time ran out. At the East Jerusalem bus station, not like the orderly Israeli central bus station, a noisy crowd thronged. "It's a hard country. You have to slip in sideways," an old man said kindly as I sat down to share a seat with him.

The little town of Bethlehem of my imagination was a bustling Palestinian city in the West Bank, predominately Muslim with a notable Christian presence. The Basilica of the Nativity was built over the site believed by the traditional Christian church to be the birthplace of Jesus, and was the oldest major church in the Holy Land. A sticky guide took my arm as I stooped to descend the steep dark stairs into the grotto. "You are my Christian sister. Don't be afraid, I don't want money. Please come. Be welcome here," he said, his body brushing mine. I pulled away from the unwelcome encounter.

"Come visit my shop. Free looking. Free drinks," another guide said as I reached out to touch the holy rock that signifies the manger where Jesus was born.

I ran from the basilica to the nearby Chapel of St. Catherine. My beliefs, or any beliefs I had skeptically guarded, were torn to shreds. In the little town of Bethlehem, I wanted to be done with all churches, doctrines and dogmas. The tortuous beliefs for which wars had been waged could not be the creation of an intelligent, benevolent God. The Biblical story would have to be a parable – a story for a better world, with Jesus a supreme teacher of love, compassion and forgiveness.

Both Israel and Egypt had shaken me. Three of the world's religions had pounded at my door. Khalid, a devout Muslim, a Jew luring me into back alleys and a Christian intent on doing business at the birthplace of Christ.

God help me.

42

The Price We've Paid

IN GENEVA, the powerful city that makes many of the policy decisions for less developed countries, Claire and I presented to the East African Task Force. In front of a group of ten impeccably dressed men and women, we summarized our six-month assignment in Djibouti. I had stuffed my experience underground, undercover, a necessary measure in the last month of travel. I spoke calmly but could not find the words to describe the profound irresolvable dilemmas of Djibouti nor the parched places of my heart.

We supported each other well in the debriefing, two nurses, two young women who had tried to make a difference against all odds. Tears overcame me as we left the impressive office of the International Red Cross.

"You are a good girl but too intense and sentimental and we are just two nurses in a big business," Claire said, more pragmatic, more matter of fact than me.

"But I was happy travelling with you," she added, appeasing my worry that my emotions had gotten out of hand.

We had a day to visit Geneva, in postcard-perfect Switzerland, a stark contrast to where we'd been. The contradictions in my own life were stark too, unanchored between two worlds: home and far away from home. I couldn't imagine settling down in Vancouver, but I needed to do exactly that. I phoned my father from the hotel. We talked in an ordinary way, as if he'd forgotten I'd been gone. I would have loved a more effusive father, but he wasn't that kind of person, my solid, practical, Scottish dad.

We flew back to Canada, first to Montreal where I had a whirlwind visit with Solange, a nursing friend from the Cambodian refugee camps. We talked about the country that had ripped through our hearts. Solange, still trying to piece her life together a year later, was sponsoring a Cambodian refugee to come to Canada. I'd had the rapid cultural transition to another disaster zone in the same year. We longed for the international life, yet we craved the stability of home.

"*Il y a un prix que nous avons payé*," Solange said. There is a price we've paid. Uprooted, scattering of self, fragmented lives. We could see in each other how we were struggling. The need for stability and a home seduced us on one side. On the other, we were living our wildest dreams. Kindred souls and brave travellers, paying the price.

"If only we were simple girls who could live a simple life. It would be easier and safer," I said.

Safer than the shooting stars that filled me with wonder then took a crash course in my heart. Like Khalid who lived in a devout Islamic world, his shining eyes and fervent views still reflected in mine.

I wrote to Khalid: "You know I was just a Canadian girl you danced a 'slow' with and kissed cautiously at the Red Sea, the day, cool as watermelon on our salty lips and hot as the Suez sun. Now I'm on a Boeing 747, a little intoxicated with French wine. 'Don't Go Breaking My Heart' plays on my headphones."

Solange and I laughed about the men who passed through our lives. She was looking for her *bon homme* too. They all had their charm, and all had their catches, our reasons not to stay.

"I need a new life. I need a home. I need Vancouver." I dreamed of riding my bike on green forest paths, gazing out to sea at Lighthouse Park and cooking exotic meals for friends.

I flew on to Toronto for a Red Cross debriefing with Lorna, the assistant to the CEO. She wore a red dress and red high heels. It was time I too bought some sexy new shoes. We caught up on the latest news, not political but personal. Red Cross gossip, our love lives, our dreams, Lorna always talkative and intensely likable. She brought me right to where I needed to be, in Canada, in everyday living, in laughter.

The phone rang. The Palestinian Red Crescent was calling the Canadian Red Cross directly, bypassing Geneva, asking for assistance. Lorna put the phone on speaker. My eyes lit up.

"Well, Ella. Interested?" she said with an encouraging smile.

I could feel the raciness of yes, I could feel my heart quicken, I could hold the ticket in my hand, fly away one more time, a nurse on the front lines, to the war-torn Middle East. Tempting. Intriguing. A dangerous unknown.

"No, I can't go," I said, in a voice that wasn't as firm as I wanted.

"Are you sure?" Lorna insisted.

"Yes, I've made a promise to myself. I'm going home."

FIVE

Full Circle, March 2019

We shall not cease from exploration
And the end of all our exploring
Will be to arrive where we started
And know the place for the first time.

—T.S. ELIOT

43

My Signature Mark

THE PLANE DESCENDS, tilting through layers of cloud, circling into India. I am side swept through time zones, anticipating the journey and praying for a soft landing. It's a conflation of time, two lives old and new colliding with their hopes and dreams, expectations and fears. My fatigue turns into a momentary panic. I need to use my head to convince my heart I want to be here.

A dusty, musty smell hangs in the air at the Indira Gandhi International Airport in this most polluted capital city in the world. It wafts over me as I stand, clutching a copy of my e-visa, trying to envision a smooth entry into the country I want to visit one more time.

Three weeks before departure I had attempted to obtain an online visa. I began the lengthy application and surmised that I best not state the birthplace of my father, India, which is now Pakistan. In 1918, the year of his birth, Pakistan did not exist, and my father was a British subject. Any association with Pakistan, past or present, would be unwise as the two countries, both having nuclear warheads, now clash.

"Have you visited India before?" the e-visa asked.

"Yes," I checked, only to be prompted to provide a former visa number, which of course I didn't have. I couldn't proceed with the e-application and phoned the Indian passport service in Vancouver. The gentleman advised me to check, "No, I have never been to India before."

"But I have been to India!"

"Not to worry, ma'am. Just say 'no.'" I'd never lied on a government application, but lie I did. Within 24 hours I received an officially stamped document: visa granted. This unnecessary bureaucratic incompetence struck my sensibilities as a denial of a personal truth, an affront to my traveller's identity.

I now stand in an indeterminate lineup, more like a mass of moving people. I shuffle forward to the airport counter where six customs officials, dressed in khaki uniforms, sit side by side. I eye each man, trying to determine which one looks the most lenient of the group. They all look dismally uninterested in their work as they ask their perfunctory questions.

"Have you been to India before?" the man I had hoped to get asks.

"No, this is my first time," I say like an eager newcomer.

"What is the reason for your visit?" he asks, a glint of recognition in his eyes. I am not a good liar.

Forty-two years ago, I left this man's country forever marked with its complicated allure. In those passing years, my life was defined by other markers – marriage, motherhood, divorce and a career – but my signature mark remained the same. Solo travel. It still is, as I travel alone, although this time on a carefully planned and prepared trip. I researched transportation, accommodation and destinations – not off the beaten path but on the well-travelled path, the Golden Triangle of Delhi, Jaipur and Agra. I won't be hiking in the Himalayas, riding second-class trains with a fraudulent pass, seeking enlightenment on the banks of the Ganges or signing up to work on a dangerous front line. I'm not as clear-sighted or as sure-footed as I once was, walking cautiously on uneven streets with my arthritic hip and unsteady gait. I am more cushioned, safe, medically insured and digitally connected than in 1977. On this trip, I carry my return ticket with me.

"I wish you'd stop travelling and be more responsible," my mother had said many years ago. She would not have known then that travelling is a responsible act, a way of living in a wider arena, an ever-changing panorama of people and experience, a journey with all possible destinations. Now she lies in her bed in a care facility, encouraging me to have a holiday, wanting the best for her daughter, fighting back tears, vulnerable and frail. "Don't worry, Mom, I'll be home soon," I whisper, kissing her goodbye.

"I've come to see the Taj," I reply, looking the customs inspector, an older man with an untidy belly hanging over his belt, straight in the eye. He smiles, my reason to visit his country accepted, a reason he must hear a hundred times a day. He even chats about his recent trip to Canada to visit relatives in Surrey just outside Vancouver, then stamps my passport, wishes me a safe journey and waves me through.

In arrivals an eager crowd is waiting, those with name signs pushing forward to the front. I find "my man," whose name is Ganesh, holding my name upside down at the end of the line. Ganesh is the jolly, fat Hindu elephant god, the remover of all obstacles. My Ganesh, a skinny man, hurries off with my suitcase at a fast clip, not once looking behind to see if I am following him in the maze of multi-level parking.

We take off into a rainy Delhi evening, in a mega-metropolis of 30 million people. The traffic darts forward in some "lane-less" fashion on a highway several lanes wide. I haven't come back to the India I once knew, with overloaded bullock carts creaking along dusty roads. Urban India is fast, intense and cosmopolitan. I'm here for three short weeks, no longer the young woman who once earnestly threw her heart into this country.

I arrive exhausted at the B & B that is dated and windowless, not "cozy chic" as advertised online. It is clean, comfortable and safe, all I desire after an interminable international flight. My hosts, Abha, a plump, soft-spoken lady, and Rupinder, her loquacious husband, have been waiting for my arrival and have an elaborate dinner prepared. I'm not hungry and can only nibble, trying to be polite, as several domestic helpers stand nearby and waggle their heads. Employers and employees lounge and linger in slow motion.

I settle in well, sleep well and eat well, helping myself to several *parathas* – Indian-style potato pancakes – for breakfast. Abha and Rupinder can't do enough to make me feel at home and give suggestions to "roam around" Delhi.

In Hauz Khas village, a Delhi suburb, I find the Blossom Tea Room, an airy upstairs lounge, where I can relax and collect myself, something I need to do as I'm seriously jet-lagged. An engraved sign hangs on a decorative wall: "A cup of tea is a cup of peace." From an extensive choice of tea, I choose rose blossom, the menu claiming it is rich in vitamins A, C and E, hydrates the skin and reduces fine lines.

A smartly dressed couple sits at a table beside me in this trendy establishment. The girl has lustrous black hair and skin the colour of creamy caramel. They do not touch each other, but their modesty burns with desire.

I sip my cup of peace, the only foreigner in the tea shop, feeling invisible, surrounded by youth, beauty and dreams. I watch them flirt with intimacy as I flirt with a new version of myself, a new kind of romance, stepping out in different ways. If the world is full of young lovers, where does an older heart land? Right here. Heart willing. With herself and the world.

I pull out my manuscript pages that I brought from Canada and set them on the table. This I love to do, write and craft my memoir, sitting in a coffee shop or the Blossom Tea Room, listening to the soothing hum of life around me. Sensations surface from my past travels – vibrant colour, oppressive heat, opulent temples, wretched poverty, the Taj, chaotic train stations and the omnipresent gods and goddesses.

There was always a chasm to jump between what I assimilated and what seemed impossible to assimilate. Memories fragment like a broken mirror, reflecting pieces of my resilience and my compassion, as well as my impatience and privilege. I try to understand my complicity in privilege, and all that comes with it – education, opportunities, comforts and, most importantly, choice. It may have been unintended, or it may have been in that glance described by V.S. Naipaul: "It is your gaze that violates them, your sense of outrage that outrages them…it is your anger that denies them their humanity." I am vaguely ashamed, but I need more than shame, maybe courage to live more consciously and compassionately.

Outside a steady rain has left the street one long mud puddle. Despite the weather, I wander through the medieval ruins of Hauz Khas, visit some sari shops and find the Naivedyam Restaurant. It's not a dine-alone sort of place, though eating alone is easy, comfortable territory for me. I choose *thengai rava masala dosai*, a crispy golden semolina pancake, even though I ate pancakes for breakfast. It's cooked with finely grated coconut, filled with mildly spiced mashed potato and served with four condiments – coriander, tomato, coconut and sambhar – each of them a savoury delight.

By mid-afternoon I find a scooter to return to the B & B. My cell beeps. A text message all the way from Canada. A well-meaning friend tells me to "take care" as Pakistan has just closed its airspace for all transit flights to and from India. Tensions recently escalated between the two nuclear powers following an attack on the Indian paramilitary, killing 40 police in the disputed region of Kashmir. International political scandals or threats of conflict pose a travel risk, but this one seems remote and my flight back to Canada is over Chinese airspace. One less thing to worry about.

On the other hand, I *am* worried as the scooter wallah careens around corners in Hauz Khas, smiling at me in his rear-view mirror, amused that his daily livelihood is the stuff of hair-raising movies. I am afraid of dying before my time, that unknown time, knowing it could be anytime. I don't need to be on treacherous mountain passes with vertical drops to sure death. Delhi is bad enough.

"Slowly, slowly," I say.

"No worrying, no worrying," he replies and drives faster.

There was a time I whirled around Delhi sidesaddle on a motor-cycle with Sanjay, the wind in my face, my arms wrapped around his warm body. The desire hasn't changed, only the circumstances. Would I dare do now what I readily did then?

I RUB MY EYES, fatigued after a sleepless night with the noise of barking dogs. Or it may be the AQI (air quality index) registering in the very unhealthy range, not quite hazardous, on the daily Delhi index. My eyes burn in my head. It's the month of March, just after winter when the city is at its worst, covered with a tox-ic haze that obscures the sky and with air pollution levels that reach catastrophic levels.

Ganesh stands on duty at the door of the B & B, ready to drive me to downtown New Delhi where I'll meet my guide for a rick-shaw tour of Old Delhi, pre-booked from Canada. The ease of dig-ital travel astounds me, compared with the sheer chanciness of travel in the pre-internet era.

Two French girls, waiting for their booked tour of the Old Delhi slums, tell me they are shaken with the numbers of gawking men. "Just stick together, don't worry, you'll be fine," I reassure them in my best French. No one is gawking at me; no one is sidling up to me, other than the tuk-tuk drivers. The advantage of being older comes with its own mixed blessings, but I settled those concerns yesterday over rose blossom tea.

My young guide, Stanley, shows up right on time. Without a trace of disappointment that I am his only booked customer, we set out on the comfortable Delhi metro to the bustling streets of Old Delhi. Off and on a rickshaw, we visit markets of spice, jewelry, street foods and flowers. Orange marigolds are in abundance as offerings for the temples. A few sacred cows loiter, though most of India's ubiquitous cows have been moved out of the densely populated cities into greener pastures, both literally and figuratively.

Descending dingy stairs to a maze of underground tunnels, I follow Stanley through a subterranean city that feels like a dark cave. People are working in tiny, enclosed, windowless rooms, eating, sleeping and feeding families. The narrow passages close in on me, my nervousness rattles me. I can't lose sight of Stanley as we climb back up several flights of stairs. I think I might pass out before reaching a rooftop.

I take a deep breath and look down into the courtyard of another community. Garbage is strewn on corrugated tin awnings, monkeys jump around and dogs lounge in the sun of a dilapidated wooden structure once a mosque. Men and women attend to their affairs on tipsy balconies, stringing up laundry or flipping chapattis on gas burners. I peer down into this contemporary mess of mankind, into an urban slum, like a voyeur, my tour costing 30 Canadian dollars, the monthly salary of many.

Old Delhi, described as the soul of Delhi, has too many people living in too little space. I am walking into the world of the "have-nots." I wonder how long "we in the West" can continue to live comfortably with our abundance.

Given more time, maybe I'd walk Old Delhi's narrow alleys, explore Chandni Chouk, India's busiest market, and be tempted to try the array of aromatic food. I *want* to be the kind of person that sees the unpredictable beauty of India, no matter how brutal conditions may be.

India has taken a great leap into the 21st century as the largest democracy and sixth-largest economy in the world. But the country is still crippled with poverty, overpopulation, illiteracy, gender inequality and environmental catastrophes of dangerous pollution, severe water shortages or extreme flooding.

Arundhati Roy, the Indian novelist, writes: "And what of my country, my poor-rich country, India, suspended somewhere between feudalism and religious fundamentalism, caste, and capitalism, ruled by far-right Hindu nationalists? The tragedy is the wreckage of a train that has been careening down the track for years." I remember the squalor, the stench of pissing walls, the beggars so deformed I couldn't look and the pavement dwellers living impossible lives. I also remember India's vitality and immediacy and splendour rising above its despair.

For now, all I want to do is return to my comfortable B & B. I'm tired and need to rest, to assimilate all that I have seen on my three-hour tour. I tip Stanley for his excellent attention and hop into a cab. A little girl, maybe 6 years old, knocks at the window-pane, rattling her tin cup. I dig into my purse to look for a coin, but the driver abruptly takes off, leaving the little girl behind.

DELHI DRIVERS have outstanding peripheral vision as they slither and slide past one another like a swarm of fish. Ganesh expertly maneuvers around a motorbike that swerves in front of us. A close call, the near collision could have sent its three riders, all without helmets, to the hospital.

We arrive at the most sublime of temples: the Baha'i Lotus House of Worship. The Baha'i faith advocates peace and unity among all races, nations and religions. The design of the temple is inspired by the lotus, the flower arising from muddy waters, the symbol of purity.

I file through the lotus petal entry along with a group of Tibetan Buddhist monks, schoolgirls from Sri Lanka and a seniors' tour from Scandinavia. A musician plays the harp inside the temple's simple interior. The music soars and resonates and tiny birds fly within its walls. The atmosphere is celestial, even among tourists.

The temple calls me to a higher enchanted place, where I know, despite all the earth's suffering, there is one imperative for our survival. Love One Another. It's at the heart of our common humanity.

It is not for him to pride himself who loveth his own country, but rather for him who loveth the whole world. The earth is but one country and mankind its citizens.

—BAHÁ'U'LLÁH, FOUNDER OF THE BAHA'I FAITH

Ganesh, a sweet man with a furrow on his brow, patiently waits for me in the parking lot beside a tour bus marked "Mysteries of India." I buy a dozen trinkets, fridge magnets, from the persistent boys who crowd around. Our next stop is Akshardham Temple on the outskirts of Delhi.

Built in 2005 and considered a Hindu architectural masterpiece, Akshardham means the divine abode of God. The information pamphlet ensures a spiritually enriching experience at this hand-carved stone temple built without structural steel. The temple grounds are extensive, larger than a football field, and my hip is aching. I open my collapsible walking pole, not caring how I look as I click along the inner courtyards of the imposing structure. Its thousand intricate details seem excessive and overbearing as I swing from rapture to disappointment in a day. Tired out, I take a swig of water and hobble back to the car.

44

Risks and Benefits

THE DECISION TO COME TO INDIA meant weighing the risks and benefits, but I don't want to live inside that equation. I want to shake up the journey and toss caution to the wind. I know how to do this; it's not an entirely forgotten skill.

I could have stayed home in my pretty bubble of a town, sheltered from a stormier world elsewhere, though of course "elsewhere" can land in my backyard anytime. There's always talk about the "Big One." The Earthquake. Or an Oil Spill. Safety is an illusion, so I remain true to myself and set off solo, the journey as bewildering as it can be liberating.

Had I imagined my trip to be a spiritual pilgrimage rising from the ashes of a former lifetime, or even an organized tour, would that have permitted more comfort and ease? It is neither of these, as I cling to my seat belt, terrified in the traffic on our way to Jaipur, an unattractive stretch of highway. Fifi sits beside me and manages to snooze. No wonder – she's from São Paulo, Brazil, the sixth-largest city in the world. I met her yesterday at Big Fat Sandwich, Delhi's trendy Starbucks. She invited me to go with her on the five-hour trip in a private car. It didn't matter that

I had a carefully pre-booked train ticket. I wanted to go with Fifi, choosing the company of a new friend over my love of train travel.

Our driver thinks he's in the Grand Prix as he races between two mammoth long-haul trucks, barely squeezing through. In the congestion a herd of buffalo meander down the side of the road. I am acutely aware of my mortality when in India. It could be a pedestrian accident, death by walking, or as my travel doctor stated blithely, it could be malaria, the number one killer, that gets me.

We drive by a variety of animals wandering in the streets as we approach Jaipur, the capital of Rajasthan – a horse, a camel, an elephant, monkeys and several sacred cows. The Kawa Guest House, where Fifi has a room, is hard to find down a long dirt path. I carry on with the driver, who stops several times to ask directions before finding my lodgings on the other side of town. I arrive at Charita Guest House wrung out, my eyes red and swollen, in a state of collapse.

Charita welcomes me into her stately home, decorated with Rajasthani art. Off the side of the garden and up a flight of stairs is a cozy room with a cherubic Lord Krishna playing his flute, looking down at me from the wall. A blast of lemongrass infuses the air.

"How was your trip from Delhi?" Charita's son Viyash asks as he helps me with my suitcase. He's hip with his pink sunglasses and slicked-back hair, and drives a motorcycle.

"I'm done in. The traffic was crazy."

"I live in Mumbai where the traffic is next-level-insane."

"Now I understand why Lord Ganesha is so popular," I say. He laughs and tells me about his studies in India's largest city.

Charita arrives in the room to check if Viyash has assisted me correctly. They exchange a rapid volley of Hindi with English catchwords popping into the conversation like "fly over," and "take-out," and "cell phone."

For dinner I eat a tasty vegetarian meal with small dishes of lentils, cauliflower and potatoes. Charita, who doesn't usually sit with her guests, takes a seat, pleased with my curiosity about

Indian cuisine, her city and her life. She's a cosmopolitan woman, wearing a sari of brilliant purple, lime green and soft peach.

"Oh, this is just my everyday sari, I have one for every occasion." She laughs when I admire her style, and she compliments my silky blouse bought specially for the trip.

I retire to my private balcony, bathed in evening sun. A restfulness washes over me as I contemplate my first week in Delhi and now Jaipur. It's the season of my life that I call autumn, mid-autumn. The colours I choose are burnt sienna, rippled gold and deep plum. Bold colours. They'll drop from the tree when the time comes. A tear moistens my cheek in this season of both solitude and deep connection.

In the early morning, the call to prayer ripples across town to Charita's neighbourhood. The get-out-of-bed-and-pray command is a strange wake-up call, more appealing than an alarm clock. The prayer is a call to the virtuous life, to a higher godly plane, to peace in a troubled world. With all due respect to Islamic tradition, I imagine a female voice calling the faithful to prayer. It would be more nurturing than the authoritative, insistent drone of the male muezzin.

The plaintive call brings forth distant memories in Islamic lands – Turkey and Egypt. How willing I was to be held in the arms of a believer, to be charmed by devotion to faith, to intellect, to passion and to love. I am not so easily seduced now, but for a moment, here in Jaipur, the passions of youth are kindled. A flame ignited.

My journal, this one with a gorgeous Indian motif embossed on its cover, I hold in my hands like I might a lover. Once I lost my journal to the river and, sometimes, I lose the stories themselves. They float somewhere in my subliminal awareness as if the life I once lived is no longer mine: the foreign lovers, exotic travels and work on the front lines.

JAIPUR IS THE HISTORIC CAPITAL CITY and gateway to Rajasthan, the land of maharajas, medieval forts and magnificent palaces. I remember the city as a provincial town. It's now a city bursting with over three million people, most on their cell phones in the wildly hectic streets of the Pink City.

The Hawa Mahal, or Palace of the Winds, is one of Jaipur's architectural showpieces. The palace, built in 1799, combines Rajput Hindu and Moghul Islamic design. It's smaller than I remember, yet exquisite with its 953 intricately carved windows, called *jharokhas*. Women of the royal family, forbidden to appear in public, could sit behind the latticed windows and peer out to the street. The women's dignity and virtue were protected, though not having the liberty to walk in the streets seemed a cruel fate. The pink sandstone honeycomb facade of the Hawa Mahal looks tired, from another era. It needs a facelift.

"Come visit my shop." "Special discount for you." "First customer of the day." Old and tired lines I've heard a thousand times before. At the sidewalk store beside the Hawa Mahal, I stop and admire the wares. A floral bedspread of scarlet red and earth ochre catches my eye. A dream bedspread, a perfect keepsake, to remember Rajasthan and its fabric art. My romantic inclination battles with my practical mind. How would I get off and on the crowded train with a heavy bedspread? Should I send it home to Canada? Practicality wins. I don't buy the spread, though I'm not happy about this.

"Another time," I say. The shopkeeper appears as disappointed as me. It can't be an easy way to make a living, dealing with tourists and their whims.

I jump back in the car with Imran, my driver, an Islamic man, who takes me to Jai Mahal, a surreal architectural attraction on the outskirts of town. The partially submerged palace sits out on a lake, floating like a swan on mystical waters. Imran and I chat back and forth about God and marriage, common subjects in India.

"I have a broken heart, now a happy heart," he says. I don't tell this earnest young man about the whims of mine.

"May I ask if your wife wears the *niqab*?"

"Oh yes, of course. The Koran tells us to cover our women to respect God. It is shameful if my wife does not obey."

"Is it the lady's or man's choice?" I ask.

"It is our natural choice," Imran says, as surely as the sky is blue. He shows me her picture on his cell phone, her head uncovered, her hair falling to her shoulders, a sparkle in her eyes, smiling for all the world to see.

"She is very pretty," I say, knowing I will not talk about gender equality with Imran.

"I am very, very happy. My life is perfect. I have a wife and two children."

I'm happy too as we "fly over" the roundabout. A man with a gigantic sack of potatoes on his bicycle cuts in front of us. Imran swerves smoothly around him as if we are all part of a choreographed dance.

45

What Matters Now

FIFI ASKS ME TO JOIN HER on a rural Jeep safari, a prearranged and misnamed tour as there isn't a wild animal in sight, only cows and goats. Our guide, Mohan, takes us to two villages and a schoolhouse that lacks chairs, desks, books and resources. The children sit in a row on the concrete terrace of the primary school. They stand up and bow, as instructed on our arrival.

"I want to capture the beauty of children, especially their eyes," Fifi, a photographer, says. "India was my dream and it hasn't disappointed me," but our visit is orchestrated, not conducive to spontaneous photography. We are both trying to be gracious guests with Mohan, who must regularly show up with foreign clients.

We wave goodbye to the kids and drive down dirt roads through patchy green fields of wheat and marigolds where women work. Traditional, rural India is only a short distance from Jaipur, a fast-paced modern society.

Mohan, who is 30 years old, has an elaborate gelled hairdo, looking like a Bollywood hopeful. He is good at his scripted explanation of Indian life, though he wants to talk about his own life, particularly about an arranged marriage, or the alternative, a "love marriage," as it is called.

"I have one condition for my marriage. I can't ever leave India. I must care for my parents. It is my duty. I am the eldest son," Mohan states, pointing out a mongoose that runs across the dirt road. He would think it shameful that we in the West put our parents into care homes, as I did with my mother when the time came. She accepted this, understanding it would not have been a happy arrangement living under the same roof with me. I attempt to explain the social and economic factors that affect these decisions. Mohan isn't listening, another pressing concern on his mind.

"If I fell in love with a foreign lady, will she stay with me in Jaipur?" He looks to us for motherly opinions.

"She will be a special girl to stay. Then one day she may go back to her own country," I say, remembering how I went back to mine.

"If a foreign lady doesn't fall in love with me, no worries. I'm happy with arranged marriage." It is an *inshallah* way of seeing the world. For Mohan, a Hindu, it is a decision of the gods.

MY ARTHRITIC HIP HURTS if I walk for more than 30 minutes. I'm drawn to sitting down, reading a book – right now an excellent novel, *When the Moon Is Low*, by Nadia Hashimi – and listening to the chatter of Hindi or Rajasthani or Marwari around me, I cannot tell. I find a space of quietness within the backdrop of human community at this rooftop restaurant. This is my travel element, feeling content at the Peacock Palace beside the Hassle-Free Silver Shop.

I drink a glass of spicy masala chai and talk to the woman sitting next to me. Her name is Antoinette, a Brit living in New York City. We quickly discover each other's *raison d'etre* in India. She works in a museum of Hindu art and visits Mumbai every year, offering art classes to children of prostitutes. "It's a small measure to break the cycle of prostitution," she says.

The women I meet are fascinating, dynamic, independent, strong, socially conscious and caring. (Where are the men?) We can be friends, travellers for a time, free spirits, unhampered with the layers of life that weigh us down. Others join us at the table; we make it a comfortable place to be.

The next morning, Antoinette and I take a tuk-tuk out to the spectacular Amer Fort in the arid hills surrounding Jaipur. Declared a UNESCO World Heritage Site in 2013, the fort, also known as the Amber Palace, attracts up to 5,000 visitors a day. The palace, constructed of red sandstone and marble, was once the opulent residence of the Rajput Maharajas.

Antoinette is an artist and dresses Indian style, in a flowing *shalwar kameez* with a soft *dupatta* draped over her head. I limp along, looking North American with my baseball cap and day pack, not wanting to lose her in the crowd. She explores every nook and cranny of the palace, as I take every opportunity to sit down and admire its magnificence.

An old and weary elephant with a royal purple saddle and a mahout dressed like a maharaja is available for palace rides. Neither Antoinette nor I would take an elephant ride, not now. We don't want to participate in his pitiful fate.

Much worse is the horrific killing of elephants for ivory. In Africa, tens of thousands die every year. We need to save these great, intelligent, endangered species. I can't imagine a world without elephants. Carbon footprints, depleted ozone or melting ice caps are harder to conceptualize, but the slaughter of elephants is a visceral wound of the earth. Save the elephants, save the children and save the planet. This is what matters now.

TODAY, ON MARCH 10, 2019, I wake up to horrifying global events on my iPad newsfeed: Ethiopian Air Flight 302 crashes, killing all 157 aboard. I later learn there were 18 Canadians on board, some young environmentalists going to the UN Environment Assembly in Kenya. One of those Canadians was an Indigenous man from a small town where I used to live. His name was Micah Messent. On his first trip to Africa, he wanted to help change the world. His life mattered and now he is dead. My heart breaks for his family, for the collective sorrow, for this senseless tragedy.

I reach for my embroidered bag in which I keep quotes on bits of paper, little hits of inspiration, resonant chords I carry with me when I travel. A quote from a Mary Oliver poem falls into my hand. It is a perfect balm for my soul.

It's a serious thing just to be alive on this fresh morning in this broken world.

As our lives unfold, we can be on either side of the paradox – in unexpected crushing pain or exquisite delight. So it is today as I indulge in an Ayurvedic massage of hot camphor and coconut oil infused with medicinal herbs. My whole body lathered and swimming in hot oil. Lovely, lovely, lovely. I am detoxified, purified and restored to vigour and vitality.

Outside the Peacock Palace, I chat with a driver and snap a photo of his polished tuk-tuk, his philosophy inscribed on the side panel:

God Has No Phone.
But I Talk To Him Every Day.
He Has No Facebook.
But He Is Still My Friend.
He Has No Twitter.
But I Still Follow Him.

He could be Hindu or Muslim or Christian, it doesn't matter. This is India.

Charita's friend Madhu has invited me to her home for tea. She sweeps up her gray-flecked hair into a knot at the nape of her neck and kindly scolds the house girl for forgetting the biscuits.

Several years ago, Madhu lost her 16-year-old daughter in an accident. As the young girl walked home from school, she was hit by a bus. "It changed my life. I could no longer work in hotel management. I asked myself over and over what could matter now. I had to find a new life after death, and for me that was road safety." I offer my condolences to this woman marked by grief and inquire about road safety, certainly a subject of pressing importance in India.

"Changing attitudes takes time. No one pays attention to the rules and signage in India. We are an unruly people on the road," Madhu sighs, filling my cup with lemongrass tea. "Unruly" is the perfect word. The disorder and disobedience remind me of wayward, willful children, determined with horn-honking theatrics to get their way.

"Fear of dying is a universal fear, however people don't connect it to road safety. Indians lack a civic sense, caring for one's city or one's nation, yet we are also fiercely patriotic. We are an overpopulated place, so we need to get on with each other. We know how to compromise, and we are warm-hearted too. Family is most important in our country," Madhu summarizes, in defense of her unruly nation.

"Which god brings you strength in troubled times?" A commonplace question in India I don't hesitate to ask.

"Durga is my goddess. Yes, Krishna is very human, Ganesh is lovable and Lakshmi is generous, but Durga is the supreme, powerful, mother goddess who gives strength and protection."

This multiplicity of gods in Hinduism can be difficult to fathom for the Western mind, yet it is the very fabric of life in India. The pantheon has three million deities, a god for every facet of life and death. As God cannot be known, he or she is known through many manifestations. Hindus may choose a personal god to whom they pray, *devas* or *devis* that represent a force of nature or moral value, or believe in one all-pervasive God, Brahman, as the eternal origin of all existence.

"I imagine all the gods as different faces of some greater indefinable mystery," I say. Madhu and I seem to agree that we do not need absolute answers and that in an intelligent universe, God cannot be of any one religion, a God that separates and divides. In a whimsical sort of way, I appreciate Hinduism's perspective. It offers nuance, diversity and choice. I might choose Saraswati, the goddess of music, art and wisdom, or Parvati, the goddess of love, beauty and harmony.

"Let's stay in touch," I say to Madhu, which seems to be another way of saying goodbye. She sees me off as I jump in a tuk-tuk for the Jaipur Junction station. I'll take the train from Jaipur to Agra, a much safer choice than the treacherous highway. I need to buy a ticket, hard-copy proof, as an online transaction is too convoluted with Indian Railways.

It's not clear which long lineup I need in the busy ticket office. A young Korean backpacker points out the #1 lineup for essential paperwork for foreigners. That completed, a kind Indian lady squeezes me in front of her in the #2 lineup and gently pushes me forward to the wicket. An older man with neon orange henna hair, who must think he's a sexier version of himself, sits behind the metal grill. He does one thing with terrific flair: selling tickets. He throws rupees into the air that land in a drawer in a heap of scattered bills like a pile of autumn leaves. He then tosses the change back to the customer as if dealing dice. Watching him is worth the wait. He issues me my ticket, a flimsy piece of paper like a city bus transfer, destination Agra.

46

The Elsewhere of Our Lives

THE TRAIN ROLLS FROM SIDE TO SIDE, a gentle rocking, as the chai wallah sells his tea in half-size paper cups. I sip the sugary tea, the national drink of India, not yet tempted to eat the gooey sweets from the mithai wallah. The countryside of dry fields is flat and uninteresting as we approach Agra. Passengers talk on their cell phones, other than a few loud Russians who I doubt are drinking tea.

I am rolling on, "over the other side," as Indians say, to the Taj Mahal, a memory of splendour. I pray to some goddess of writing, maybe Saraswati, that the Taj will hold the story, something transcendent or transformational, an epiphany of sorts.

Train stations in India require a certain travel savvy, a mix of patience, pushiness and grit. My excitement at being in Agra outweighs the commotion of the station. A man is waving a flimsy piece of paper with a barely decipherable name on it in what looks like Hindi script. He's the B & B private driver, a small luxury I'm relieved to have.

The boldly painted Coral Homestay is nestled in a jungle-like garden of bougainvillea and frangipani. My room has tangerine walls decorated with Bollywood posters and Hindu art. Pratibha, the hostess, has created a funky, warm and welcoming décor.

Pratibha, dressed in tight jeans and a T-shirt, juggles an international group of a dozen people, some just departing, some just arriving. I make myself at home, exchanging stories with other guests over a scrumptious vegetarian Indian dinner. Conversation comes easy with young tourists or with seasoned travellers. We are a tapestry of colourful tales. I sip a cool beer then retire to my pretty room.

The Islamic muezzin of Agra, a city that is 10 per cent Muslim, wakes me up early in the morning, the call to prayer emanating from the beginning of all time. I rub my eyes awake, happy to start my day, which doesn't have a single scheduled thing to do other than visiting the Taj.

Noisy India implodes and explodes around me as I stroll down the street, wood smoke and pollution in the air, to a wonder of the world. Shops have set up their goods on the sidewalks, canned products, sandals, beauty creams, chapatis, cigarettes and signs for foreign exchange, the money-changers already looking for customers. The tuk-tuk drivers are out early too, trying to scrape a living off the tourists.

"Please madam, only 50 rupees. You are my best customer. I am #1 Helicopter India."

"No, I want to walk. No, No, No," I say with a smile and carry on contemplating the uncertainty of their lives. These men are the interface with everyday, street-level India, sometimes so insistent and infuriating; other times, they can't do enough to ensure you have a comfortable ride.

After buying my ticket at the Taj tourist office, I walk to the East Gate, where I file through the lady's lineup in a police-patrolled cordoned area. No packsacks, no smoking and no food allowed. A man on a noisy lawnmower tends to the manicured lawns.

I walk through the Great Gate toward the Taj, majestic in the morning sun. She is entirely feminine, with polished marble that glows a delicate rose, her cupola, breast-shaped, and her minarets, celestial arrows. Every superlative for the Taj has already been written. I cannot find an original word: sublime, heavenly, magnificent, divine. The mausoleum is a masterpiece of symmetry and harmony and represents the finest of Mughal architecture.

"Please may I be of assistance for your tour of India's greatest monument?" a guide asks. I don't want history; I don't want details; I want the silence of the Taj to be my muse, my inspiration and *my divine.*

"Can you take my picture, and I will take yours, please?" a Japanese girl asks. She is one of a few hundred tourists here, snapping pictures or taking selfies. We pose and admire each other's shots. I wish I had dressed in Eastern elegance for the occasion, a once-in-a-lifetime photo op.

That young woman of long ago was probably dressed in jeans and a T-shirt, as she sat for hours gazing at the Taj, my journal said. The memory is a blur. I can only sense her, alone at the Taj, as I am today, among families, friends, couples, tour groups and guides. I walk my solitary path and mingle with the crowd. It seems to me that we are all smiling.

A MILD PANIC SKITTERS across my logical mind as I realize I only have five days left before returning home. I've just scratched the surface, and India is a country to plumb to the depths, or at least appreciate a layer of its richness. My driver, Nazim, a likable, mild-mannered, skinny man wearing a knitted white *topi*, the circular cap worn by Muslim men, will take me to the Agra Fort and the Baby Taj this morning.

"Do you have a husband?" he asks, though his English is minimal.

"No, not now."

"I'm very, very, sorry," Nazim says, shaking his head as if this is an extremely sad fate in life. He may think I am a widow or never married, though I have no way of discerning his response in a culture that values marriage as the highest good and perhaps the only respectable option. But marriage is changing in India too, as women, both Muslim and Hindu, stand up for their lives, leave bad marriages and claim a different life than their mothers led. This I read in books, see in films and learn in my travels.

Whether Nazim speaks from deeply held traditions, from sexist attitudes that permeate the Indian subcontinent or from kindness, it doesn't matter to me now. I only get excited when I see the brilliant spread of saris drying on the riverbank below us. He insists on stopping the car on the busy bridge so I can jump out and take a picture.

Agra Fort is an imposing walled city built in 1573 under the reign of Akbar, one of the greatest of the Mughal emperors. Akbar's grandson, Shah Jahan, added marble terraces and intricate latticework to the red sandstone fort. It is rumoured that Shah Jahan, disposed of by his four sons, died in the tower overlooking the Yamuna River, his beloved Taj Mahal in the distance.

After 45 minutes of wandering around the extensive grounds, I'm exhausted, hot, satiated, done. There are only so many Moghul forts I can visit, and the day is too hot to enjoy myself. At the roundabout outside the gate, the traffic darts madly. I am stranded, unable to step into the mayhem until a traffic control officer takes my hand and helps me across the hectic road. I imagine I'm not the first foreigner in distress that he has reached out to, held their hand and safely delivered to the other side.

Nazim waves from his car. I jump in and gulp some water as we drive back across the river to visit I'timad-ud-Daulah. This Mughal mausoleum is known as the Baby Taj, a precursor of the Taj, built for the grandfather of Mumtaz. I love the Baby Taj almost as much as the Taj and revel in the silence of its inner chambers. Hardly a soul is here, just as I remembered it four decades ago. Light shines through the carved marble, illuminating the delicate inlay art of lapis lazuli, onyx and topaz called *pietra dura*.

Outside the gate, Nazim is leaning against a crumbling wall smoking his cigarette. I am grateful for his presence, knowing someone is waiting for me to drive me home.

AN ATTRACTIVE SOUTH ASIAN WOMAN is sitting on the terrace over-looking the Taj in the late afternoon at the five-star Oberoi Hotel.

"Lovely view," she calls out in a demure English accent. I am sitting at the far end of the terrace drinking fresh ground coffee, not the usual Nescafe in India, and eating superb cardamom cookies.

"Yes, it can't be beaten," and we call out the usual inquiries. "Where are you from?" "How long have you been in India?"

"May I join you?" I ask.

"Of course. Please do," this sparkling, hip young woman responds. I imagine there is nearly half a century between us.

Mez and I discover things we have in common: our fathers were born in India, we are left-handed, love coffee, are independent travellers and we both think India has something to teach us. Tolerance, perhaps, in our troubled world.

She has travelled from Yorkshire to Pushkar, in Rajasthan, to study classical Indian dance. Dance is her spiritual practice. Her upbringing was Islamic, her mother a devout Muslim, but Mez is not a traditional Muslim daughter.

"Your relationship with your mother intrigues me. I was about your age when I first came to India. My mother didn't approve."

"My mother is the eternal mother who embraces all that is love. As long as I am loving, she accepts her liberated daughter. My parents had an arranged marriage, but they love each other very much," she tells me and waves to the waiter for more cardamom cookies.

"My marriage was not arranged. I have left my husband back in England for three months. I'm here to study," she adds. "There is space for us all."

"I love your free spirit," I say to Mez.

She looks at me and replies, "But look at you!"

"The free spirit in me is also a restless heart looking for a home," I say.

"I came to India to connect with my ancestral home. My greatest discovery is that my roots are in England, where I was born and bred. The auntie who lives down the street, the flowers in the garden, my favourite coffee shop, my friends and my family. It's where I belong."

"I have my trustworthy landmarks too, in a charming city with pink cherry blossoms in the spring." But home has been a moving landscape of multiple houses, neighbourhoods, communities and friends. Moving on became my territory. It was in leaving that I could come back changed, it was in travel that I could reinvent myself, it was in motion that I felt most alive. At least, that was my romantic version of self.

Leaving home, be it geographical or metaphorical, means longing for something left behind or longing for something yet to be experienced. Leaving somewhere and anticipating somewhere else was full of possibility and promise.

"Maybe home is where we live, and our spiritual home is where we travel," Mez says.

"Home is where we know ourselves, not *terra incognito* but *terra firma*. It can be found anywhere and everywhere, in the unlikeliest of places," I say, thinking both of us have arrived at some deep truth.

We sip our coffee and admire the view; it is the Taj after all. It feels we have arrived at a place of deep contentment yet still holding all our "what-ifs," alternate realities and sought-after dreams. It's the elsewhere of our lives.

John O'Donohue writes: "Longing is the deepest and most ancient voice of the human soul." This is our understanding as we say goodbye. We give each other a hug, then she walks away, khaki pack slung over one shoulder, camera over another. She's off to catch a train for Khajuraho. I walk back to the Coral, followed by the local tuk-tuk drivers, lighter and happier, holding a space for us all.

THREE MONTHS LATER, I am holding that space for my mother and me. She lies on her bed, starting to slip away, letting go of her life in this world. Not only is she holding on by a fine thread, I am too, facing the final goodbye.

I didn't know that one day I'd be at my mother's bedside, her caregiver, bridging the chasm that once existed between us. So many reckless words were hurled across that divide, but now none of that matters. I have come to love this lady, my mother who could be generous and wise, tough and exacting. Her life stories shaped her into a complex woman, a strong woman, then fading, exposed in her old age. I see her for who she was, running full force into life, aching to be loved like all of us, like her daughter who never really stopped trying. To love and be loved. I'm learning as my mother dies how much we need each other – family and friends, cultures and countries. We need each other to be a civil, sane and caring society.

"Finish your book," my mother whispers, her words so quiet I'm not sure I hear her correctly. This isn't my mother giving advice; she is expressing her love. It is the day she slips into unconsciousness. "I will, Mom." Her concern for her children's welfare held her till she could no longer hold on. Our time is precious together. I squandered that time for so many years and now I have a few moments left.

It's a lovely warm June day when my mother dies. And there is a loveliness in that single breath between living and dying. In my torrent of tears, in all the fraught stories, in being present till the end, till life quiets into a deep forever sleep. Death is the great settling of affairs, of arriving at an exhausted peace, as my mother does and I do that June morning.

I leave my mother's care home and walk downtown. After a profound loss, it's startling that life carries on, people chatting at sidewalk cafes, on their lunch breaks, on their cell phones, and I am suspended in a state of disbelief, though I know my mother has just died. I think I might faint, and I have only fainted once in my life, 42 years ago in India. I need to hydrate myself and sit down on a bench on a busy street, the kind of place to sit and watch the world go by as I drink a bottle of kombucha.

Sitting lasts a few minutes or maybe it's an hour. Time loses its parameters. Space becomes spacious, an altered, motherless space. A childhood memory surfaces – camping trips with Dad. Sometimes Mom came along, though she preferred to stay home, cook and clean, and have some quiet time for herself. Mom liked things orderly, while Dad let us run wild. When he took us out fishing for salmon in his small boat, all five of us pushed and dared and jumped into the chilly Pacific. Always without life jackets. Mom must have shuddered with fear.

How difficult it was for her in our disorderly family, her children acting out, getting into trouble or travelling off to remote corners of the world. Now these stories are stripped bare to something essential where I hold a glimmer of awareness. No, it's more than a glimmer; it's a flash of lightning. Understanding Mom. Understanding Me. We are all connected, all born and torn from our mothers' wombs. We live our lives on this fault line of love, then cracked open when death comes. It's time now, I need to get up from the bench, find my car and drive my way home.

47

Of Light and Shadow

ON MARCH 15, 2019, another horrific act of violence pops up on my iPad. "Fifty people killed in New Zealand terrorist attack. Another fifty injured." The rampage was during Friday prayer at a Christchurch mosque. This hate crime committed by a white supremacist is a terrifying act of alt-right extremism.

I don't know what to feel or think or do when I hear of such incomprehensible acts. I feel disgusted and angry about the world at large, teetering on a perilous path of environmental destruction, oppressive regimes, idiotic leadership and global inequities. All I can do is get dressed as birds chirp outside my window.

Downstairs Pratibha is serving breakfast to her guests from Argentina, Denmark, Belgium and England. We sit at a common table, inquiring about each other's plans for the day interspersed with comments about the tragic morning news. Travel is our bridge to conscious engagement. In some small way, we are caring about "the other." We need this, more than ever, on our wounded bloody Earth.

I set out to taste a flavour of India, though it feels like "tourist flavour" as I am visiting the popular sites of Bharatpur Bird Sanctuary and Fatehpur Sikri. I have a headache and am much less energetic than the Belgian couple, Ulrike and Carl, who join me. I met them last night at the Coral. They could be my children.

At the bird sanctuary, a guide takes us round a dry scrub brush track of land by bicycle rickshaw. We view the snake pits, the turtles and the birds – a purple sunbird, a spotted owl and many egrets basking in the sun. Our guide, a knowledgeable ornithologist, tries to disguise his trouble getting off and on the rickshaw, which I spot immediately as I'm doing the same. We share our arthritic hip stories as he points out birds I'd never have spotted on my own. The sanctuary boasts over 300 species and is best known for its herons and storks. Men and women, whom our guide refers to as "gents and ladies," squat at the side of the dirt road digging a ditch with hand shovels and crushing stones, a stark image of crushing poverty.

After lunch, Ulrike, Carl and I carry on with yesterday's driver, Nazim, to Fatehpur Sikri. This perfectly preserved deserted city was built in 1569 by Emperor Akbar and is considered, second to the Taj Mahal, the greatest achievement of the Mughal dynasty. The manicured gardens and stately courts were designed to accommodate Akbar's three wives. Pre-monsoon fields as dry as dust surround the mighty fortress.

Traipsing around this impressive imperial palace makes my headache worse. I waver between exploring a place as grand as Fatehpur Sikri and the discomfort of the long, hot walk. If I'd wanted effortless travel, why didn't I take a packaged getaway, an all-inclusive or a cruise? I never have and wonder if I ever will.

INDIA IS A VAST INDEFINABLE LAND, not a single voice but a tangled voice, as tangled as the electrical wires, a mess of circuitry on the street corner. Then, with a flick of the switch, there is light and everything sparkles in strange ways. Like my ATM encounter. The simplest of tasks frustrates me, like trying to find an ATM that works. I walk to four, two are out of order and one won't accept my PIN (could I have forgotten my PIN?). I've walked a good distance and my patience is wearing thin.

"May I assist you, ma'am?" a thin young man holding a tattered bag of books asks. I let him into the booth, ready to trust anyone who can help. He hits a key and discreetly turns his head the other way as I enter the amount and withdraw the cash. Five thousand rupees ($100).

"Thank you so much for your help."

"It's no bother, ma'am. Our ATMs are a cumbersome task for the foreigners."

"Yes, it was a cumbersome task," I say, laughing at the absurdities of travel. The gracious, gangly man returns to the line, where another man hacks and spits into the ditch.

I wave down a tuk-tuk. The driver gives me his hand as I climb aboard and takes me the short distance to the Oberoi. I crave fine things like quiet and cleanliness and drink a mango soda with a sprig of mint. It's a refreshing pause on a hot afternoon. A time to write and reflect on this cumbersome country, yet the unexpected kindness of its people never ceases to astonish me.

With only two more days left in Agra, I decide to visit the Taj again. There are thousands of visitors to the Taj Mahal daily, and hundreds are here now. Despite the crowd, there is a subdued rustle among us, a certain kind of reverence, an unspoken agreement. We are all part of this experience, appreciating great architecture or dreaming our private dreams, like Fifi, who bought expensive earrings in a shop nearby, a memento of the iconic love story of Shah Jahan and Mumtaz Mahal. I bought my star ruby pendant, *this one teardrop*, though I'm sure the skilled vendor sold me the sentimental piece at an exorbitant price.

A younger woman is walking toward me, shimmering in and out of light and shadow. I think I'd like to say hello. I have met her before, somewhere along the way, then she moves aside and disappears in the crowd. I know she's there watching me.

At the Great Gate, I look back, one last glance at the Taj, and see her lingering in a faraway place, the distance between us held in a shy sweetness. "Have I fulfilled her youthful expectations? Am I the desire of her girlhood dreams or have I fallen short?" I think both as I rearrange my skirt that is too tight and raise my hand to wave. Like a mirage, she is gone.

I have become an older woman. I never imagined or dreamed or planned to be her. With no exclamation point, no great fanfare, I have arrived. It's new territory not yet travelled, somewhat like the weather, changeable with the light slanting in sideways.

Coming face to face with the older woman is a reckoning of life's joys and sorrows. I am suspicious of those who say they have no regrets. My regrets, the heartaches where I was holding on or letting go on some proverbial, precarious cliff, were many. I had all the common markers of a woman's life – a marriage, a child, a career, family and friends. There were small and large losses – divorce, deaths, friendships gone astray, crushing sorrows. The thousands of experiences that mark a life.

I juggled life at home and abroad, a solitary and relational life, seeking and accumulating experience the way some women accumulate clothes. My younger self, preoccupied with finding the missing piece, thought it would be a man. How ordinary and human I was, looking for love with men who came and went like bolts of lightning.

I haven't changed much, still getting excited with different places and people, but see myself through new eyes: the traveller, the mother, the nurse, the writer, the young girl, the older woman, the lover and the other. Not entirely one or the other, I am all. Derek Walcott, the Saint Lucian poet, wrote:

The time will come when, with elation, you will greet yourself arriving at your own door, in your own mirror, and each will smile at the other's welcome

I leave the Taj and take the free shuttle bus that scoots up and down the East Gate Road, not a wild and dangerous ride but pleasant, and I am comfortably content. From the terminus, it's a short stroll back to the Coral. Pratibha, who was in jeans yesterday, is wearing a gorgeous sari of robin's egg blue. This efficient, competent, graceful matriarch of her homestay and I drink tea together on the terrace and talk about life in India.

"Attitudes change slowly, especially in the villages. I grew up in a village, but my parents made sure I had an education. Everything depends on education, especially for the girls who need to get out of lives of hardship."

"I see the young girls working while the boys play."

"Boys are valued more than girls in my country. And girls are blamed for things that go wrong. It is hard for a girl to remarry if her first marriage fails. Even if there was abuse, the police do not listen to the girl. The family needs to resolve the problem."

"I'd like to believe the world is changing and, one day, girls and young women will be educated, valued and contributing, even leading the way. Just like you. I'm impressed with how you do what you do."

"It is my opportunity to meet the foreigners. Opportunities are coming slowly. At the same time, change is coming too fast," Pratibha says, adjusting the long trail of her sari over her shoulder, the gesture so natural among Hindu women. The draping and tucking and pleating of eight metres of fabric would seem an impossible task to Western women. I envy her grace.

The next morning at Café Coffee Day, India's other franchise, I meet Aniti. Just like Pratibha and Mez, she is the quintessential Indian woman, bridging the traditional and contemporary world. An American, she has a degree in developmental economics and comes regularly to India to "give back." She works in rural Rajasthan, helping women start micro-businesses.

"I want to effect real sustainable change. Most of all I'm concerned about the unprocessed trauma of women's lives," Aniti says.

"Do the village women speak to you about their trauma?" I ask.

"The women want to tell me their worries. They live under the weight of poverty and oppression," Aniti says, sipping a latté. "Young women are our hope for humanity, though it is hard for them to rock the patriarchal boat," she states, her voice clear and assured and righteous.

"You are a strong role model for them. A true feminist," I say, admiring her convictions.

"I only do what needs doing for women in rural India. Humanitarian aid is messy and simple solutions don't always work, but it's the simple acts that make a difference for people who are traumatized," Aniti says.

"I would like to do more," I add, feeling a pang of guilt with the doers and activists and humanitarians I meet. I was once working and contributing to the complex arena of aid in disaster or conflict zones in Lebanon, Cambodia and Djibouti. I examine my life now – the grand and infinitesimally small – and fall into doubt. I tell myself my reflections, as a traveller and a writer, are the truth of my life and not separate from my work in the world. They mirror each other. Writing is my new front line.

"I wish I could spend a day with you in the village. Your work is important," I say as we finish our lattés.

"Rural India is deeply traditional and change can't be fast or imposed. I receive more from the villagers than I give. That's how I learn to do what I do."

48

The Long Way Home

SEVERAL GOVERNMENT GUIDES stand about at the ticket gate, waiting for a customer, on my last visit to the Taj. A young man with hair falling over his eyes and pants falling from his gaunt frame approaches me. He talks too fast, his English hard to understand.

"Please talk slowly," I say.

"You old woman," he responds.

I am instantly old, my purple sunglasses hiding my eyes that well up with tears. I want to slap this insolent, snotty-nosed kid in the face. He doesn't know how to say *older* woman, which I might have let pass.

"I walk slowly," he says, pushing aside the other guides all needing a late afternoon customer. Maybe he misunderstood "talk slowly" for "walk slowly." I do walk slowly and carry my fold-up pole that right now I resist the urge to crack over his head. Catastrophizing the entire trip, I follow him to the East Gate, wondering why I am here for the third time in five days. For my last precious hour at the Taj, it's suddenly clear. I decline his services and walk through the gate.

Wiping away the tears from my once-pretty face, I sit on a bench, not the same one Princess Diana sat on but off to the side under a leafy tree, and gaze at the Taj. I get it – I got hit in the gut with a backhanded gift. Didn't I want to embrace the younger and the older me? A couple on the bench near me asks if I want my picture taken in front of the Taj. I decline this too, holding my star ruby pendant in the palm of my hand.

On the shuttle bus back to the Coral, my forever-young myth blows away. I glide past the tourists, the street vendors, the tuk-tuk drivers, the everyday people, and come full circle into my new world. Sometimes I count on the kindness of strangers and sometimes I too need to be kind with poor, young men scrambling for work, pushing to be seen and heard.

I settle for a good dinner and time to rearrange my bags before my return to Delhi the next day. Plans change over dinner. I meet Kate and Nuala, sisters who have just arrived from Britain, who invite me for an impromptu walk down to the riverside behind the Taj. "Yes, I'd love to see the Taj one more time."

They are a feisty two, hardly off the plane, already sampling the street food, and have *bindis*, bright red spiritual eyes, stamped on their foreheads. We walk from the Coral down the East Gate Road and through the narrow streets to the river Yamuna behind the Taj. The Yamuna, a tributary of the Ganges, is one of India's holiest rivers and is sadly among its most polluted. At a small stone temple, women chant and sing, celebrating the arrival of Holi, the Hindu festival of colour. Nuala and Kate join in, clapping time as if we're at a jamboree. I do too, a little less boisterous, a little more reserved. The fragrance of sandalwood drifts in the air.

We sit on the stone ghats waiting for the sun to set. Someone gongs a bell, a cow chews its cud and a scrawny, gray horse arrives out of nowhere and pulls up tufts of grass. A few women are doing photo ops and three uniformed men, police or army, stand at a casual guard smoking cigarettes. The boys of Agra race about on bicycles up and down the uneven steps to the riverside. An old man scatters crumbs to the ravens, perhaps his evening ritual, a simple act in a busy world where he no longer matters. Maybe he does.

Everything is a *maybe* as the sun sinks into the western sky, silhouetting the Taj in translucent pearl. For one glorious moment, I believe in timeless, eternal, immortalized love, till this one jewel, *this one teardrop*, falls into the river of time. I remember that young woman, that brave girl, seeking her true path, stumbling in and out of love. I have learned to welcome her and hold her in good hands.

All I need do is say goodbye to India – blessed, intriguing, disturbing India. When I was young, I thought this country was the ultimate travel experience. It still is. Spiritual metaphors lurk everywhere, in the sacred river, in the myriad of gods and in the beauty amid the unrelenting hardship of people's lives.

THE AGRA RAILWAY STATION is thronged with people. I see a head of blond hair down the platform and, as I've always done, walk over and say hello.

Helena is from Sweden and glances up frequently at the departure board for the train to Delhi that is 30 minutes overdue. We ask a few people passing by if we are in the right place for the right train. We laugh at our respective needs for certainty and schedules we can rely on. I am no longer the girl who hopped a freight train many years ago.

The crowd surges forward as the New Delhi Shatabdi Express pulls into the station. I struggle with my suitcase as Helena, knapsack on her back, climbs onto the train with ease. She strikes me as a courageous woman, having travelled alone in Asia for six months. Just as I did many years ago. For this trip, I had a planned three-week itinerary. Helena's travels are impromptu, deciding by the day where to go. Even in Sweden, where she lives on the Arctic Ocean, she cross-country skis into the wild all by herself.

"Aren't you scared of polar bears?"

"No, all the polar bears live in Norway. And there are no wolves in the north of my country."

"I came face to face with myself in Agra," I say to Helena, who is a few years younger than me. I tell her my old woman story.

"Indians often ask my age. Am I married? Am I alone? They are always shocked. They move their heads one way and another way." She wiggle-waggles her head, not knowing those words in English.

"India was kind to me," she says, sipping a cup of aromatic chai. "Once I left my camera in a tuk-tuk and the driver took it to the police station. He talked to other tuk-tuk drivers who found me at my hostel and returned my camera. That was my lucky day."

"It was kind to me too. No one pestered me, not even the tuk-tuk drivers. Come to think of it, my drivers were the kindest of all. India makes me look in many mirrors." I pause for a moment's reflection. "India makes me look at my soul."

"That is good philosophy," Helena says in her straight-faced Scandinavian way. "Will you come back?"

"Maybe," is the most certain I can be as I look out the window at a dreary countryside littered with garbage along the backside of squat houses. Building after building of unfinished construction as we approach Delhi stands abandoned mid-project, so unlike Fatehpur Sikri, an abandoned city of grand class. The land rolls by as I roll on. I catch myself longing for that magical travel experience, no matter how often I stumble into it, discovering that this *is* the moment.

What matters now is everything I see and feel and experience, not just the grand moments but something more delicate, like the fragrance of flowers, or the memory of a kiss, or the arrival of warmth after winter. It may be the nod of recognition from a chai wallah or an airport official, or the kindness of a new friend. Helena invites me to visit her arctic shore.

"Why not?" I reflect. I'd never considered the far north of Sweden.

Tomorrow she is off to Darjeeling and I am going home. The journey back is the journey forward, the beginning is anywhere along the way. The train is at the station. I can pack or unpack, immerse or rearrange myself. There are no absolute destinations. There is only the truth of my life that shapes and shifts like clouds billowing under a burning sky. ◉

– Acknowledgements –

My story began several decades ago. I travelled over four continents, meeting strangers and making friends along the way. Every one of them enlivened my travels and contributed to bringing this book into the world.

I appreciate the mentorship of my two editors: Jennifer Kaddoura for her deep reflections in the early stages of the book, and Claire Mulligan for her astute suggestions, including getting the action on the first page! Their belief in my work meant a lot to me. Don George, former editor for Lonely Planet, offered some encouraging words too.

My beta readers Catherine Lang and Wendy Brown read earlier drafts and with their sharp editing eyes provided excellent critiques.

Sending gratitude to my community of writers, whose enthusiasm and insights were sincerely valued: Norah Wakula, Ramona McKean, Kelly Ditmars, Dalyce Joslin, Alison Gear, Beth Hawkes, Lisa Kuzma, Francine Volker, Hannah Horn, Jeff Dwyer and Woody Wheeler. Many thanks to Pamela Gutrath for her photographic assistance and all my other friends (you know who you are) for your kind and steadfast support.

Much appreciation to the Writers' Union of Canada and the Federation of British Columbia Writers for their terrific Zoom webinars. Writing workshops with Alison Pick at Sage Hill Writing in Saskatchewan and Alison Wearing at Under the Volcano in Mexico were wonderful creative retreats. And special thanks to Karen Connelly for her inspiration in the Courage Room.

Last but not least, I am forever grateful to Don Gorman and his talented team at Rocky Mountain Books. Thank you for choosing me to be one of your authors.

– About the Author –

Ella Harvey's diverse career and her adventurous spirit have taken her to remote regions of the world, with experiences in Asia and Africa contributing to her world view. She has lived on five continents and worked on four. Along with *A Time of Light and Shadow*, she is also the author of *Encounters on the Front Line: Cambodia – A Memoir*. Ella lives in beautiful Victoria, on the west coast of Canada, yet is frequently found dreaming of elsewhere.